New Spring in China?

By the same author:

FLAME FOR GOD, JOHN SUNG

COME WIND, COME WEATHER

RED SKY AT NIGHT

URGENT HARVEST

A PASSION FOR THE IMPOSSIBLE

A WORLD TO WIN

THREE OF CHINA'S MIGHTY MEN

New Spring in China?

A Christian Appraisal

by

Leslie T. Lyall

HODDER AND STOUGHTON

LONDON SYDNEY AUCKLAND TORONTO

British Library Cataloguing in Publication Data
Lyall, Leslie T.
    New Spring in China?
    1. China — Social life and customs
    I. Title
    951. 05'092'4   DS724

ISBN 0-340-24549-2

First published 1979

"Stoop, and there it is;
seek it not right and left.
All roads lead thither,—
One touch and you have spring!"

from "Taoism" by Ssu K'ung-t'u (A.D. 834–908)

Dedicated to my wife who shared many years
in China

Acknowledgments

In compiling what is virtually a digest of available information about China, I gratefully acknowledge my indebtedness to the Christian China Study Group (London) Reports, the Bulletin of the China Study Project (British Council of Churches), China Notes (Division of Overseas Ministries, NCC/U.S.A.), the China Quarterly (1920–35), Asian Outreach (Hong Kong), Pray for China (Hong Kong), Current Scene in Mainland China (Hong Kong) and the Lutheran World Federation Information Letter (Geneva). Footnotes in the text refer to books consulted.

I also wish to thank Miss Joyce Baldwin and Mr. Martin Goldsmith for their expert advice and my wife for the many hours of typing and retyping involved.

Contents

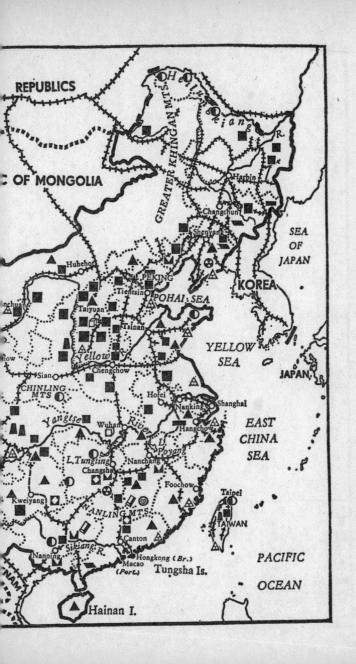

Author's Introduction

In the ancient Chinese calendar, which divides the lunar year into fortnightly periods, *lih ch'uen* or "beginning of spring" marks the end of winter storms and the advent of new life and promise. In 1979 China celebrates thirty years of Communist rule—thirty stormy years of uncertainty, indecision, impulsive leadership, tragic mistakes, adolescent hero-worship, changing moods of optimism and pessimism, emotional outbursts and irrational behaviour. The People's Republic of China has passed through a phase of what the German classicists called "Sturm und Drang" with its ebullient enthusiasm and unbridled passion. Is the winter of China's storms now to give place to a new spring of hope and progress?

Recent visitors to China have gained the impression of a country coming to terms with itself and the modern world, a country still learning the basic facts of life, a nation in its immaturity. For centuries China has suffered from retarded growth. Now she is in danger of outgrowing her strength—a nation in a hurry to attain adulthood and to take her rightful place in the family of nations, a country so potentially rich and yet so poor, having such a long national history and yet so backward by comparison with the "outside kingdoms", as she calls them.

Hopefully, China is at the end of the beginning, the end of the nightmare of uncertainty and incessant internal strife, the bewildering changes of direction and the childish parroting of contradictory slogans. China's period of "storm and stress" may be ending. Are we witnessing a new beginning —the beginning of China's spring? The wonderful Chinese people deserve a hitherto unknown stability, a strong and wise leadership, liberty to think for themselves and to exchange ideas free from ideological straitjackets. These they must have if they are to progress in the way they hope. It is time for the "new China" to proceed from adolescence to maturity. And all who love China will wish her well. Welcome spring!

Most of all, those who are concerned for China's highest interests will pray for a change of heart in the matter of religion. The freedom of religion, to which China pays only lip-service, must become a reality. Christians ought to be free to follow their convictions and to practise their beliefs without fear of official disapproval and the crippling discrimination they now endure. These are their human rights.

This book is an attempt at an honest appraisal of Communist China from a Christian point of view. A vast and ever-increasing volume of books on China by the experts is available for the serious student. This volume is for the reader who may be bewildered by the Chinese puzzle and is looking for a simple outline of Chinese Communism in theory and in practice and its effect on the Chinese people. Marxists and socialists see all socialist regimes through their pink spectacles—even Cambodia! —and they make it their business to portray these regimes in the best possible light. A Christian appraisal, however, must above all be honest, fair and constructive. It must avoid the simplistic attitude that argues, "All Communists are atheists and therefore incapable of anything but evil!" A Christian "proves all things" and "holds fast that which is good". May the Spirit of truth help the readers of this book in their understanding of China and inspire them in their intercession for the Chinese people.

CHAPTER I

Cri de Coeur

"MAO IS DEAD" . . . "MADAME MAO ARRESTED". The second banner headline following so soon after the first astounded the world. Then came the details of a plot by the "gang of four" to seize power—a plot which was defeated by the determined and prompt action of Hua Kuo-feng, the Premier so recently appointed by Chairman Mao himself. Mme. Mao's three fellow conspirators were among the highest officials in the land, promoted to eminence by the late Chairman for their loyal activities during the Cultural Revolution. They had been the heroes of the "January Storm" which marked the turning-point in that tumultuous upheaval. Now they had been caught red-handed, about to stage a coup d'état. They were arrested by Chairman Mao's personal bodyguard. Almost at once they suffered the supreme ignominy—expulsion from the Chinese Communist Party, a disgrace which they had once helped to inflict on the former Chairman of the Republic, Liu Shao-ch'i. The tables were certainly turned.

Was the fall of the "gang of four" not a divine judgment on those who, in the Cultural Revolution, commissioned the youthful Red Guards to destroy all religion, and Christianity in particular? Mme. Mao was the patron of the Red Guards who did their utmost to carry out their commission. An Old Testament prophet would most certainly have related the two events as cause and effect. Sooner or later, God will vindicate His faithful people. He is the One who, as the prophet Isaiah declares, "brings princes to naught and makes the rulers of the earth as nothing". So it proved for the "gang of four".

Challenge of a vast population

But when, oh, when will the Christian Church wake up to the greatest challenge to its faith in all its long history? When will it turn its attention from lesser domestic concerns to the one great burning issue of the day—China? Never before in history has the Church been confronted with a totally un-evangelised population of 950,000,000 in one country—one fifth of the human race—and most certainly included in the Divine compassion and redemptive purpose. The masses of China are encircled by the tough horse-riding nomads of Mongolia, the hardy tribes of Central Asia, the sturdy Tibetans on the roof of the world and as many as 150 tribes in the mountain massif of the south-west. Here are 950,000,000 individuals who face an eternity with or without Christ. They present a task totally unprecedented and un-paralleled in the world today. But who gives them more than a passing thought?

Challenge of an atheistic ideology

The Church has in centuries past met the fierce and bloody opposition of Islam, but her own offensives have made very little impression on that stronghold. Hinduism remains a well-nigh impregnable enemy redoubt, scarcely breached after centuries of assault. Buddhism, too, presents a scornful face to Christianity, confident that her strength is enough to resist all attempts to replace her. But never before has the Christian Church looked on from outside the ramparts at a nation where "no-god" reigns supreme, where for a whole generation of thirty years all religion has been scorned as superstition and where there is now no religious vocabulary in use, no word for "God" or "soul" or "salvation" and where a generation that never saw a missionary has grown up with atheistic materialism as its only "truth". One can at least discuss the concept of God and the nature of religious experience with Muslims, Hindus and Buddhists, but not with the devotees of Marxism–Leninism–Mao Tse-tung Thought. In China Christianity confronts the most intractable problem of all time in trying to communicate its message. But who is grappling with the problem?

Challenge of a virtual inaccessibility

Then, never before has a land of so many Christless people, in the firm grip of such a powerful pseudo-religion, been so inaccessible to God's messengers. For centuries the world has been wide open to travellers, explorers and missionary pioneers. In the world of today, with its rapid travel and international communications, one can buy a ticket to go where one wills—with one exception—China! Diplomatic personnel, business people, scientists and engineers on special missions, groups of sympathisers on skilfully-guided propaganda tours, and recently tourists, have been visiting China since 1972 in growing numbers, but certainly no official church representatives have been able to enter. To the Christian who wishes to preach Christ the vast tracts of China are firmly closed. Only a few Chinese Christians, mostly on the pretext of visiting relatives in the south-east, are able to gain easy admission. China is opening her doors to the world, to trade and technology, but definitely not to the Gospel.

A strategic challenge

And never before has the Christian Church faced such a strategic challenge. China has vast natural resources of every kind, vast manpower and infinite skills. Given peace, stability and sensible government China has the potentiality, as historians like Toynbee have prophesied, of becoming one of the most powerful nations in the world early in the 21st century. If at that time China is still ruled by militant atheists committed to world revolution she might exclude the Gospel from Asia, as Russia threatens to do in Africa, and be a dire menace to the whole world. But, if God were to move in power among China's millions, the permeating leaven of the Gospel might transform Chinese society and make China a blessing rather than a curse. But time is short, and the matter is desperately urgent.

China and Russia

But where in the world is the most stupendous challenge ever to confront the Christian Church being taken seriously?

The Russian Christian lobby is strong, but while the Russian Church has a history of one thousand years, the Chinese Church has a history of only about one hundred years. And whereas the Russian Church has deep roots in Russian culture and is virtually indestructible, the Chinese Church has never taken root in Chinese culture. Russia still has 20,000,000 church-going Christians sixty years after the Revolution. China has none! There are now no church buildings available to them. While a part of the Church in Russia is operating "underground", the entire Church in China was driven "underground" in 1966—the only Communist country in the world (with Albania) where this has happened. Yet who cares? One Georgi Vins in Russia sends Christians onto the streets of London to demonstrate. But who demonstrates on behalf of hundreds of Chinese "Georgi Vins"? President Carter attacks Russia for its denial of human rights in that country but makes no issue of comparable denials in China. Why? Why? we ask.

The answer is, in part, that a curtain of silence has fallen around China and her Christians. China has no voice like that of Richard Wurmbrand to alert us to the sufferings of Chinese Christians. No Chinese Solzenytzin has emerged from China to describe China's "Gulag Archipelago". On China ignorance prevails. The "greatest challenge" is unrecognised. Few in the West show concern and few give themselves to intercede for these 950,000,000 souls in spiritual darkness.

What must be done?

What, then, must be done? First, the absurd notion adopted by many Western theologians at Louvain in 1974 that China with its material improvements, its alleged social justice and its moral slogans about "fighting self and serving the people" is no longer in need of the Gospel of Jesus Christ, must be firmly refuted. The myth of the "new man" in China must be exposed. The error promulgated by these theologians must be corrected. The Biblical truth that all men are in fact lost and guilty sinners under the judgment of God until they come to faith in Christ must be restated and re-emphasised. Paul, in writing to Timothy said, "God desires all men to be saved and to come to a knowledge of the truth, for there is one God and one Mediator between God and men, the Man Christ Jesus who gave Himself as a ransom for all." And that includes all the 950,000,000 people of China who have an equal right with us to be told the truth about their Saviour and ours.

Is there a Church?

Secondly, the true facts about China and the Church in China must be made known. The curtain of silence must be drawn aside. That Church must be given a voice. The Christian Church in China may have a very short history comparatively speaking. It may have been a pathetically small Church in 1951, when the missionaries left after a century of toil and sacrifice—a mere 1,000,000 Protestants, compared with 15 million Protestants in Latin America won in only sixty years and up to 100 million Protestants in Africa. And yet, in 1949, when Chairman Mao declared the founding of the People's Republic of China, there was a living Church of born-again, Bible-loving, prayerful believers, with fine spiritual leaders—the very salt of Chinese society. Moreover, the Church had been renewed by the visitation of the Holy Spirit in each of the first five decades of this century. It had already suffered in the fires of persecution, especially in the Boxer massacres of 1900 and the Communist-inspired anti-Christian movement of the twenties and thirties. But what of the present?

After 1966, when the Cultural Revolution began, there was total silence from the Chinese Church for six years and even now an almost total silence from the vast interior of China continues. The four south-eastern coastal provinces, where the Gospel first obtained a foothold in 1842 (and where most overseas Chinese originate, allowing them to come and go with some freedom), are the only ones from which regular news emerges. But what news! Conversions, baptisms, church growth—in one county amazing growth —pastoral ministry, healings, short training schools for converts, mountain retreats and leaders' conferences. But also, frequent arrests, the constant fear of the labour camp and invariable discrimination against Christians and their chil-

dren in education and employment. All religion is still regarded as superstition due for total elimination. Bibles, which
were confiscated and destroyed on a mass scale in 1966, are
still in desperately short supply. At best the Church is a tiny,
persecuted, hard-pressed minority, in a vast sea of atheism
and materialism. It is more desperately in need of loving
concern and prayer fellowship than any Church in the world
today. Humanly speaking, it is, like the churches of Asia
Minor founded by St. Paul or those of North Africa, in
imminent danger of being wiped out.

Who is concerned?

But who is really concerned? The Christian and secular
press carry reports of the churches in Russia, Romania,
Yugo-Slavia and other East European countries and Christians have come to feel a deep concern for our brethren
there. But after the missionaries left China in 1951 news of
the churches steadily dwindled and prayer correspondingly
withered away. China is seldom mentioned in the Christian
press. Who is concerned? God most certainly is concerned
for 950 million of His creatures who have never heard of the
salvation and liberation which Christ came to bring through
His death and Resurrection. And if God is so deeply concerned, should not every Christian share His concern? No
task is more urgent today than to mobilise the prayers of the
Church worldwide for China and God's people there. God
must surely act, in His own time, on behalf of one fifth of
the human race. When He does it, it will be through His own
Church in China which He is even now preparing for that
day. The Church in China must therefore become the focus
of powerful worldwide intercession while awaiting the day of
Divine intervention. At the moment, the Chinese Church
might well complain, as Jerusalem once did of old, "Is it
nothing to you, all you who pass by? Look and see if there is
any sorrow like my sorrow . . ." Shall we not reply, "God
forbid that we should sin against the Lord is ceasing to pray
for you!"

CHAPTER II

China Revisited

Two Communist nations

A visit to two Communist countries, one in the West and one in the East, within two months, has been a revelation. The Yugo-Slavian socialism of Tito's variety and the austere socialism of Mao's China are in stark contrast. In Yugo-Slavia there is evident prosperity, even affluence. The village chalets of the Julian Alps differ little from their Austrian neighbours—neat, freshly painted and a blaze of geraniums, fuschias and carnations: privately-owned dwellings in which the owners take pride. Churches remain open and the village shrines and crucifixes are everywhere, well-kept and lovingly tended. Private cars are normal rather than exceptional. Advertised entertainments in the towns suggest a degree of lingering bourgeois decadence! China is another world and surely Chairman Hua, on his visit to Yugo-Slavia must have been struck by the contrasts: China is the only country in the world where no-one is allowed to own a private car, even if they could afford it—and few could; no display of the least affluence, for such does not exist; no modern, roomy, comfortable, private housing, for that awaits a distant future day; and certainly no night clubs or similar varieties of frivolous entertainment—just films, plays and operas of ideological merit and often boringly repetitive. As for religion—no churches remain open for the "people" and every sign of organised religion has disappeared. In other words, a prosperous blend of Marxist socialism and Western capitalism contrasts with an austere socialism which has yet to produce the prosperity for which the Chinese people have laboured for thirty years. Both countries are rebels against Russian "hegemony" and both are world tourist attractions on a large scale. President Tito's visit to China in 1977 and Chairman Hua's visit to Yugo-Slavia in 1978 may well have a far-reaching significance for both countries.

A new Peking

Peking is not the Peking I knew thirty years ago. Austerity has taken the place of charm. The ancient walls and most of the towering, noble city gates have gone, together with the old narrow thoroughfares. Peking is stretching out in all directions. Broad, straight thoroughfares run at right angles to one another as in Marco Polo's time but on a much larger scale, many of them with tree-lined grass verges. They compose a vast, orderly network of wide roads, underpasses, fly-overs and architecturally attractive bridges, all built, presumably, for a so far non-existent car traffic. More than anything else, Peking at present resembles a vast construction site with building materials piled high everywhere: mountains of gravel, huge piles of bricks, concrete slabs, timber. The old, mud-walled buildings are rapidly disappearing and giving place to fourteen-storey blocks of flats, government buildings and educational institutions of every kind, some in the early and ugly Russian style, but the more recent ones in a pleasing Chinese style of architecture with its curved and green-tiled roofs. The eighty-metre wide Ch'ang An Boulevard runs from east to west bisecting the city. It proudly passes the Tien An Men or Gate of Heavenly Peace on the north side and the Tien An Square on the south—a vast square, with a capacity to hold two million people, containing the Monument to the People's Heroes and the more recent Chairman Mao Memorial Hall. The railway station, where a now rare statue of the late Chairman dominates the forecourt, is a very impressive building. It is totally free of litter, even of cigarette ends, and that in a nation of smokers!

No, Peking is not the Peiping of pre-liberation days, but it promises to become a fine and worthy capital city when all the reconstruction is complete. And, who knows, the two and a half million bicycles, the only privately-owned means of transport, which now clutter up the streets at rush hour, may one day slowly give place to the so far non-existent private car. For the present, bicycles dominate the scene, though

there are government-department-owned cars and cars for
government officials, curtained to prevent prying eyes from
seeing the occupants. And, of course, there are Chinese-
built trucks, military vehicles and buses contending with the
non-traffic-conscious cyclists.

Peking airport is a pleasant place north-east of the city
and approached along a tree-lined avenue — not just one line
of trees but at least six deep on either side. After the strict
security at other world airports, it was a relief to board and
leave our plane to Manchuria with no baggage or body
checks of any kind. It was the same when we left Peking for
Tokyo. China must have great faith in her internal law and
order system. No-one travels in China for pleasure or personal reasons, so all the Chinese we met on the planes or
railways must have been cadres and officials on army or
government business. It was fascinating to watch the departure boards at the station and airport: planes and express
trains bound for Tihwa, Kunming, Taiyuan, Tatung, Chungking, Kaifeng, Loyang, Shanghai, Canton, Hankow, Sian,
etc., etc.

The north-east

Manchuria or "the north-east" still bears the stamp of a
pioneer region. Changchun, the capital of Kirin province,
has a history of only a hundred and seventy years and of
both Russian and Japanese occupation. Our Lakeside Hotel
was almost sumptuous and, used chiefly by high-ranking
cadres, had every modern convenience and was carpeted
throughout with lovely Peking-style carpets. But the city's
chief claim to fame is that it has China's Number One automobile works. All visits to institutions begin with a "meeting" in a room with portraits of Marx, Engels, Lenin and
Stalin at one end and Mao and Tua at the other (Stalin is *not*
out of favour in China!). Sitting around a table and served
with Chinese tea we are welcomed by the manager, then
follows mutual handclapping. Next the manager explains
the history of the factory, school, institution or whatever
with the inevitable reference to the iniquitous "gang of four"
who tried to sabotage all progress, and to the new day of
progress under Chairman Hua. More clapping and then a

N.S.C.—2

tour of the premises, in this case a huge factory covering one and a half million square yards; it was certainly impressive—25,000 girls and men working together in the foundry and on the assembly line, which turns out 60,000 trucks a year. At the meeting, I asked if the automobile industry in China was plagued with the kind of labour troubles we expect as normal in Great Britain. No! although the right to strike is written into the Constitution, there has never been a strike so far, the manager told us. They deal with disputes in a democratic way by discussion. "Do you have trade unions?" I asked. "Yes, but they serve only a welfare purpose such as caring for the families of sick or injured members and arranging various forms of entertainment."

A visit to the factory kindergarten was to be overwhelmed with well-orchestrated shrieks of welcome from hundreds of little voices and waving hands, followed by a highly skilled, perfectly precisioned and very charming performance of folk songs and dances by gaily dressed kiddies. In the same city we had already watched highly professional performances of ice figure-skating and Chinese martial arts in the local physical education institute. Here, too, we were told of the interference of the "gang of four" and the new day that has dawned since they were arrested. In Kirin we stayed at a hotel on the banks of the Sungari River and visited the dam, reservoir and power station some miles up-river. The Russian frontier is not so far away and we could not help noticing the anti-aircraft guns guarding the dam. War, for the Chinese, is an obsession and every precaution has been taken against a possible attack, including the construction of vast underground caverns beneath Peking and other major cities as protection against aerial and even nuclear attack.

View from a train

The journey by train back to Peking was long—nearly twenty-four hours. But, after a red carpet send-off, we enjoyed "soft class" (2nd class) accommodation which was luxurious compared with British Rail. The People's communes through which the train passed were impressive—large fields of cultivation, scientific agriculture, modern sprinkler systems and huge plastic cloches covering acres of land; few tractors however and labour-intensive cultivation with teams of twenty or so working together in hoeing, weeding or harvesting the maize crop. Red brick farm houses are gradually replacing the old mud-walled houses and light industrial plants are associated with the rural towns. Great attention has obviously been paid to improving irrigation and building reservoirs to provide a steady supply of water. As the train passed through Tangshan, two years after the disastrous earthquake which may have claimed 700,000 lives, the damage was still evident: half-crushed locomotives, collapsed factories, tilting water towers and ruined homes of the people. Then Shanhaikuan, where the Great Wall meets the sea, Tsinghwangtao and Tientsin before returning to Peking.

Frank discussion

The most valuable part of this journey was the opportunity to talk freely with a very open and well-informed guide who spoke excellent and idiomatic English and without the presence of the political watchdog who normally accompanies the guides. I confirmed many of the things I had read and impressions I had gained. He too criticised the "gang of four" (szi ren pang) and the "new-born things of the Cultural Revolution" as being altogether unbalanced and negative in their consequences. But the highlight was a frank exchange about religion. Why, I asked, are religious believers in Russia and Eastern Europe growing in numbers and able to meet for Christian worship in their own buildings, while the Red Guards had closed all churches in China and Chinese Christians do not enjoy the freedom promised to them in the Constitution? Mr. Yen's answers were the stock answers. But when I challenged him about the manifest nonsense that "labour created the world" and the arrogant claim that "man can conquer nature", despite the earthquakes and floods and drought from which China suffers, he was both courteous, interested and not at all offended. He was however sceptical when I told him about Chou En-lai's Christian connections and sympathies and the existence of many practising Christians in other parts of China. Mr. Yen had evidently been informed of the fact that

I had been a missionary, but, far from being suspicious or antagonistic, he said before we parted, "Mr. Lyall and I have become good friends!"

Back in Peking, we followed the tourist route to the Summer Palace and the Forbidden City, conceived and built on such a colossal scale and once the exclusive residence of emperors and empresses who eked out a lonely and uncomfortable existence surrounded by intriguing courtiers, eunuchs and concubines. The towering terracotta walls, the red pillars, the golden roofs above painted and decorative eaves, the priceless treasures of gold, jade and porcelain are today the property of the "people". They throng the many courtyards every day of the week to admire the exquisite skills and artistry of their predecessors—achievements which a new generation must match if China is to build a greater, finer China than the great empire of Genghis Khan or the magnificence of the Sung and Ming dynasties—a China for every man and not just for the proud emperors and mandarins of bygone days. We also visited the ancient Ming Tombs in a charming valley whose beauty has been enhanced by a new reservoir lake and the Great Wall, built three centuries before Christ to keep out the Tartar invaders, still magnificent in its magnitude.

Tourism

But China is being invaded once again—not by the barbarians from the north but by people of all nations. The Friendship Hotel is but one of several huge hotels accommodating foreign tourists: it consists of an intricate complex of buildings and annexes with all modern facilities. Just one of its half-a-dozen dining rooms contained twenty round tables to seat twelve at each and served two six-course Chinese meals a day of *real* Chinese food: an embarrassing kind of entertainment when we thought of the simple fare of most of the people, even in the capital city and its neighbouring communes. China Travel Service also laid on an unforgettable farewell Peking Duck dinner in the historic two hundred-year-old restaurant. Peking literally swarmed with East Europeans (no Russians!), Americans, Canadians, Australians, New Zealanders, Japanese, Germans, Italians and

Chinese from overseas. All had come, thousands of them, and continue to come in a ceaseless tide every month of the year as the welcome guests of the Chinese government to see the new China. China welcomes tourism, which she plans to extend even to Lhasa in Tibet. American hotel chains are being consulted about the best means to accommodate the hordes that are expected. Already the China Travel Service is a model of efficiency, punctuality and hospitality. Peking alone has over one hundred guides speaking (very well) some fifteen foreign languages, all friendly, courteous and patient —sometimes they need to be! The Friendship Store is a large emporium exclusively for foreigners where most of China's traditional arts and crafts are available at a price. Yes, China has jumped on the tourist bandwagon in a big way. The foreign invasion could reach astronomical heights.

What, one must ask, do all these tourists and visitors make of the "new China"? The mere world tourist would love the old China of bygone days, but would find the "new China" light years behind Japan, Hong Kong, Singapore, Malaysia and other countries on their itinerary in material progress. Her roads and transport (except the railways) bear no comparison. Her hotels are improving, but from the Friendship Hotel in Peking to the Ginza Dai-Ichi in Tokyo is to move from one world to another. China has a long, long way to go to "catch up with the rest of the world" and this goal will scarcely be attained by the year 2000.

Friendliness

But for those of us who were looking beyond the externals to discover the real China, the Chinese people rather than material evidences of progress, our first and last impression was one of friendliness and warmth, not just on the part of the guides but from the people in general—in that Changchun department store where we mingled freely with the shoppers and chatted to the attendants and others, the people taking their leisure in the parks and Forbidden City, the young people in the schools and factories. Talking to them in their own language one sensed an immediate warm reaction as though they were hungry for friendship and understanding—PLA soldiers, a waitress from Pingyao in my old province, the air hostesses, parents and children, an old man from Changsha on a railway station. Our guides and their political watchdogs, initially correct and efficient, thawed with every hour and were soon conversing freely on any topic introduced. Liu, aged 25, told me why he was not yet married and freely discussed the question of sex relationships in present-day Chinese society. Yen, our Manchurian guide, was a model of frankness and a fund of information.

The people have changed

I remembered what a life-long resident of China who had lived under the old regime and for nearly thirty years under the new (and now living in the U.K.) said in 1976: "If you missionaries were to go back to China, the greatest changes you would notice would not be the material changes but the change in the Chinese people themselves." I can now confirm this. In particular, the young women of China were impressive — the guides, the waitresses, the factory workers, the air hostesses, the school teachers: they are disciplined, dignified, neatly dressed, self-confident, cheerful and often very charming. Men in the mass appeared less cheerful and the spontaneous smile not so common. Nevertheless, they too, as Chairman Mao said in 1949 "have stood up"! After centuries of oppression by their own people and exploitation by foreigners a new air of self-respect and abounding confidence in their future is apparent. A remarkable change in a nation's morale has occurred. The essence of China is its people — warm, generous, courteous to a fault, punctilious, methodical and incredibly numerous. As for other visitors, so for me, the people themselves were the main joy of my trip. Chinese youth is as attractive as youth anywhere — whether the lovely children of the car factory workers in the kindergarten or the immensely skilful student figure-skaters on ice or the group of "young pioneers" out for a holiday trip and in high spirits. The old are conspicuous by their absence: they stay at home to look after the grandchildren while the parents work.

A spiritual desert

"One thing thou lackest" is the phrase that comes to mind in visiting China today. Material progress there has been and will be. People are adequately nourished and clothed. A variety of simple necessities is available at the department stores. Housing falls far behind acceptable standards at present, but even here progress is accelerating. And yet one's impression is of a spiritual wilderness. Few have heard the name of God or Christ and if they have, the very names are a part of the superstition they believe religion to be. Tim Brown, who was a student in China from 1974–76 comments: "Folk religion may be far stronger than I or Chinese friends realise . . . But China is a nation where a larger and larger section of the population lives without any overt observation of religion. Buddhism is no longer the force mitigating the violence of the natural world and in a land of paddy agriculture the floods and the droughts can be violent indeed. Taoism is no longer the call of brotherhood against the oppression of the imperial throne. And Christianity has become a limited and private fellowship. Only Islam still flourishes with a public life. Institutional reform has done away with the social and economic bases on which the traditional religions of China have relied. Somewhere beneath the carapace of urban China the young may still give the old a religious burial. But the trend over the past thirty years is decline. The Cultural Revolution seems to have brought the gods of China to death's door and I see no-one who will call them back. That time, it appears, has passed." That is a point of view which ignores the sovereignty of Almighty God, whose saving purposes for the Chinese people will come to fruition in His chosen time. But it is an outlook from which it is hard to escape in the China of today.

CHAPTER III

Farewell to Mao Tse-Tung

The death of Mao Tse-tung occurred on 9th September 1976, in Peking at the age of 83. He had "gone to see God" as he sometimes told foreign guests that he would. It was the end of an era.

Youth

Born in 1893 into a well-to-do peasant family in Shaoshan, Hunan, the young Mao was an early rebel by nature. In 1911 the eighteen-year-old schoolboy witnessed with great emotion the capture of Changsha by Sun Yat-sen's revolutionary troops. After a year in the army Mao went on to gain the equivalent of a degree in education. He was well-read in the Chinese classics and in the eighteenth-century rationalistic writers. In 1917 he helped to found the radical New People's Study Society. As World War One came to an end Mao took a post in the Peking University library where he was caught up in the student-led "May 4th Movement" of protest against Japan. By 1920 he had become a committed Marxist and was present in July 1921 at the secret first Congress of the Chinese Communist Party held in Shanghai.

Collaboration with Nationalists

The Chinese Communist Party decided to collaborate with the Nationalists in support of the "National Revolution". Mao joined its leaders, Chiang Kai-shek and Chou En-lai, in Canton and soon showed an exceptional grasp of organisational problems. But, criticised by his own party, he returned in 1925 to Hunan where he discovered the revolutionary potential of the Chinese peasantry, whose cause he now espoused in face of opposition from the more orthodox Marxists.

Returning to Canton Mao took part in the 1926 Northern Expedition which was designed to unify the nation. By August the Wuhan cities and Hunan were in the hands of the revolutionary armies. But when Chiang Kai-shek felt that his own leadership was being threatened he led his forces to Shanghai where the Chinese city was handed over to him by left-wing workers. The subsequent execution, on Chiang's orders, of hundreds of these same workers, as Communist sympathisers, precipitated the break with the Communist wing of the Kuomintang. The long and disastrous civil war began.

Retreat to Chingkangshan

The failure of the "Autumn Harvest Uprising" under Chou En-lai at Nanchang drove the Red forces to set up a mountain fortress in the Chingkang mountains. Mao was joined by Chu-teh, the founder of the Red Army. Using guerilla tactics they repeatedly fought off the Nationalists, but Mao was at odds with the orthodox left wing of the party which, like the Russians, disapproved of his radical agrarian policy as being un-Marxist. Nevertheless Mao succeeded in establishing the first Chinese Soviet Republic in South Kiangsi, in face of continuing criticism. But he only maintained his authority by the ruthless suppression of any revolt. Even so, in the early thirties his leadership was under constant criticism and he was finally dropped from the Central Committee.

The Yenan Years

By 1934 the Red armies were encircled and blockaded. Without Mao's leadership they were facing defeat. In July 1934 the Politburo decided to retreat to North China in what came to be known as the Long March (see Chapter V). During the retreat Mao's leadership of the Chinese Com-

munist Party was firmly re-established at the celebrated
Tsunyi Conference. Once in Yenan in Shensi Mao continued
to resist the Kuomintang on the one hand and Soviet
attempts to dominate him on the other. In 1936 he forced
Chiang Kai-shek to suspend the civil war and to join in a
united front against Japanese aggression. During the eight-
year war the Communists gained in prestige both as successful guerilla fighters against Japan and as revolutionary
nationalists. When Japan surrendered in 1945 Chiang Kai-
shek rejected every suggestion for further collaboration. The
civil war was resumed, the Nationalists were defeated and
their government took refuge in Taiwan.

The People's Republic of China

On 1st October 1949, from the Gate of Heavenly Peace in
Peking, Mao Tse-tung declared the inauguration of the
People's Republic of China. China had been "liberated".
Mao, already Chairman of the Party, was now appointed the
first national Chairman. Two main tasks faced the new regime: to consolidate its political control and to lay the
foundations for economic development in a poor and backward country already ruined by a calamitous inflation. In
the next thirty years real progress was made in six directions.

1. The Economy

Between 1939 and 1949 all prices in China rose eight
million million fold! But within months after "liberation"
inflation was halted. The new "People's Currency" has
proved completely stable ever since. There has been little
increase in consumer food prices, while a rigid rationing
system has ensured an equal distribution of all essentials
both in urban and rural areas. The poorer Chinese have experienced a revolutionary change for the better in their living
standards, though by world standards these are still very low.
And, in some areas, the peasants still endure periods of
hunger and some oppression.

2. Education

In 1949 illiteracy in China was as high as ninety per cent.
In 1978 it had been reduced to less than thirty per cent. But

universal education for so vast a population requires resources of funds and teachers which are very difficult to find in so poor a country. Yet many obstacles have been overcome and, in spite of its politicisation, literacy has made great strides in thirty years.

3. Public Health

Health care for a population the size of China's is an enormous problem. Before 1949 medical treatment was an expensive luxury for the urban minority. For the poor, good medical treatment was prohibitive and virtually unavailable. The first National Health Conference in 1950 set out the priorities.

1. Health care must serve the common people.
2. Priority must be given to the prevention of disease.
3. Western and traditional medicine should be integrated.
4. Health campaigns should be co-ordinated with other mass movements.

The first of these campaigns attacked "the four pests"—rats, flies, mosquitoes, and bed-bugs—with great success. The desperate shortage of doctors led to the training of large numbers of para-medicals, known as "bare-foot doctors", because they also worked bare-foot in the rice paddies. They functioned within the "rural co-operative medical services" system and their role is still crucial. They are found everywhere today—on the steppes of Mongolia and in Tibet, among the mountain tribes and even at sea with the fishing trawlers. They have a basic knowledge of first-aid and common diseases, carry out mass vaccinations and give advice on family planning. In spite of many admitted shortcomings, the achievements in public health are impressive. Professor John Gurley of Stanford University, U.S.A., wrote in 1970, "the prevention and control of many infectious and parasitic diseases which have ravaged China for generations, e.g. typhoid, T.B., malaria, cholera, syphilis and schistosomiasis (snail fever) etc., have resulted in their near elimination. The improvement of the general environmental sanitation and practice of personal hygiene is phenomenal." [1]

[1] "Maoist Economic Development; the New Man in the New China", by John Gurley in *China Notes*, VI, VIII, No. 4.

4. Communications

Since 1949 railway mileage has been doubled. The Ch'engtu-Paoch'i line (676 km.) was opened to traffic in 1975 and the spectacular Ch'engtu-Kumming line (1,085 km.), which runs through wild mountain terrain, completed a year later, is one of the greatest engineering feats of our day. Railways carry more than 850 million tons of freight annually.

A network of new motor roads covers the country: 750,000 kilometres today compared with 100,000 kilometres in 1949. The Yunnan–Tibet highway was completed in 1974.

Shipbuilding has made great strides. In 1974 the merchant fleet totalled three hundred vessels weighing 2·7 million tons. China has seventeen ports, all of which are being modernised and prepared for container traffic. Chanchiang, the terminal for the Manchurian oil fields, is being enlarged to take 50,000-ton tankers.

In 1949 China lost her entire civil aviation fleet to Taiwan. Since then she has developed 107 domestic routes serving 73 major cities and 16 international routes connecting 32 countries. Her aircraft include Boeings, Tridents, Ilyushins.

5. Status of Women

The New Marriage Order of 1951 abolished child marriage, polygamy and concubinage and gave divorce rights to both parties. Today Chinese women enjoy full equality with men and are employed in all walks of life.

6. Morals

China today is a society in which very serious crime is comparatively rare and where sexual puritanism prevails. Petty crime is handled within the community through group criticism and sanctions. Re-education in labour camps is a last resource. One observer writes: "The intense use of small peer groups which exert pressure together with anticipated pressures has enabled the authorities effectively to influence the overt behaviour of people but not so much their attitudes and aspirations".[1] Crime, drugs, banditry, prostitution, gambling and pornography have largely been eliminated.

[1] *Lost Chance in China*, by John Server.

Mao has also popularised the ideal of selfless service to the community. The Little Red Book says, "We should be modest and prudent, guard against arrogance and rashness and serve the Chinese people heart and soul."

Professor Gurley again comments: "Communist China is certainly not a paradise but it is engaged in perhaps the most interesting economic and social experiment ever attempted . . ." The Christian applauds every change for the better in China, but he must also feel a certain sadness that these achievements are the fruit of a materialistic philosophy which gives no glory to the Creator and believes that in satisfying man's material needs all his needs are thereby satisfied. The Christian knows that "man does not live by bread alone but by every word that proceedeth out of the mouth of God". Without the Bread of Life man remains spiritually destitute. The worst famine of all is the famine of the Word of God. Chairman Mao is known to have read the Bible, but in offering to his people the cold stones of materialism for the satisfying Bread of Life he was depriving them of the highest good.

Mao was among other things a poet and a poem written in 1925 expresses his wistful agnosticism.

> Standing alone in the cold autumn,
> Where the Hsiang River flows north,
> On the tip of Orange Island,
> Looking at thousands of hills,
> Red all over,
> Row after row of forests, all red,
> The river is green to the bottom,
> A hundred boats are struggling,
> Eagles striking the sky,
> Fish battling the currents of clear water.
> All creatures fight for freedom
> Under the frosty sky.
> Bewildered at empty space,
> I ask the great grey earth;
> Who controls the rise and fall?
>
> *Autumn 1925.*

Mao as a leader

Mao Tse-tung's long career proves him to have been a successful leader who, despite increasing criticism and opposition, retained his authority to the end. He possessed the unique force of character to lead a revolutionary movement full of other strong characters. He was, according to Stuart Schramm, "relatively conservative", and constantly opposed both right and left deviations. Schramm also says, "He was the most effective manipulator of men in the political world . . ." Edgar Snow described Mao as a man of intellectual depth and peasant shrewdness with a power of ruthless decision. His life style was always one of spartan simplicity and self-discipline. He cared nothing for personal comfort or luxuries.

Mao was undoubtedly at the peak of his success in 1956 and had he stepped down then his reputation in Chinese eyes would have been almost untarnished. The naïve "Hundred Flowers" invitation, the reckless Great Leap Forward, and the chaotic Cultural Revolution which followed 1956 would have destroyed entirely the prestige of any lesser man. Nonetheless his place in history is secure; he brought his immense country out of the Middle Ages into the nuclear era. His achievements were considerable. But now in 1978 his fatal mistakes are being frankly assessed by the very people who once regarded him as a well-nigh infallible god. *Sic transit gloria mundi.*

CHAPTER IV

Two Revolutions

China's autocratic tradition

Western style democracy is completely alien to Chinese tradition and ways of thinking. In so far as Christian missionaries desired to see a system of democratic government introduced into China together with the acceptance of Christianity they showed a culpable ignorance of a civilisation which had developed over the centuries in almost total geographical isolation from the rest of the world. China's progress in education, government, religious concepts and the arts owed nothing to outside influences, Greek or otherwise, as was the case in the West.

China has always been an autocracy, with the emperor, the "son of heaven", being both a ruler and a priest. "Divine monarchy," writes C. P. Fitzgerald, "thus became at an early period the set pattern of Chinese government." Confucius, a court official in one of the feudal states comprising the loose federation of the Chou dynasty, believed that man was born good and that there is a moral order to which rulers must conform. In due course the Confucian classical writings which advocated high moral standards of conduct became the text-books for examination for entry into the civil service. For centuries scholar mandarins, who were expected to be exponents of the "princely man", governed China. A dynasty survived as long as it conformed to these standards and when it ceased to do so "the Mandate of Heaven" was withdrawn and the dynasty fell.

Scholars and peasants

C. P. Fitzgerald has argued the case well that no rebellion has ever been successful in China without the support of both the scholars and the peasants. Agriculture, after all, has always been the fundamental occupation of the Chinese people and it was for centuries very successful. The Chinese are still the most efficient farmers in the world. They have to be in order to maintain a fast-growing population. The need has increased, especially in the last hundred years when the population has more than doubled. This accelerating population growth is China's greatest problem, but in the nineteenth century the scholar-politicians could find no answer to the imbalance of population and food supply. It was no longer enough to live in a past philosophical Utopia which stressed harmony and balance in human society while hunger and starvation stared the country in the face. Should China, therefore, turn her back on her ancient culture and be re-shaped on a Western pattern as some early revolutionaries maintained? Should China join the world's industrialised democracies in order to become strong enough to resist the threat posed by the world's great powers? This was China's dilemma.

Human rights

The "democracy" of Greece and Rome was really an autocracy. The idea of democratic freedom only arose in Europe as a result of its many wars to win independence from foreign oppression. Human rights are now an issue fundamental to Western democratic thinking, but they are less so to Asian thought. China, at least, has never had to fight for her political freedom from foreign powers. Moreover, the idea of the rights of the individual have been submerged by the Confucian emphasis on the individual's place in the family and the clan; the rights of the clan took precedence over a person's individual rights. So the soil of China was not well-suited to the seeds of Western democracy. "There is no place for freedom as the West understood it, no place for salvation as the Christian understands it and no place for individualism as the liberal would have it." [1]

[1] *The Birth of Communist China*, by C. P. Fitzgerald, p. 42.

Failure of the first revolution

Largely for these reasons the first revolution failed. The Republic which was established in 1912 was destined to end, not in democracy, but in chaos. The elected Parliament proved to be a travesty of democracy. But the brief and abortive attempt by the President, Yuan Shih-k'ai, to restore the Empire was no remedy. During the first World War a weak China was in no position to resist Japan's outrageous "Twenty-One Demands" made in 1915. These demands aroused the Chinese people to anger and alarm. But the Peking Government lacked authority and the Republic became the victim of avaricious rival warring generals. Inevitably it was the peasants who suffered from the oppression both of the lawless soldiery and of the rapacious landlords, without any protection from the law. Armies pillaged and robbed and everywhere banditry ruled. Lawlessness prevailed. Rural reconstruction under such circumstances was an impossibility. The lot of the peasants steadily deteriorated as flood and famine also took their heavy toll. Scholars and peasants alike were in despair. It was not that democracy had been tried and found wanting; it had never (like Christianity) been tried. In desperation Dr. Sun Yet-san in 1921 set up a new republican party in Canton and repudiated the powerless government in Peking.

The appearance of Communism

The first World War and the Treaty of Versailles, which rewarded Japan with territory and privileges in a sovereign China and gave a cold shoulder to China herself, completely undermined the prestige of the West in Chinese eyes. China began to blame all her troubles on foreign aggression and designs on her sovereignty. These were available scapegoats for her own tragic failure. On 4th May 1919 pent up nationalist feelings burst out in student parades protesting against China's shabby treatment at the Peace Conference in Versailles. The Chinese rightly felt that China had been betrayed and was now greatly endangered. The young Mao Tse-tung was one of those caught up in the nationalistic fervour. Meanwhile, one of the first international gestures of the new revolutionary government in the Soviet Union was to extend a hand of friendship to China, sore at her treatment by the other Western powers. Russia voluntarily surrendered the extra-territorial rights which had been enjoyed by all foreigners since 1842 and also offered to give up her special privileges in Manchuria. Nothing could have pleased China's intellectuals more or been better calculated to create sympathy for Communism than this gesture. The Western powers, on the other hand, erred again in failing to recognise the new would-be democratic regime in Canton. These are among the reasons why China eventually turned to Communism.

The Renaissance Movement

But first two distinguished scholars, Dr. Hu Shih, a disciple of John Dewey, and Ch'en T'u-hsiu, once fellow-students at Peking University, initiated a literary revolution which came to be known as the Renaissance Movement. It started in Peking University in 1919 and was primarily concerned to get away from the classical tradition in literature and to popularise the colloquial dialect as a medium for spreading modern ideas more widely. It was nothing less than a literary and intellectual revolution. Its watchwords were "science" and "democracy". The publication of the Bible in the vernacular was widely hailed as a fine example of the popular trend and made this book more widely acceptable to millions of readers. But the Renaissance Movement soon became involved in a conflict of political theory. Dr. Hu Shih was a humanist, but not a Marxist, and later withdrew to the United States to become a leading anti-Communist intellectual. Ch'en T'u-hsiu on the contrary was won over by the Third International and elected the first leader of the Chinese Communist Party. Both men envisaged a fundamental reconstruction of society. Dr. Hu Shih listed poverty, disease, ignorance, corruption and destitution as the five great evils of China, not capitalism and imperialism as the Nationalists would have it. A new era in student movements began; the students switched their concern from earlier burning issues to that of the fundamental reconstruction of society. To give them credit the Peking, and later the Nanking government, did initiate schemes for rural reconstruction, the improvement of the educational system (illiteracy was still ninety per cent) and the upgrading of the status of women. Farmers' unions and mutual aid groups certainly existed. At least ten thousand co-operatives of every kind functioned. The National Association for Mass Education and a Women's Rights League both did what they could. The Thousand Character Mass Education Movement, centred on Tinghsien in Hopei, was started by Dr. James Yen, a prominent Christian. The movement was based on a kind of basic Chinese—a thousand selected characters in which a wide variety of books was produced. The movement was highly promising and educational authorities took it up. But, in the end, it was the Communists who profited from it most, for it facilitated their campaigns against illiteracy both in their armies and among the peasants. The effects were revolutionary, because mass education makes mass indoctrination that much easier.

A spiritual vacuum

As the more radical Marxist ideas gradually became better known, through skilful propaganda and through books (often banned by the Nationalist Government), the younger generation turned from Dr. Hu Shih's "Sickle Moon Society" to the rising Red Star of Communism as the only viable alternative to the feeble one-party Republican Government in Peking. Military oppression, exorbitant taxation and the grinding poverty of the masses were fertile soil for the seeds of Communist ideas and ideals. Dr. Stanley Jones, one of several foreign evangelists who visited China about this time, commented: "The soil of educated China is a great moral and spiritual vacuum." Many Christians were at that time engaged in creative social thinking and were involved in rural rehabilitation experiments, rural education schemes and in relief work of every kind. But the Christian Church had too few leaders to meet the current crisis and to present any strong challenge to the existing social system.

A misapprehension

Dr. Jonathan Chao is surely mistaken when he writes, "Missionaries sought to implement social reforms, but their isolated and spotty efforts hardly made a dent on the bastions of tradition and power." This reveals a misunderstanding as to the true function of foreign missionaries. Missions never sought any such thing. Social reform was never their responsibility. Nor was it the responsibility of the Chinese Church. Only a government with powers to pass appropriate legislation can effect social reforms. All the Church and missions could do was to enunciate Christian principles of justice and compassion and, on a very small scale, to provide examples of what the government ought to be doing on a nation-wide scale. This they did to the limit of their resources —in education, medicine and welfare. The Christian universities and the Peking Union Medical College, for instance, set high standards of excellence for the nation in the education of students and the training of doctors.

Nationalism and the Kuomintang

In Canton the Kuomintang re-organised itself on the lines of the Russian Communist Party and began to talk of a Party dictatorship rather than a democratic republic. The Kuomintang thus turned away from democracy and directed the attention of the nation to foreign imperialism and the abolition of the "unequal treaties", believing that these were the prime cause of China's troubles. It was to nationalism and the recovery of national sovereignty that the Kuomintang made its appeal. Social revolution, land reform and the rule of law were now secondary issues. Communist Party members were permitted to join the Nationalist Party in a strange alliance. Chiang Kai-shek and Chou En-lai became close colleagues. Mao Tse-tung was made responsible for propaganda and mass organisation. Chance events then played into the hands of the Nationalists. On 30th May 1925 a British police officer ordered his men to fire on a student demonstration in the International Settlement in Shanghai and a student was killed. The reaction throughout the nation was violent. Anti-foreign feeling reached boiling point. Missionaries hurriedly left the interior. Boycotts of foreign firms and of goods from Hong Kong caused serious commercial losses. Violent anti-foreign sentiments were only matched by the vicious expressions of anti-Christian hatred. The incident was the spark which touched off the powder keg of Communist revolution and ensured its ultimate success.

The moment seemed to the men in Canton ripe for unifying the nation. The Northern Expedition of the revolutionary armies set out from Canton in 1926 under the command of General Chiang Kai-shek. Their march to the Yangtze carried all before it and by the summer they had taken the three Wuhan cities (including Hankow) and were threatening Nanking. Social revolution followed the victorious progress of the armies. Mao Tse-tung had done his work well in preparing the peasantry to rise up against the landlords. But it soon became clear to Chiang Kai-shek that, as the Communists made their bid for power, his leadership of the Kuomintang and of the Nationalist movement were both alike in jeopardy.

Parting of the ways

At the beginning of 1927 a Nationalist Government was established in Wuhan and hopes were high that all eighteen of China's provinces would be brought under the control of that government and that the warlord era would be brought to an end. But the violent anti-foreign propaganda which accompanied these military successes alarmed the Western powers. They hurriedly sent an expeditionary force to protect the International Settlement in Shanghai and ordered warships to sail up the River Yangtze to protect foreign nationals in the river ports. Undeterred, the Communists in Hankow incited a mob to overrun the British concession and to plunder the homes of foreign residents. Then, on 24th March, left-wing forces, determined to embarrass the Kuomintang and the Government and so bring about an open breach between its left and right wings, attacked and captured Nanking, where they indulged in indiscriminate killing of foreigners. Deaths included that of Dr. Williams, the greatly respected vice-president of the University. Even before these events a horrible massacre by left-wing elements in Canton had provoked an even more violent counteraction. Chiang Kai-shek knew he was in a very dangerous situation and must take drastic action. He therefore postponed any onward drive to Peking and diverted his forces

instead to Shanghai. There the massacre of workers precipitated the final breach with the Communists. At the same time
a part of the Fourth Army under Chu Teh mutinied in Nanchang and joined the Communists. This unit formed the
nucleus of the Red Army which by the early 1930s numbered
more than 60,000 men. The breach between the Nationalists
and the Communists was now complete. In 1928 the united
Nationalist armies finally drove north to Peking and expelled
Chang Tso-lin, the last of the warlords and on 4th October
transferred the central government of China to Nanking. The
Wuhan government expelled its left-wing members and the
two Nationalist governments were then re-united. A long,
bitter and ruinous war was about to begin. The tragic failure
of the first revolution had made a second revolution—this
time a Communist one—inevitable.

Critical Year for Christianity

1927 was a critical year for Christianity in China. The
rising tide of nationalism and the growing power and influence of Communism were accompanied by a violent
antagonism to religion. While missionaries were refugeeing
at the coast in the safety of the foreign concessions, their
stations in the interior were being looted and damaged. Some
three thousand missionaries left China never to return. It
seemed to many like the end of the road for missionary work
in China. Chinese Christians suffered intensely and were
generally reviled as the "running dogs of the imperialists".
The missionaries took stock of the situation, knowing that
things would never be the same again. They saw clearly that,
if the Church was to survive in the difficult years ahead, it
must become independent of the missionary societies and
attain a genuine autonomy. For two years they waited,
engaging in prayer for the Church and the nation in its
tragic divisions. Most missionaries were pro-government in
their sympathies and instinctively against the Communists
who were so opposed to Christianity. They generally referred
to Communist military units as "bandits". Few of them
thought very deeply about the great social and economic
issues which were at stake or related Divine justice to the
prevailing conditions in the country.

Dark days for the Kuomintang

As for the Kuomintang, it seemed to have no clear revolutionary aims, no unity of purpose and no ideology to cement the new society. Chiang Kai-shek's sole aim now seemed to be the destruction of the Communist enemy. Actually, his best way to oppose the Communist revolution would have been to carry out a policy of genuine land reform, which he did later in Taiwan. If he had then reduced rents, dealt with the unscrupulous landlords, provided loans for the peasants and redistributed the land—measures all of which were feasible—he might possibly have hindered the spread of Communism. Nationalism and the banner of anti-imperialism alone provided no solution for China's problems. And, as time went on, corruption in the government, at all levels, became rife, while the war against the Communists dragged on without success. The Kuomintang failed both to stabilize society and to win mass support. The phase of unity between peasant and scholar was over. The peasants rallied to the Communists while the scholars, believing that the Kuomintang stood for national independence rather than subservience to Russia, rallied around the new Nationalist regime in Nanking.

Conversion of Chiang Kai-shek

Then an extraordinary event, unprecedented in Chinese history, astonished the world. On 22nd October 1930, Generalissimo Chiang Kai-shek was publicly baptised on his confession of faith as a Christian. This was a very bold act at such a crisis in China's fortunes. Christianity was still, in the eyes of most Chinese, not least the scholars, a despised "foreign" religion and, in the eyes of the Communists, mere superstition. Where political motives and religious conviction begin and end is hard to determine, but Chiang Kai-shek never ceased to practise his Christian faith during the rest of his long life. His understanding of the Christian faith may at first have been very inadequate, but his funeral in 1976 was an outstanding testimony to his firm Christian convictions and it made a tremendous impact on the whole of Taiwan.

Further catastrophes

In 1931 the political and economic stress in China reached an appalling magnitude. It was a crisis unprecedented since the Revolution. Half-a-dozen wars raged in North China, while China had to look on helplessly as the Japanese carried out a lightning occupation of Manchuria, the three provinces so vital to China's existence for their oil reserves and industry. A Japanese attack on Shanghai followed in September. A catastrophic flooding of the River Yangtze affected fifty million people. A Muslim revolt and a famine in the north-west left millions dead. And, to crown it all, the Nationalist forces failed again to defeat the Red armies in Kiangsi and Hunan; in fact the Communists were overflowing into neighbouring provinces. Wherever they went hundreds of civilians died, Christians among them, as victims of the Red terror.

Mao's peasant revolution

Unlike the Nationalists, the Communists had a clear aim and their operations were well co-ordinated. Gradually, the arguments of Mao Tse-tung prevailed against the orthodox Marxist policies of the left wing of the Communist Party. Russian advice was spurned as well as that of the Russian-trained Chairman of the Communist Party, Li Li-san. Mao Tse-tung insisted on concentrating on the peasant masses rather than the small industrial proletariat in the cities. For this "error" he was expelled from the Central Committee and, it may be, even from the Communist Party itself. But Mao remained undeterred. By hunting and killing the landlords, often with great cruelty, by putting Kuomintang officials to death and by treating all opponents with great severity Mao sought to demonstrate that the Communists were the real friends of the peasants. In so doing, however, he antagonised the educated classes, while the peasants accepted his leadership as for centuries their predecessors had accepted the authority of the emperors.

The success of the Communist movement was due to the appalling corruption of the gentry and absentee landlords, the illegal taxation and the cruel exploitation of the peasants.

The Nationalist army generals and officers were as corrupt as any. On the other hand, the violent excesses perpetrated by the Communists alienated many early sympathisers, while Christians at least believed that there must be a better way of changing society. Generalissimo Chiang himself acknowledged the gravity of the situation and provided his own diagnosis of China's ills: "years of misgovernment in many provinces, matched only by a serious moral deterioration. The consequence was that the Nationalist Revolution which had been intended to give freedom and uplift to the masses had provided conditions under which," Chiang said, "life and property were far less secure than under the old regime." But for the insane butchery of multitudes of civilians the Communists would have swept all before them. Even as it was the peasants regarded them as deliverers from the tyranny of the warlords.

Nationalist military successes

In 1934 Chiang Kai-shek launched a "final extermination campaign" against the Communists who had been effectively blockaded in their strongholds in South China. The Communist leadership recognised that the military odds were now heavily against them, so the Central Committee ordered a full-scale withdrawal to North China, ostensibly to form an anti-Japanese vanguard to fight the Japanese. The Long March followed. The remnant of the large force that set out from Kiangsi finally reached Yenan in North Shensi and set up a new base in the loess hills of that region. In the first fifteen years of its existence, the Chinese Communist Party again and again almost destroyed itself by internal dissensions. Now, in Yenan, a new era was about to begin.

New Life Movement

For the Nationalists the situation remained desperate. Chiang Kai-shek had to act and act he did. He issued an order for all his military officers to be retrained, and gave strict instructions to his forces that the welfare of the people was to be their main concern. Simultaneously, in 1935, he launched the New Life Movement, the aim of which was to

restore China's traditional Confucian moral standards.
General and Mme. Chiang personally met a number of missionary groups to invite their co-operation in promoting the
movement. The Christian Church took the opportunity to
emphasise that real "new life" can be found only in Christ.
In fact, all over China, in the early thirties, the Church was
experiencing the purifying and renewing fires of revival and
with it an unprecedented growth in membership. Temporarily, at least, the people of China seemed to gain fresh hope.
Furthermore, government attempts to improve the economic
conditions of the people were not entirely fruitless. A new
spirit was abroad.

Ultimatum to Chiang

Late in the year 1936 Chiang Kai-shek planned to launch a
drive against the new Communist base in Yenan with a view
to exterminating it. Instead, he found himself a victim of
kidnapping in Sian and was forced to bargain for his life. In
exchange for a promise from Chiang to abandon the anti-
Communist war in order to fight against the common enemy
Japan, the Communists undertook to suspend land confisca-
tion and distribution and agreed to the Red Army becoming
the Eighth Route Army under the supreme command of
Chiang Kai-shek. The pact marked a turning point in the
Communist fortunes. From his now legendary base in
Yenan, Mao Tse-tung began to issue patriotic appeals to the
masses who flocked to his standard by the tens of thousands.
The educated classes in particular were impressed by the
character and charisma of Mao Tse-tung. The Revolutionary
University in Yenan became a Mecca for students from all
over China. Now, again, peasants and scholars were united
in their support of the Communists. The conditions were
therefore once more right for success.

War with Japan and aftermath

Mao anticipated that a war with Japan would probably
mean defeat for the regular Nationalist forces, while his own
guerilla troops would survive. In the event, the Nationalist

armies won world esteem for their heroic battles against the Japanese in defence of Shanghai and in Shantung, but eventually they were inexorably driven back to West China, leaving the Communist partisan armies to bear the brunt of the fighting in the Japanese-occupied areas. By the end of World War Two the Communist armies numbered 900,000 men. The longer the war continued the firmer became the Communist control of the "occupied" areas. Dissension between Chungking and Yenan grew and finally military cooperation broke down completely. When the war ended the Communists were in control of most of North China, an area with a population of ninety million people. They were the true liberators from the Japanese enemy of the millions of Chinese north of the Yangtze River.

After the war, both American efforts to achieve a truce between the Nationalists and the Communists and internal efforts by Chinese generals to effect an agreement on a coalition government were all blocked by Chiang Kai-shek. So the civil war was resumed. The Soviet leaders were dubious about the real strength and potentiality of the Chinese Communists and consequently gave them little material support. Indeed, they added their voice to the advice that the Communists should co-operate with the Nationalist Government. But the well-trained, well-disciplined and seasoned Communist armies, following major military victories in Manchuria, captured Peking in 1948, Nanking and Shanghai in the same year and were in complete control of the whole of China by 1949. Chiang Kai-shek's American-equipped but demoralised armies were routed and the Nationalist Government took refuge in Taiwan.

Communist victory

Mao Tse-tung's policies had triumphed. On 1st October 1949 he mounted the giant rostrum erected on Tien An Men or the Gate of Heavenly Peace in Peking and proclaimed the inauguration of the People's Republic of China. "The Chinese people have stood up!" he declared. Neither the Nationalists nor the Communists offered to the Chinese people democracy in the Western understanding of that word. Communism is totalitarian, but so was the old Empire and so was the first Nationalist Revolution. And like the Empire, Communism is absolute, hierarchic and doctrinally uncompromising. It is as if a new order has arisen to restore the Chinese Empire in the form of the People's Republic.

CHAPTER V

Terror and Heroism

Civil war

Although there were local wars on his hands in six or seven provinces, in 1930 Chiang Kai-shek decided to concentrate on defeating the Communist armies in Central China. In all, he conducted five "extermination campaigns", the first four of which failed. Between the rival armies which settled like locusts on the countryside, the ordinary people of China suffered intensely. From their base in Chingkangshan in the Losiao mountains on the Hunan–Kiangsi border, the better paid, better organised, more enthusiastic and determined forces under Ho Lung, Chu Teh, Hsiao K'eh, P'eng Teh-huai and Yeh Ting fought agains the 300,000 better equipped Nationalist forces. Kiangsi, once the quietest of provinces, became a battlefield between the opposing Red and White Terror. City after city fell to the Communists and Mao Tse-tung set up the first Chinese Soviet there.

A directive from Party Headquarters to the Communists in Hunan and Hupeh in early December 1927 ordered the killing off of as many "bad gentry", reactionaries and big landowners as possible. As a result 150,000 civilians are estimated to have been killed. Half a million fled and 100,000 homes were put to the flames. Twenty to thirty Chinese Christian leaders were killed and others lost all their possessions. Church buildings were occupied by soldiers and great damage caused. For the Christian Church it was a fearful ordeal—a foretaste of suffering to come for the whole Chinese Church.

Missionary martyrs

Communists were also instructed to mobilise the masses to "attack the foreigners". The Fifth Army troops murdered three Finnish missionaries in February 1929, the Misses Cajander, Ingman and Hedengren, as they were travelling on the Kan River. Surely not "imperialists"! In March Yuanchow in West Kiangsi fell into the hands of General P'eng Teh-huai. Mr. and Mrs. Porteous, the China Inland Mission Superintendent in the province, and Miss Gemmel had no time to escape. They were captured and accused of being capitalists, imperialists, propagandists for foreign culture, of denationalising the Chinese Christians and of spreading superstition. The ladies were released after eleven days, but Mr. Porteous was held while Christian go-betweens tried to obtain his release without paying the huge ransom sum demanded. These men ran tremendous risks and were complimented by the Communist general for the devotion and courage they showed. "There must be something in this Christian religion!" he said. Finally, in response to a petition presented by Pastor Eo-yang and other Christians and a substantial gift of urgently needed medicines, Porteous was released on 26th June. A small sum of ransom money sacrificially raised by the Chinese Christians was returned to them by the Communist General. Other Chinese prisoners were less fortunate. They were executed.

Meanwhile in Kweichow Communist units held the C.I.M. superintendent captive for a while and another C.I.M. missionary was killed. In Honan in North China, five C.I.M. missionaries were held by "brigands" and then released. All missionaries were declared to be agents of imperialism and so enemies of China deserving of execution.

As large Red forces under Ho Lung operated in Kiangsi, many missionaries had near escapes. Everywhere Chinese Christians and missionaries faced danger, perplexity and distress. In the eighteen months after 1st January 1930 many missionaries were held for ransom and seven Roman Catholic missionaries, and one Protestant, were killed. At the end of July 1930 the Red armies captured and sacked Changsha, the Hunan capital. Church buildings were either destroyed or suffered severe damage. Ferguson of the C.I.M. was engaged in famine relief work and was carrying relief funds. He was captured and the money confiscated. The Communists marched him from place to place and put him on show in village after village, though he often took the opportunity to preach to the villagers. In spite of the earnest pleas of the Chinese people he was finally executed.

In 1932 the Nationalist 52nd and 59th divisions were wiped out and many government soldiers defected to the Communists. The carnage was terrible. The central government was fighting an uneven war. In 1932–33 sixty counties of Kiangsi were under Communist control and the first Chinese Soviet there issued its own currency and postage stamps. Large land holdings were confiscated from the landlords and land reform was introduced. Landlords, rich peasants and wealthy merchants were "liquidated"—sometimes as many as five hundred in a single night. All opposition and any signs of rebellion among Red troops were ruthlessly crushed.

Decision to retreat

Then in 1934 Chiang Kai-shek launched his "final extermination campaign". The Communist leadership recognised that their situation was now desperate. The economic blockade was at last crippling the Red armies. So in July 1934 the Central Committee of the Politburo decided on a strategic retreat from encirclement. When the crucial decision was reached Mao Tse-tung had been expelled from the Central Committee, was probably under house arrest and was also gravely ill with malaria. His influence in the decision-making process at the time was nil.

This withdrawal or retreat, known as the Long March, is a high point in Chinese mythology. It belongs as surely to the history of Chinese Communism as the Exodus does to the history of the Jewish people. To have taken part in it is still, forty-five years later, a strong qualification for leadership in the Party and in the Government. But, as in the case of the Exodus and the wandering in the wilderness, there are two aspects of the Long March—one of great heroism and bravery, the other of appalling suffering endured and inflicted. Large areas of the west and north-west were ravaged by the Red armies. The Fourth Front Army based in Szech-

wan decimated the civilian population of Pachow in a savage
slaughter and laid waste the villages. The scars of burned-
out villages remained for many years afterwards. In 1934 the
First Front Army was driven out of Kiangsi into South
Anhwei. The C.I.M. authorities judged it safe therefore for
John and Betty Stam to proceed to their appointment at
Tsingteh where they were to assist the church and its out-
station at Miaoshan. John and Betty were married in October
1933 and their daughter Priscilla was born the following
September. No sooner had they settled in at Tsingteh than a
Red unit of 2,000 men suddenly attacked the city, inflicting
heavy casualties. They picked up the Stams and their baby
girl and took them on to Miaoshan. When an unknown
farmer pleaded for the child the reply was, "All right, your
life for hers!" and the man was promptly struck dead with a
sword. Early the next morning, the Stams were bound and
led up a small hill as green as Calvary. Calmly, amid the
ridicule of the soldiers and bystanders, they knelt side by
side and were beheaded. A Christian doctor who pleaded for
their lives died with them. The date was 6th December 1934.
Miraculously, baby Priscilla was overlooked, rescued,
lovingly cared for by Chinese Christians and eventually taken
to safety.

"Tools of imperialism"

In early August 1934, the Sixth Red Army under General
Hsiao K'eh began the official retreat. He had orders to join
General Ho Lung's army at his base on the Hunan–Kweichow border. The whole Communist community of soldiers
and civilians under the supreme command of General Chu
Teh and Otto Braun, his German military adviser, numbered
100,000 persons. Of these, 85,000 were soldiers and 15,000
Party and Government cadres. Uncertainty prevailed as to
their final destination. The first 300 miles of their march were
disastrous. After a week-long battle, the force finally succeeded in crossing the Hsiang River in northern Kwangsi
under heavy fire. But the loss of half the army strength (over
40,000 men) was a terrible price to pay. Disagreement ensued
as to the best direction in which to move. Mao Tse-tung
finally gained support for his plan to move into Kweichow

where the opposition was likely to be weaker, rather than to face another major battle in Hunan.

On October 1st Hsiao K'eh unexpectedly arrived at the city in Kweichow where Mr. and Mrs. Bosshardt, Mr. and Mrs. Hayman, their two small children and Miss Emblen, all of the C.I.M., happened to be together after a conference. The usual accusations of being "spies for an imperialist government" etc. were made and the general ordered his prisoners to write letters to various people demanding a ransom price of $100,000 for each person, or $700,000 in all. The women and children were soon released because they were too much of a liability for an army on the march. But Bosshardt and Hayman were ordered to go along with the army. Looting, the slaughter of civilians and the torture of prisoners went on incessantly in one town after another. The two men, while frequently threatened with death themselves, were often the horrified eye-witnesses of the deaths of their fellow-prisoners and many terrible deeds. Teen-aged youngsters became bloodthirsty fiends. A seventeen-year-old was nicknamed "the executioner" because of his expertise in the use of his sword. Hsiao K'eh at last made contact with Ho Lung's Second Front Army and handed over his prisoners who followed their new captors into Hupeh. The army kept moving from place to place under constant bombing from Nationalist planes.

Hermann Becker, a German C.I.M. missionary, was known to Ho Lung personally. Ho Lung had received help and kindness from him in the past. Becker now took up the negotiations for the two captives' release. On 17th December they tried to escape but were betrayed, recaptured and cruelly beaten as a punishment. At other times they also experienced some compassion from their captors. At last, Becker's negotiations succeeded in obtaining the release of one man—Hayman only, after 413 days of captivity. Bosshardt was left alone. His last words to Hayman were, "Pray that I may recklessly preach Christ." From Hupeh the Second Front Army moved into Hunan with their foreign hostage and crossed the Yuan River back into Kweichow where Bosshardt was on familiar ground. The army hurried west again into Yunnan under constant Nationalist bombing. Not far from Kunming, the Yunnan capital, the army halted.

The "judge" invited Bosshardt to dine with him, showing every courtesy to his guest. He told him that because he was a Swiss national and therefore not an imperialist he was to be released. The release took place on Easter Monday, 14th April 1936, after eighteen months of captivity.[1]

Mao's authority recognised

As the year 1934 ended, the First Front Army crossed the Wu River in Central Kweichow following a remarkable action. A few picked men first crossed the broad stream on rafts under heavy fire and scaled a sheer rock cliff to capture the Nationalist strongpoint guarding the ferry. Then, by a ruse involving the use of captured KMT uniforms, they took the city of Tsunyi virtually without a shot being fired. In January 1935, the Politburo held the celebrated Tsunyi Conference which at last placed Mao Tse-tung firmly in control of the Chinese Communist Party. Henceforth the real power belonged to him.

Deeds of daring

The next possible step was for both armies to make for the northern parts of Szechwan and to join forces with the Fourth Front Army there. But strong Nationalist armies barred the way. So Mao began a "sinuous motion" around northern Kweichow and won a major battle against local troops at Loushan Pass. This victory inspired Mao to write another poem—

> Keen is the west wind;
> In the endless void the wild geese cry at the frosty
>   morning moon,
> The frosty morning moon.
> The clatter of horses' hoofs rings sharp,
> And the bugle's note is muted.
> They say that the strong pass is iron hard,
> And yet this very day with a mighty step we shall
>   cross its summit,

[1] Bosshardt has written in detail some of his experiences under the title of *The Restraining Hand* (Hodder & Stoughton).

We shall cross its summit!
The hills are blue like the sea
And the dying sun like blood.

Assessing the strength of the opposition, Mao decided not
to proceed but to recross the Wu River at Tsunyi and to
make a detour through Yunnan and Sikang provinces into
western Szechwan. He made a feint at Kweiyang, the Kweichow capital where Chiang Kai-shek had his Headquarters
and then suddenly led his armies west straight across Yunnan. Feinting again against Kunming, the Yunnan capital to
their south, the Red armies marched northwards towards the
River of Golden Sands (Chinsha), a tributary of the Yangtze
which marks the border between Yunnan and Szechwan.
Once more a few men crossed the turbulent stream in small
boats disguised as KMT scouts, policemen and tax-collectors
to occupy key points in the village which lay at the ferry
crossing. Then, in the course of nine days, the entire army
was ferried safely over. Chiang Kai-shek thought the Red
Army was playing into his hands in a very difficult terrain
and flew to Chungking to direct operations.

The next obstacle was the Tatu River, a roaring torrent
flowing through deep gorges. Its crossing is a part of Red
legend. It began, like the Wu River crossing, with a surprise
attack on a small force guarding the ferry. A small boat was
captured and this enabled an assault to be made by eighteen
picked men on an enemy position in blockhouses at the top
of a sheer cliff. The First Division continued to cross by
boat, but because the current was too swift to permit the
building of a bridge, Mao ordered the main force to drive on
to capture the suspension bridge at Luling, 110 kilometres
away. The Red force had to march over precipitous tracks
along the sheer cliffs in constant danger of bombing, and
fighting occasional skirmishes with Nationalist units. They
finally reached the heavily fortified city of Luling on the
opposite bank. Between the two banks of the river stretched
thirteen heavy iron chains sealed into the rocks, the two
outer ones serving as handrails. The other nine originally
supported a floor of planks, now removed by the Nationalist
troops. At four a.m. on the 25th May 1935 twenty-two
volunteers carrying machine-guns, swords and hand-gren-

ades began clambering across the swinging chains followed
by another company carrying planks to rebuild the bridge.
Some of the assault party were killed but the others inched
forward and finally dashed through the flames where the end
of the bridge had been set alight. By dusk the Red Army had
defeated two KMT regiments and was in firm control of the
city.

Dissension

This was virtually the end of the actual fighting for Mao's
troops. But tremendous natural obstacles lay ahead, not to
mention arguments between the commanders. Mao wanted
to proceed to the Shensi–Kansu border area with a view to
fighting Japan. Chang Kuo-t'ao, on the other hand, proposed
withdrawing to Sikang or even Tibet to escape the Nationalist armies. This was a strong challenge to Mao's authority
and the two men parted company. Chu Teh, a Szechwanese,
chose to go with Chang and so to remain in his home province. (Later this former coolie found his way to Germany to
study at Heidelberg University!) Wherever the Red Armies
went they spread alarm and confusion because of the reputation for terror they had established for themselves.

Costly progress

Ahead of Mao lay the terrible grasslands, an area of
dangerous swamp where many of his men were sucked down
and perished. The Man tribes were also hostile and deprived
the Red armies of food and in every way opposed their progress. They were even reduced to eating their precious
horses, their leather boots and their belts. To make matters
worse the weather was bitterly cold at night and the poisonous mud produced agonising sores. In southern Kansu some
enemy opposition was encountered, but following a feint at
Tienshui Mao's army passed through Muslim territory to the
Liu Pan mountains, the last major natural barrier before
reaching Shensi. Mao again expressed his feelings in verse:

The sky is high, the clouds are pale,
We watch the wild geese flying south till they vanish:

If we reach not the Great Wall, we are no true men!
Already we have come two thousand leagues.
High on the crest of Liu Pan Mountain
Our banners idly wave in the west wind.
Today we hold the long cord in our hands;
When shall we bind fast the grey dragon?[1]

Throughout this epic retreat the Nationalist armies were
never able to guess what were the immediate objectives of
the Communists nor their ultimate destination. Nevertheless Chiang Kai-shek repeatedly announced the "utter destruction" of the "red bandits". Fighting almost every step of
the way for the first months, the Red Army and its civilians
altogether trekked six thousand miles. They crossed eighteen
major mountain ranges and twenty-four rivers and passed
through the territory of ten hostile provincial warlords. Of
the hundred thousand personnel that started out from
Kiangsi only seven to eight thousand men and women survived. In October 1935, a little more than a year after the
march began, three decimated Communist forces converged
in North Shensi.

The arrival of the Red Army in Shensi is usually considered to mark the beginning of the "Yenan Period". Actually Mao did not establish his headquarters in the loess caves
of Yenan itself until the end of 1936.

Terrorism

The story of the Long March is undeniably one of human
bravery but also one of appalling savagery. The Old Testament is also, in parts, a record of terrible atrocities and
massacres. But, as in the case of Jehu king of Israel, those
evils were the direct consequence of the horror that the vice
of Jezebel and the weak sinfulness of Ahab had brought
upon the troubled land. "A moral law was in operation then
as now—a moral law woven into history and working out
inexorably to its fulfilment. 'Those who take the sword perish
by the sword,' said our Lord in Gethsemane and men reap
what they sow. Violence always begets violence." [2] Jezebel

[1] i.e. the Japanese.
[2] Professor E. M. Blaiklock.

died because she thought (as many since have thought) that might is right and fear stronger than love. She died for an evil cause as many misguided Chinese Communists have done. Such is the tragedy of fallen man.

Heroism

An epic of military history the Long March may be. But what are we to think of the terrible suffering inflicted on a helpless population during the ten years of civil war and the desperate year-long fight for survival? Christians, along with countless numbers of their fellow-citizens, "were tortured, refusing to accept release . . . others suffered mocking and scourging, and even chains and imprisonment. They were stoned . . ." and, we may truthfully add, were buried live, dragged behind trucks by their feet until their skulls were fractured ("cracking the walnut"), thrown into stinking cess pools to drown and died a hundred other horrible deaths— "of whom the world was not worthy . . ." [1] So the heroism was certainly not confined to the Communists. Many Chinese Christians and some missionaries "loved not their lives unto the death". And surely theirs was a far greater and more praiseworthy cause for which to make the supreme sacrifice. "These are they who came out of great tribulation; they have washed their robes and made them white in the blood of the Lamb. Therefore are they before the throne of God . . ." And the blood of the martyrs is the seed of the Church.

[1] Hebrews 11. 35–38.

CHAPTER VI

China's Theory and Practice of Government

The masses deified

In Peking's Tien An Men Square a prominent slogan defines Mao Tse-tung's basic concept of democracy: "People and people alone are the motive force in world history." The famous fable of the Foolish Old Man who removed two mountains, so popularised by Mao in the Little Red Book, tells how "God" came to the aid of a man and his son who were attempting the impossible task of digging away the mountains barrow-load by barrow-load. "God" for Mao meant the Chinese masses whose wisdom and power alone could remove the mountains of imperialism and feudalism. The "people" is a collective god. Mao himself never believed in his own divinity and, once the need for a personality cult during the Cultural Revolution was over, he deliberately played down the cult of Mao worship. Mao always regarded the masses of the Chinese people, workers and peasants, as the infallible source of all wisdom and skill. They alone are sacred and sovereign. They can do no wrong. The people are the source of all power and authority. The masses are the creators of history. One's attitude towards the masses is the basic criterion for distinguishing Marxists from anti-Marxists. This belief lay behind Mao's constant insistence on "self-reliance" and the need to respect the initiative of the masses. In the masses, Mao firmly believed, resided the potential wisdom and strength to enable China to cope on her own without external assistance. This principle, known as "the mass line", Mao sought to apply at every level. In so doing he was departing from the Soviet model.

Mao recognised long before his more orthodox colleagues the revolutionary potential of the rural masses or the peasants who form eighty per cent of "the people"; but it meant a long, hard struggle to bring his colleagues around to share his convictions. Mao's theory of the Chinese revolution was a new development of Marxism–Leninism and has proved to be important for the Communist revolution in the Third World where rural populations predominate.

The "New Democracy"

The "New Democracy" united "peasants, workers, petty capitalists and national capitalists" under the leadership of the Communist Party. It was a development of Marxism–Leninism which seemed to offer all these classes a way out. Not "Workers of the world unite!" but "Peasants, workers, petty and national capitalists of China unite!" It was an admission that many features of capitalism must survive for a time. The essence of the doctrine was that in China and other semi-colonial countries sudden revolution in the Russian manner is neither possible nor desirable. The Chinese national flag with its four smaller stars and one large one against the red background symbolises the new and original association.

This "democracy"—not very democratic by Western standards—is a grass-roots democracy in which every citizen is drawn into debate about his own immediate concerns, state concerns and international concerns. Their meetings which are held regularly in every unit of society—the street, the office, the school, the hospital, the factory etc.—are skilfully guided by the local cadres, but free expression of opinion, within limits, is encouraged. Ultimately, according to theory, the Government at every level only acts in response to the will of the people. The people themselves are "God" and nothing against the will of the people can ultimately triumph.

Back in 1950, early in the Communist occupation, American films were still attracting large audiences in Shanghai cinemas. It would have been a simple matter to ban their import by decree. But that would not have been the "democratic" way of doing things. No! meetings were encouraged all over the city at street level at which people were encouraged to speak out as to the bad effects on them of the emphasis on sex, violence and luxurious living portrayed in the films. Area meetings followed and finally a huge mass rally was held at which vehement denunciations of American films were made by selected spokesmen. A resolution was duly passed by the ordinary people of Shanghai requesting the Government to prohibit the import of American films in future. Then and only then did the Government, "in response to the will of the people", place a ban on all American films. That is how China's "people's democracy" works — carefully stage-managed and yet with the semblance of personal participation in the processes of government. Chinese democracy is a "guided democracy". There can be no stepping outside the guide-lines. China's "democracy" is, in fact, totalitarian.

Why did missionaries leave China? Not because the Chinese Government ordered them out. No such order was ever given. But the churches, through their representatives and under Government direction, drew up a "Christian Manifesto" condemning imperialism and the alleged use of the churches made by the imperialists. When the Manifesto was finally published in the Chinese press the local cadres called on the local church leaders to discover their reaction; those leaders were at once under severe pressure. Soon they were putting it to the missionaries, reluctantly, in most cases, that their continued presence was no longer a help but an embarrassment. Thus it was not long before the missionary societies took the inevitable step of advising the withdrawal of their members from China — a "voluntary withdrawal"! This is another example of the way in which a carefully manipulated "people's democracy" works.

Class warfare

"The people", however, are not *all* the people. The "people" includes those of the four classes mentioned. There are also others who are "enemies of the people" or "class enemies" — landlords, bureaucratic capitalists, reactionary supporters of the Kuomintang and even Christians. These play the role of the Devil in the new theology. "The people" are represented by the Communist Party just as the Emperor used to be the agent of "Heaven" to rule the earth. The Communist Party is every bit as autocratic in its rule as the emperors used to be, although the spirit in which the Party leads is very different. Most Communist leaders appear to be genuinely concerned about the well-being of the ordinary people. The historian C. P. Fitzgerald writes: "The religion of the Communists is not all one-sided; with belief goes performance and the nature of the Communist good works is as closely related to the central doctrine of their faith as Christian charity is to the Sermon on the Mount ... To help the people is more than an act of kindness; it is almost a religious rite ... This is a religion not of personal salvation but of collective improvement." [1] And the Communists, many of whom were brought up in the Confucian tradition, derive their ethical principles from that source.

Democratic centralism

But who really leads—the People or the Party? In 1975 the revised Constitution no longer described the Chinese People's Republic as "a people's democratic state" but as "a socialist state of proletarian dictatorship". "Democratic centralism" is a combination of mass democracy or the "mass line" and central control—"from the masses to the masses in an endless spiral". First be a student of the masses, then become their leader. Vice-chairman Yeh states: "Our Party is organised on the principle of democratic centralism which means centralism on the basis of democracy and democracy under centralised guidance ... a combination of collective leadership with individual responsibility." Mass ideas must be assessed by the brains at the centre where policies are finally determined and the proper course of action crystallised. Then those policies go back to the masses to be tried out. This may be some safeguard against bureaucracy, but a dichotomy between the "mass line" and "centralism" is always present. The emphasis periodically swings from more centralism to more regionalism—i.e. decisions made, not at the centre, but nearer the people. In fact power in China is very concentrated in the Politburo. In his speech of 27th February 1957 relating to the Hungarian uprising

[1] *The Birth of Communist China*, by C. P. Fitzgerald, p. 149.

Mao said: "Within the ranks of the people, we cannot do without freedom, nor can we do without discipline; we cannot do without democracy, nor can we do without centralism . . . Under democratic centralism the people enjoy a wide measure of democracy and freedom, but at the same time they have to keep themselves within the bounds of a socialist discipline." Mao's old friend Siao-yu, in *Mao and I were Beggars*, likened such "freedom" to that of a chicken in its run.

The Communist Party

The Communist Party historically came first and remains the highest arbiter of national policies. The effective control of the State apparatus is vested in the Communist Party. It is the highest unit of government and the key lever of power. Theoretically it is the instrument by which the supreme people rule themselves. It is the true representative of "the people". The peasants, not the workers, are the real foundation and chief support of the CCP and make up eighty per cent of its membership — a strange Marxism!

Local Communist parties elect their own committees and this process is repeated at different levels right up to the highest level of all — the Central Committee which may have over a hundred members. The Politburo, the core group, may consist of between twenty and thirty members. The Politburo appoints the powerful Standing Committee which consists of less than ten members. In 1977 this committee was reduced in size from nine to five members. Thus the CCP is essentially hierarchical. It is significant that the senior members of the CCP in 1978 nearly all took part in the Long March and are therefore elderly; but it also means that they are men of long experience whose loyalty has been firmly proved. The Chairman of the Central Committee of the CCP, with the Standing Committee, virtually rules China politically and the Chairman is at the same time the Commander-in-Chief of the armed forces.

Article Five of the Constitution says: "The whole Party must observe unified discipline; the individual is subordinate to the organisation; the minority is subordinate to the majority, the lower level is subordinate to the higher level and the entire Party is subordinate to the Central Committee." The highest leading body of the Party is the National Party Congress which normally meets every five years. The official voice of the CCP is the newspaper *Red Flag*. If, as observers of China tell us, Communist doctrine has established itself as a religion in China, then the Communist Party is the sacred priesthood or the incarnation of the leadership of the people whose programme will ultimately lead to an earthly Paradise. But this, according to Mao, may take "a thousand years" to attain. This new religion makes no pretence of democracy or free will.

The People's Liberation Army

After the Party came the Army. The People's Liberation Army won the victory for Communism on the battlefields. Its guerilla or partisan tactics, associated with Mao Tse-tung and based on the strategy of Sun Tzu, the 500 BC military writer, have been the classical pattern of guerilla warfare the world over. In brief the principle is:

> The enemy advances, we retreat;
> The enemy camps, we harass;
> The enemy tires, we attack;
> The enemy retreats, we pursue.

This celebrated four-line slogan was invented in the Chingkang mountain base.

Without the Army the Chinese Communists could never have come to power. "Political power," said Chairman Mao, "grows out of the barrel of a gun." The Chairman of the Communist Party is also the Commander-in-Chief of the armed forces. Thus, "the Party controls the gun and the gun must not be used to control the Party." In the Cultural Revolution, however, the Army gained power and influence and dominated the revolutionary committees which replaced the old Party apparatus. Lin P'iao's traitorous attempt to seize power in 1974 followed. The priority of the Party had then to be restated at the National Congress of 1975. Power was thus more than ever concentrated in the Party, and the regime became, if anything, more authoritarian than ever.

The regular Army, which numbers about three million, is

recruited largely from among the peasants and is regarded as an élite corps of model citizens which can be used in civilian as well as in military activities. Its functions are both military and social. It is the national pace-setter and is supposed to manifest all the political virtues. PLA men mingle and work with the people in a most informal way and are generally popular. At an early stage they earned the respect of the people by their discipline and good behaviour. The old bad image of the Chinese soldier is a thing of the past. Public order in China is maintained through the army and the militia. The latter provide personnel for the locally-run workers' picket teams who carry out both patrol and guard duties in industrial areas. Security cadres and police function in residential areas. In 1965 the PLA abolished all formal ranks and insignia. Officers from Marshal downwards are indistinguishable from the ordinary soldier, except by the number of pockets on their uniform.

The Army operates some state-owned farms, factories and transport services and plays a vital economic role as the builder of roads and railways. It built Peking's underground railway and the Tan-Zam or Tazara railway in Africa. It also plays an important part in border development. The soldier spends fifty per cent of his time on military duties, thirty per cent on political studies and activities and twenty per cent on productive labour. The Army produces eighty per cent of its own food. Just as China has her model commune in Tachai and model industrial centre in Taching, so the Army has its "model unit"—the "Hardbone Sixth Company", a title conferred in 1964. A young soldier, Lei Feng, renowned for his selflessness and good deeds, is held up for individual emulation.

In addition to the Army proper, China has placed about two-thirds of all Chinese citizens under fifty years of age under part-time military training. They are armed and trained by the Army and constitute a powerful and influential militia. The "gang of four" attempted to win the allegiance of the Shanghai militia in support of their own aims.

The Chinese insist that their armed forces are solely for defensive purposes; they point to the fact that they have never been used for aggression outside their own borders—Tibet being regarded as an integral part of China. The fear of war with Russia which has a million men and nuclear weapons deployed along the five-thousand-mile frontier, is genuine. The Chinese Army, while having a small nuclear arsenal, is largely equipped with an older generation of conventional Russian weapons and army leaders are demanding the modernisation of the Army. Teng Hsiao-ping approves of this but would argue that modernisation can only take place as a result of large-scale industrialisation. He promises that modernisation of the economy will lead to modernisation of the armed forces, but that the economy must come first. Army leaders do not all concur and some strong army opposition to Teng exists. A debate is also continuing as to whether an army trained and deployed to fight a "people's war" can at the same time be equipped and structured to fight a modern war. Teng Hsiao-ping has sketched out his plans for the future shape of the PLA as a smaller, more streamlined body with advanced weaponry, tougher discipline and a centralised line of command. But foreign arms purchases will not immediately solve China's defence problems. A settlement of China's dispute with Russia would be the obvious solution, but such a thing is unlikely in the near future.

The State Council

The third organ of government is the State Council which corresponds roughly to the cabinet of the British Parliament. It is the administrative machine and operates under the indirect control of the central leadership of the Communist Party. The Premier and as many as twelve Vice-premiers together with the ministers responsible for finance, defence, industry, trade, education, health etc. are all appointed by the Politburo and are generally, though not necessarily, Party members. In any case they carry out the policies of the Politburo. Formerly, for many years, Mao Tse-tung was Chairman of the Party and Chou En-lai Premier of the State Council. It was a happy, strong partnership. In 1979 Hua Kuo-feng holds both offices and is therefore, on paper at least, in an even stronger position than both his predecessors.

The highest organ of state power is the National People's Congress which normally meets every five years. However, its meeting in the past has been very irregular due to internal political conditions. China has twenty-two provinces, five autonomous (minority peoples) regions [1] and three directly administered cities. As with the Party, so citizens elect members to the Congress at local levels and they in turn elect members to provincial congresses; finally provincial congresses elect delegates to the National Congress. Communist Party members, therefore, are found in increasing numbers at higher levels.

The second house is the National People's Political Consultative Conference. The approximately one thousand representatives include virtually every association in the country and even religious representatives. Several Christians are members of this Conference which, however, is merely consultative and wields no real power. Nevertheless, theoretically, power resides in the will of the people, who have the opportunity to make their wishes known through this Conference. China calls herself a "People's Democracy".

The following chart summarises the various organs of government:

Communist Party

The Chairman is also the Commander-in-Chief of the PLA.
Several Vice-chairmen.
Central Committee or Politburo.
Standing Committee.
Congress meets every five years.

State Council

Premier
Vice-premiers—as many as twelve.
Departmental ministers.
National People's Congress meets every five years.
National People's Political Consultative Conference.

[1] Actually there are 54 distinct minorities totalling 38 million or 6 per cent of the population, inhabiting 50 per cent of the total area of China, including Tibet, Inner Mongolia and Central Asia.

People's Liberation Army

Commander-in-Chief is Chairman of the Party.
Subservient to the Party.
For defence, not aggression.
Militia.

A cadre is one entrusted with formal leadership power within an organisation, or an official of any kind. Originally they were mostly army people. Cadre schools are intended to be a safeguard against the emergence of a ruling class.

The Constitution

The original Constitution of the People's Republic of China differed little from the Russian Constitution and had one hundred and six articles. In 1970 the draft of a revised Constitution was circulated for discussion and then formally promulgated in 1975 at the Fourth National Congress, the last at which Premier Chou En-lai appeared before his death. The number of articles was reduced to thirty. With regard to the structure of the State the Constitution reads: "The Communist Party of China is the core of leadership of the whole Chinese people. Marxism–Leninism–Mao Tsetung Thought is the theoretical basis for guiding the nation." This leaves little room for real democracy. Article Thirteen describes the Four Rights of citizens as, "Speaking out freely, airing views fully, holding great debates and writing big-character posters." But the Constitution sets certain conditions for these Four Rights: "The State shall ensure to the masses the right to use these forms to create a political situation in which there are both centralism and democracy, both discipline and freedom, both unity of will and personal ease of mind and happiness and so help consolidate the leadership of the Communist Party of China and the State and consolidate the dictatorship of the proletariat." Article Twenty-eight says: "Citizens enjoy freedom of speech, correspondence, the press, assembly, association, procession, demonstration and freedom to strike and enjoy freedom to believe in religion and freedom not to believe in religion and to propagate atheism." Article Eighty-eight of the original

Constitution read: "Citizens of the People's Republic of China enjoy freedom of religious belief." Compare this with the Constitution of the Republic of China (the Nationalist Government) which, after endless drafts, discarded and re-written, was finally promulgated in 1936. Article Fifteen of that Constitution also read: "Every citizen shall have the freedom of religious belief; such freedom shall not be res-trained except in accordance with law." Not so very different from the Constitution of the People's Republic of China pub-lished in 1954! At the Fifth National Congress in 1978 further minor constitutional changes were made.

The Legal System

Barristers and solicitors have no place in China, lucrative professions though they may be in the democratic world where the legislature and the judiciary are separated. There it is the responsibility of lawyers to interpret the law and to apply it both for the protection and the conviction of citizens.

The People's Republic of China does not have a written code of law. The original law code which included the con-cept of an independent judiciary was swept aside in the anti-rightist campaign in 1957. Then, in 1966 Chairman Mao urged the Red Guards to "rebel", that is to flout the law, including the Supreme People's Court. Chiang Ch'ing (Mme. Mao) denounced the then existing legal machinery as bureaucratic and bourgeois. The Procurator General was himself attacked and forced to attend a criticism rally. The Red Guards became a law unto themselves. After 1966 the "radicals" frequently acted outside the law and held un-authorised trials.

Without a legal code the people are uncertain about their rights and only the Communist Party can decide what is and what is not permissible behaviour. Thus politics are in com-mand of the entire legal process and political considerations commonly influence court decisions. It follows that the Politburo can take action against political opponents with-out reference to any law code or law court. So the arbitrary arrest, torture and possible execution without trial of thou-sands of political opponents have been normal in the constant "line" struggle. One thousand six hundred "counter-revolutionaries" were arrested and executed in 1966. A larger number of "ultra-leftists" were similarly arrested and executed in 1976–8. The "gang of four" are still alive but have so far never faced any kind of trial.

In fact, where the State is a single entity, the law is really just another method of administration. Law enforcement is carried out either by the Public Security Bureau (the police), of which Chairman Hua was the head before succeeding Chairman Mao, or by the PLA. Most cases of petty crime never get to court but are settled at the work unit or neighbourhood committee level. Thus the offender is kept in his community. Matrimonial disputes are handled by social welfare institutions on the basis of one of China's few written codes, the Marriage Law.

More serious crimes are the responsibility of one or other of the four courts: the Supreme People's Court, the High People's Court, the Intermediate People's Court and the Primary People's Court. Judges are chosen from the masses and picked for "high political consciousness". Courts may sit for an hour or two, two or three times a week. The real enquiry into guilt or innocence is conducted by the "procuracy" which is supposed to be separate from the police and which decides whether to bring or continue a prosecution. The court merely decides on the appropriate penalty. Thus in twenty-five years, in the case of one court, no-one brought before it was ever found innocent. To add to the confusion about what constitutes a crime, some courts have cited the draft laws circulated at a low level in 1963 but which were never even discussed by the State legislative organs.

In the Cultural Revolution, the Supreme People's Procuratorship was, like the original law code, swept away. It was restored in 1978 by the Fifth Congress of the People and written into the Constitution.

Most of the crimes that reach the courts are offences against property—theft, embezzlement and "hooliganism". There are two types of capital crime, one "which gravely offends the masses" and the other which is "serious" but does not "gravely offend the masses". Summary execution by firing squad is the penalty for the first and a two-year suspended sentence of death for the second, during which time a changed "attitude" can result in a commuted sentence.

Mass participation in trials is sometimes allowed when clearly public opinion or emotion is a key element in deciding punishment. So, too severe penalties are often imposed and at other times too lenient ones.

At the centre of the prison system is the network of labour reform camps, the population of which is several million. A French citizen is the only man ever to have left such a camp to tell his story to the world. Life in the camps is one of strenuous work, meagre rations and continuous ideological indoctrination. Prisoners who complete sentences, even after twenty to thirty years are pressured to remain in the camp for the rest of their lives. Those who do so include very many Christians, some of whom are known to have made the "voluntary" choice in order to continue their Christian witness there.

In August 1978 the *People's Daily* stressed the importance of strengthening the socialist legal system with additional laws. Chao Tsang-pi, the present Minister of Public Security has stated that both a Criminal and a Civil Code are alike urgently needed. He has publicly condemned earlier practices of arbitrary arrest and torture. The Institute of Law and the Judiciary are in fact preparing new civil and criminal codes of law. These actions reflect an increased respect by the present leadership for legal procedures as a bulwark against the kind of anarchy caused by the "leftists" during the Cultural Revolution and a desire to upgrade China's human rights position. So far, not only has justice not been done, but the people of China have seen that it has not been done. The future must witness a reversal of this situation.

Human rights

Understandably, leading up to the full diplomatic recognition of China by the U.S.A. on 1st January 1979, the U.S.A. said nothing about human rights in China, while making them an issue in relation to Russia. In any case the subject is viewed differently in different parts of the world and in different circumstances. The more advanced countries emphasise civil, political and religious rights, while the developing countries emphasise social and economic benefits or welfare rights which are included among the thirty articles of the United Nations "Universal Declaration of Human Rights" (1948). For the first time in modern history the Chinese people are enjoying the elemental rights of health care, food, housing, employment, education and security which tend to be taken for granted in the developed countries. The Chinese frankly admit that the five per cent of "class enemies" in China enjoy very limited rights to speak and act as they please, but claim that ninety per cent of the people of the U.S.A. are themselves deprived of their rights, while only the other ten per cent enjoy the "bourgeois rights" and privileges of a financial élite! In China, as distinct from the West, human rights are thought of in a collective rather than in an individualistic context. Community rights must come before individual rights.

As to whether any Chinese citizens really enjoy the freedoms promised in the Constitution there must be a large measure of doubt. "Class enemies" and "labelled persons", including Christians, who number perhaps forty-five million (five per cent) certainly do not. The seven non-desirables are:

1. Landlords;
2. Capitalists;
3. Rich farmers;
4. Rightists;
5. Anti-revolutionary elements;
6. Capitalist roaders in positions of power;
7. "No-gooders".

These are at best second-class citizens and have been deprived of even such human and civil rights as their fellow-citizens may enjoy: e.g. the right to higher education on merit and the right to employment for which they may be well qualified. In these spheres there is discrimination against all "labelled persons" including Christians.

But what about those citizens who are not "class enemies"? Even for them freedom of movement is strictly limited by the food-coupon system, ration coupons being valid only in the locality where the person is resident. Movement of population in and out of the cities is in this way strictly controlled. There is no freedom to choose a job or a career; the Government decides on all employment. Nor can we take "freedom to speak out freely and to air views fully" at its face value. The "Hundred Flowers" experiment in 1957 clearly showed the danger of attempting to exercise any such freedom. No criticism of the Party or the regime is permissible. Such could lead to execution. The Li-i-che poster protest of 1974 (see Chapter IX) was also a protest against the denial of democratic rights to the people. And so long as the constitutional freedoms are denied so long will the voice of dissent continue and grow, especially among the disillusioned Red Guard generation and among the politically independent Chinese refugees in Hong Kong and in the U.S.A. The voice of Christian "dissent" has yet to be heard, but it will undoubtedly come in time.

The place of religion

As far as religion is concerned there is no pretence of separation of church and state as in Russia. The Christian Manifesto of 1950 pledged the obedience of the Christian Church to the Communist Party. In the 1975 revision of the Constitution the limitation on freedom was clearly increased. There never was any religious freedom promised beyond the freedom of belief and the freedom to assemble in registered places of worship—certainly no freedom to propagate their belief, a right now reserved for atheists who also enjoy the right to oppose Christian belief. Since the regime is clearly committed to bring about the disappearance of all religion, the Constitution is quite logical and the action of the Red Guards in 1966 equally logical in their attempt to destroy all religion.

Christians have every right to complain. The Government has never apologised for the "left-extremist" actions during the Cultural Revolution when all religious buildings were closed and confiscated, religious literature such as Bibles systematically destroyed and violent attacks made on individual Christians. Since 1966 when the Christian Church was driven out of sight as an organisation there have been no official, legal or visible activities of the Christian Church in China. In 1979 the Church in China remains, as in the days of the Roman Empire under the Emperor Nero, a "church in the catacombs".

Nor are Christians the only religious group to suffer. Although the Chinese Government set out to woo the racial minorities, so neglected by the National Government, by establishing the Minorities' Institute in Peking and by preserving their culture and language, this was not true of the large Muslim minority. No doubt the Muslims had been the fiercest opponents of the Communists in the early days and have for centuries been a troublesome element in China's north-west, but their religion is their culture. As far as the Muslims generally are concerned, freedom of religion was an empty promise, except in the north-west where Muslims are in the majority. Elsewhere their slaughter houses and restaurants were closed, their mosque land confiscated and Muslims were forced to live and work in the communes with non-Muslims and to eat the same food. The Arabic script was replaced by the Cyrillic script and Muslim children were forbidden to learn Arabic. Daily prayer and Friday worship at the mosque were also impossible because of the demands of the work. Thus, again, basic human rights have been denied in China to Muslims as well as Christians. The systematic destruction of lamaistic Buddhism in Tibet is yet another example of the experience common to religious believers of every kind. The appearance of a few ageing Church leaders and a few Muslims and Buddhists at the last National People's Political Consultative Conference in 1978 was meaningless and purely symbolic. If the Communist leaders of China continue to follow their present policies then there is no possibility of genuine freedom of religion in China.

In 1928 T. S. Shen, a Christian leader, said: "Marxism as a religious force is even more intolerant and oppressive than those systems which are so often indicted." This statement is as true today as then. Nevertheless, the Apostle Paul insists that Christians pray for all in authority. In his day they included tyrants like the Emperor Nero. Prayer was essential in order that ordinary citizens, especially Christians, "might lead a quiet and peaceable life, godly and respectful in every way". Such prayer is urgently needed in the case of China.

CHAPTER VII

Land Reform and the Communes

China's oldest problem is how to feed her multiplying millions. In the nineteenth century her population grew from sixty millions to three hundred and fifty millions. At first migration from China proper to Manchuria and South-East Asia enabled food production to keep pace with the need, but when, towards the end of the nineteenth century, the economy ceased to respond to the growth of population, civil disorders resulted. Unlike Japan and Great Britain, China, lacking exports and needing to import foodstuffs, found it too difficult to make the transition to an industrial economy. Her conservative society and leadership also resisted change. After the Revolution of 1911 there were some changes and some progress, but the lack of national unity, widespread disorders and the failure to make sufficiently radical changes in the countryside left the door wide open for, and indeed made inevitable, a second revolution.

China's population

The last official census was conducted by Peking on 30th January 1953. It revealed a total population of 582,603,417 of which 13·26 per cent lived in urban areas and 86·74 per cent in rural areas. The next published figure was 646,513,000 for 1957. These figures show an annual growth of two per cent. During the Great Leap Forward, when Chairman Mao favoured unlimited population growth, and the Cultural Revolution, when the sexes freely intermingled, the birth rate increased to three per cent. At a World Population Conference in Bucharest in 1974 Huang Shi-tsi, the Public Health Minister, stated that China's population had increased by sixty per cent in the twenty-two years since the foundation of the People's Republic. Even if the annual population growth has been reduced to one and a half per cent or even to one per cent in the cities, the population of China in 1978 must be about nine hundred and fifty million. With forty million Chinese living overseas the total Chinese population of the world will soon exceed one thousand million, if indeed it has not already done so.

After early hesitation, because Mao Tse-tung believed that a large and growing population was good for China's developing economy, the Chinese Government is now pushing population-control policies and family-planning schemes. Late marriage is encouraged—at twenty-eight for men and twenty-five for women. Couples are expected to have no more than two children. Abortions are encouraged and are both legal and popular, while seventy per cent of women of child-bearing age use contraceptives. But despite what is being done the rate of population growth is still too high and should be reduced to point six per cent per annum, which is the present goal.

Arable land area

A group of America's foremost agricultural scientists visited China in 1974 and published their report in the *Scientific American* in June 1975. They ascertained that, while the total land area of China is larger than that of the forty-eight American States, or about the size of Europe and Western Russia, arable land is only fifteen per cent of the whole compared with twenty per cent in the States. Eighteen per cent of the rest is non-arable land, twenty-eight per cent grasslands and eight per cent forest. Two-thirds of China's land area consists of the arid steppes and deserts of the north-west and the high mountain ranges and plateaux in the west. Of the fifteen per cent arable land only ten per cent was being cultivated in 1974. Irrigation in China amounts to thirty-three per cent compared with ten per cent in the U.S.A. and this percentage is unparalleled elsewhere. The main grain crops are rice, wheat, soybean, millet, maize, barley, oats, rye and buckwheat—in that order. Thanks to high-yield dwarf grains, multiple cropping, the use of fertilisers and extended irrigation, China attained agricultural self-sufficiency in 1971. Besides the phenomenal increase in grain production, the communes are also responsible for huge increases in cotton production—four hundred and seventy per cent between 1949 and 1974, though cotton is the only item in which China has not yet achieved full self-sufficiency.

Land reform

The new regime wasted no time in tackling the problem of food in 1949. The Land Reform programme of 1950–52 came first. Land which had belonged to the rich peasants was distributed among the poor peasants who also formed mutual aid teams to share agricultural tools and machinery. In contrast to the Russian annihilation of the entire landed class, the Chinese left the "middle peasants" alone. This was the class to which Mao Tse-tung himself belonged. Land reform was the first stage in the "overthrow of feudalism". But the pleasure of the peasants was short-lived, for, in 1953 their plots were confiscated without compensation and combined into agricultural co-operatives. Land reform itself had not solved the problem of increasing productivity and widespread famine affected many provinces in 1953. At this time many rich peasants and land-owners were tried by "people's courts" and killed. Hysteria and violence were characteristic features of the denunciation meetings. Stuart Schramm writes: "There is no evidence whatever that Mao, like so many who have wielded absolute power (Stalin in particular) takes pleasure in killing or torturing the enemies of the revolution or of his own power. But he has never hesitated to employ violence whenever he believed it necessary." [1] "He gave no quarter and he asked for none." The earlier massacres of the 1930s were only a prelude to the larger massacres later, in the course of the greatest revolutionary upheaval of all time. But, for the record, it should be recalled that, back in 1927, Mao had resisted directions from the Central Committee of the Party to use violence and terror as

[1] *Mao Tse-tung*, by Stuart Schramm, p. 153.

a means of revolutionary agitation. That programme of mass violence clashed head on with Mao's alternative strategic conception of the use of military force. Now, however, in the early days of victory, Mao urged the peasants to rise and kill, not merely one or two, but a goodly number of landlords. At the same time he warned the cadres against "indiscriminate killing". Mao regarded violence as a measure for altering the balance of forces and psychological relationships in the countryside. Thirty per cent of ex-landlords and ex-rich peasants are still, in 1978, denied normal commune membership.

The terror

The number of victims in this first revolutionary upheaval was relatively limited—one half of one per cent of the total number of landlords. The real wave of terror was still in the future. But, after the Korean war broke out in 1950, a sharp increase in the amount of terror was employed by the regime in its effort to establish its power and to root out all opposition. This took the form of a succession of mass campaigns aimed at "counter-revolutionaries, Nationalist agents and other class enemies". Long lists of those publicly executed were published—from one to three million according to the most reliable estimates in the first six months of 1951 alone. (Mao himself only acknowledged eight hundred thousand.) Through 1951, during the "Three Anti" (corruption, waste and bureaucracy) and the "Five Anti" (bribery, tax evasion, fraud, theft of government property and theft of state economic secrets) campaigns, a real climate of terror reigned throughout the country, resulting in many suicides as well as the executions among businessmen facing ruin, including some Christians. The much larger estimates of executions presented by the Taiwan lobby to Congress in 1972, the purpose of which was to prejudice President Nixon's Peking visit, can be discounted. It was the Government intention that only some of the "reactionary elements" were to be destroyed. Others, the intellectuals, were to be reshaped by the harsh methods of labour camps and thought reform.

Re-education

So, the period of violence over, the Communist Party set about the process of reform by the "democratic methods" of "criticism and self-criticism" on a nation-wide scale. The purpose was to re-educate and to convince "the people" as distinct from the "enemies of the people" that the policies of the Government were right. This method revealed Mao's style of leadership; it was the fulfilment of his lifelong ambition to be known as a teacher and his desire to harmonise "conscious action" by individuals and impeccable social discipline. "Brainwashing" (or group dynamics as it is known in the West) was certainly a less violent method than the open terror but "thought reform as practised by the Chinese Communists was nevertheless a shattering experience of identity-destruction and identity-reconstruction. It was tragic for some, emotional and intellectual security for others and for yet others a mixture of acceptance and inner revolt." [1] With this went a movement for the intensive study of Mao Tse-tung Thought. Thought reform continues to be an essential ingredient of Mao's China.

The Soviet model

The first Five Year Plan started in 1953 and until 1955, when the details of the plan were spelled out, the economic policy of the Peking Government showed considerable moderation and was based on the Soviet model. In the countryside the beginning of the plan was marked by the transition from mutual aid teams to co-operatives. The co-operatives, consisting of thirty to forty families, owned the land, the animals and the implements. Each family was also given a private plot to cultivate and a share of the total harvest. But many co-operatives were badly managed and so inefficient. Nevertheless there was a surge in the formation of co-operatives at the end of 1955 and by 1956 almost the whole of China was divided into co-operatives — now with one hundred to three hundred families in each. But, with the advent of larger, more impersonal units, many farmers lost

[1] cf. R. J. Lifton: *Thought Reform and the Psychology of Totalitarianism: a Study of Brainwashing in China.*

interest in their work and production slumped. To meet peasant hostility, the animals, the trees and the implements were returned to individual ownership and the private plots enlarged. Free markets operated to sell the privately-produced crops. Mao naturally saw this tendency as conflicting with the thinking of the CCP in Yenan. Basically, he was ignoring the fatal example of the Russians and the fact that collectivisation can only take place successfully over a long period of time. He had gambled on early results, lost his gamble and the economy collapsed.

The "Hundred Flowers"

From the outset of the new Republic Mao was plagued by worsening relations with Russia and the point of no return was reached when Kruschev denounced Stalin as a tyrant and advocated non-belligerent competition between Communism and Capitalism. The denunciation of Stalin was an act which, to the Chinese, seemed to reflect on the Communist movement as a whole, while the economic rivalry seemed to threaten a return to capitalist economic policies.[1] Kruschev was following the "capitalist road"! After the crushing of the Hungarian uprising by Russia in 1957 and also to defuse dissent at home Mao issued a challenge: "Let a hundred flowers blossom and a hundred schools of thought contend!" It was an invitation to indulge in a free-for-all expression of public opinion. But, instead of producing a mild debate between slightly differing viewpoints, it became the occasion for the nation's "intellectuals" (i.e. people with at least a high school education) to attack the basic principles of the whole system and the monopoly power of the Communist Party. Mao was deeply shocked and sent many thousands of his critics to "thought reform" camps. He also launched "rectification" and "anti-rightist" campaigns to correct the nation's thinking. Mao was in desperate mood, uneasy as he was with his Russian allies and with his own people. His second visit to Moscow to obtain military aid was a failure. And so he was driven to yet another desperate gamble.

[1] Stalin is still honoured in China and his portrait everywhere hangs with those of Marx, Engels and Lenin.

The Great Leap Forward

In 1958, at the Eighth Congress of the Communist Party, the sixty-five-year-old leader launched the Great Leap Forward and enunciated the principles of "continuous revolution". At first an almost millenarian enthusiasm swept the country. The Great Leap Forward was certainly the largest scale social upheaval in the history of the world. Its hallmarks were the "people's communes" and the principles of self-reliance, illustrated by the backyard steel furnaces. In fact its emphasis was on industrial expansion at the expense of agriculture. In August the Government organised China's vast rural population into 26,578 communes, each an autonomous unit averaging about four thousand six hundred families or households (but, in some cases, as many as ten thousand). Unfortunately, the edicts were hastily issued without first undertaking the essential research to discover if there was any material foundation for the communes and without providing the necessary psychological preparation of the people involved. Many of the small local industrial enterprises were ill-conceived—notably the "backyard" steel furnaces. Ownership of the land which had hitherto been at the co-operative level was now established at the commune level and private plots were curtailed. The commune also became the accounting unit. Thus, initially, the communes were extremely impersonal and the gap between the leaders and the peasants was very wide. Manpower was seasonally regimented for the purpose of irrigation, road building and light industrial work. Working hours were very long and exhausting. Communal day nurseries enabled women to work full time while communal kitchens and dining rooms relieved them of household chores. There were some experiments with communal housing. But the whole vast scheme went badly wrong.

From time immemorial the vagaries of the monsoon cycle have made farming, especially in north China, a hazardous occupation: rainfall is variable and drought alternates with floods. The monsoon rains decrease the further north and west you go. After one good harvest in 1958, which led to some optimism, adverse weather conditions, three years of poor harvests, gross mismanagement and the wrong use of manpower combined, led to famine and economic disaster. The winter of 1960–1 was a bitter one in China. Rationing spread the hunger equally over the entire population, but relatives abroad flooded China with food parcels. China had to make large grain purchases from Canada and Australia in February 1961 to minimise the effects of the famine. The new methods failed; the new machines did not work; the backyard furnaces became a liability; and morale sank to the lowest level yet. Many peasants felt deeply resentful at the treatment they had received at the hands of the Government. The Great Leap Forward collapsed. The policy of giving priority to heavy industry was abandoned and the Chinese leaders again took agriculture as the "foundation".

The whole venture was a typical example of Mao's "revolutionary romanticism". Its humiliating failure forced Mao to stand down from his position as State Chairman and to turn over the day-to-day administration to Liu Shao-ch'i, one of several prominent critics of the whole commune experiment. In the years that followed Mao went onto the defensive.

On his way to Lushan (Kuling) to attend the fateful Eighth Congress in 1957 Mao had envisaged the coming communes as initiating "a thousand years of happiness" after "two years of toil" and wrote the following poem in anticipation:

The lonely peak soars abruptly beside the great river,
I leap towards the summit, winding four hundred times
      through verdant nature.
Calmly and coldly I turn towards the sea and gaze at the
      world,
A hot wind scatters rain over the river to the horizon,
Clouds cross the Nine Branches and float over the Yellow
      Crane pavilion,
White mist rises from the waves rolling towards the coast.
Where has Magistrate T'ao gone now?
Can one cultivate the land in the Peach-blossom Spring?

How bitter must have been Mao's disappointment! And the nation's initial optimism was doomed to profound disillusionment.

The communes reformed

The failure of the first commune experiment was only temporary. The Government profited from its mistakes. It was prepared to listen to the scientists and a total re-organisation took place. The size of the communes was reduced and their number increased from 26,578 to 76,000. Each commune was divided into production brigades (corresponding to prefectures) and production teams (corresponding to villages of about fifty families) with a revolutionary committee as the top administrative body. This committee superintends the system of collecting taxes from the commune, the banks, the granaries, the free markets, deals with law and order, the militia, travel permits and is registrar for births, marriages and deaths. The production brigade owns the heavier tools and engages in light industry, while the production team, where everyone knows one another, owns the land, does all the accounting, calculates the work points and pays the workers.

By 1962 eighty per cent of China's population was living in the re-organised communes. Ninety per cent of China's agricultural land is owned by the communes; five per cent is held in garden plots and the remaining five per cent is nationalised as state farm enterprises largely worked by the Army. Edgar Snow comments: "China's communes are still very poor by material standards of Western land-owning farmers, but the livelihood they provide is 'adequate', however, beyond the former dreams of . . . the hungry illiterates who were most of the peasants in pre-revolutionary China." [1] The American agricultural experts previously mentioned were at first sceptical about China's claim to be feeding her people, but they satisfied themselves that, for the present, the Chinese people are healthy and adequately nourished. Two questions were left in their minds, however: 1. How effectively can a government bureaucracy influence eighty-five-per cent of the population who are farmers? 2. Can the birth rate be lowered before growth cancels out the benefits of increased production?

[1] *China's Long Revolution*, by Edgar Snow (1971), p. 120 (Pelican Books).

Wages

Meanwhile, peasants are all paid according to a work points system. Payment is made monthly by the production team according to the number of work points accumulated. This accords with the Marxist principle "from each according to his output, to each according to his work". The stronger and more skilled peasants can earn as much as forty per cent more than others. Some peasants are therefore better off than before, while others may be worse off. But this system of mutually productive effort now works reasonably well and a commune worker earns an average of 60 yuan or £20 a year. The total family income could be as much as 300 yuan or £100 a year. But there is no personal income tax and wages are in addition to almost all food, which costs about 6 yuan (£2) a month, utilities and virtually free medical care and education. Many peasant houses are privately owned. So that cash earned can either be saved up or spent on commodity goods such as clothing, household implements, bicycles (£50), watches (£25), fountain pens, transistor radios etc. The peasants also enjoy guaranteed employment.

Private plots

Further, thanks to Liu Shao-ch'i, the practice of allotting private plots of land to every family to be cultivated for their own use and profit is universal. Village fairs are held every six days and enjoy a legalised free market, though profiteering is forbidden. Nevertheless, a black market does frequently operate. The conservative peasants would not be as contented as they are without those plots: they are essential to retain the political support of the peasants who are all-important in the drive to increase food production. But to Chairman Mao they were always anathema. He regarded them as the thin end of the wedge of capitalism.

Thus, while the commune system was not abandoned, it lost its original character and the changes sharpened the debate which came to a head in the Cultural Revolution. Mao thought that there was too much land and work being given to individual farmers in the private plots. Actually the plots, which take up five per cent of all arable land, produce thirty per cent of all China's vegetables.

Further changes

In 1975 the number of communes was reduced to about fifty thousand, each containing an average of ninety thousand members. While the population in the twenty-two years of the People's Republic up to 1974 increased by sixty per cent, the annual grain output had more than doubled. The living standards of the people were therefore higher though still low by world standards. The communes are no longer completely autonomous. The central government now pays the school teachers and doctors, each commune having its own school system and network of clinics and hospitals. Only the "bare-foot" doctors are paid by the commune itself. Most communes today have light industries where they manufacture their own farm implements, tractors, harvesters and fertilisers. Manpower is increasingly drafted for work in the factories or for work on road building and irrigation schemes. Workers are encouraged to be self-reliant and inventive.

Commune life

Life in the communes is hard, though housing is slowly improving. Working days are long: in the Lou K'ou-ch'iao commune they used to be from four-thirty in the morning to seven at night. But there are also opportunities for entertainment—visiting cinema and drama shows, acrobatic troupes and musical groups. The peasants undoubtedly enjoy levels of health, security and material rewards undreamed of generations ago. Enormous variation marks rural conditions. Some communes are therefore far richer than others. There are wealthy communes in favoured environments and others which must extract from a harsh environment some degree of prosperity. The most famous commune in China is in the northern province of Shansi: Tachai was a poor village of three hundred and sixty people in the mountains, which had repeatedly been hit by disaster. But, by dint of great enthusiasm, strenuous endeavours and good leadership, the barren hillsides were terraced, water was brought to the village by irrigation channels and improved strains of seed were introduced. Tachai now has more than two hundred acres of semi-irrigated land and produces about eight metric tons of grain per hectare. This is a success story which has made Tachai the model commune, one to be emulated by every other commune in China and with a worldwide fame, as visitors from many nations are taken there on conducted tours.

Christians in the communes

The majority of Chinese Christians have always lived in the rural areas and they continue to do so. They have experienced the many changes and vicissitudes of the past thirty years. As loyal citizens they are pulling their weight in the life of the communes and have shared their prosperity in good times and the suffering in bad. Some Christians have, on merit, been elected as cadres. In a few cases it is known that an entire production team or village is Christian. Firsthand reports tell of how the Christian communities have often earned a reputation for conscientiousness and hard work and in this way have made a good impression on the authorities and the non-Christians around them. There is probably less anti-religious prejudice in the rural areas than in the cities, though conditions seem to vary greatly from one area to another. In some communes public baptisms have taken place without opposition, while Christian weddings and large impressive funerals are a continuing evidence of the vitality of the Christian Church in rural areas and afford opportunities for a powerful Christian witness.

CHAPTER VIII

Contradictions

The theory of contradictions

In 1957 Chairman Mao made a speech entitled "The correct Handling of Contradictions among the People" which was to become historic. "We are confronted," he said, "by two types of social contradictions—those between ourselves and the enemy and those among the people themselves. The two are totally different in nature." By the "enemy" Mao meant either the "class enemy" or those actively opposing the socialist revolution in China. Such people, he said, should be firmly suppressed. He went on to describe what he meant by the legitimate contradictions among the people themselves: "... contradictions within the working class ... within the peasantry ... within the intelligentsia ... between the working class and the peasantry ... between the workers and the peasants on the one hand and the intellectuals on the other ... between the working class and other sections of the working people on the one hand and the national bourgeoisie on the other ... and so on ..." Other similar contradictions were listed as "between the government and the people", including "contradictions among the interests of the state, the interests of the collective and the interests of the individual; between democracy and centralism; between the leadership and the led; and the contradictions arising from the bureaucratic style of work of certain government workers in their relations with the masses".

The "contradictions" idea has been singled out as a major contribution made by Mao Tse-tung to the philosophy of Communism. It is actually a parallel to the Marxian "dialectic"—the thesis, antithesis, synthesis concept. The concept of opposing forces was not unfamiliar to the Chinese whose

Taoist philosophy has from ancient times influenced their thinking. The *yang* (male) and *yin* (female) principle implied the inter-reaction of opposites such as heaven and earth, north and south, positive and negative etc. Now this principle has appeared in a new guise as taught by China's modern philosopher. Mao said: "If there are no contradictions within the Party nor the thought of struggle which solves such contradictions, the Party's life will come to an end." In the fifty-seven years since the Chinese Communist Party was founded there are said to have been fourteen "line" struggles. Hardly a year passes when some Party leaders are not purged or criticised and most of the present leaders, at some time or other, have either been removed from office or accused of error.

Resolving contradictions

How then should questions of an ideological nature or controversial issues among the people be settled? Mao's answer was "by the democratic method of discussion, of criticism, of persuasion, of education and not by the method of coercion or repression". He welcomed this form of continuing debate as providing a valuable creative tension out of which fresh ideas could arise.

Up to the time when Chairman Mao made his speech on "Contradictions", the Communist Party had enjoyed a virtual monolithic unity under his leadership. But then the contradictions began to surface. Leader after leader, close colleagues all, challenged Mao's ideas and actions and one by one were swept aside into disgrace with typical Mao ruthlessness: Liu Shao-ch'i, the State Chairman, Ch'en Yuin, the Foreign Minister, P'eng Chen, mayor of Peking, Wu Han, deputy mayor of Peking, P'eng Teh-huai, veteran of the Long March and Army Commander-in-Chief, Teng Hsiao-p'ing, Communist Party Secretary, and others who had given their all for the revolution. What then was all the argument about? None of these men were "enemies of the people", so the "contradictions" must have been over differing policies and emphases or "lines" among the people. The issue goes to the heart of China's theories about the right road to socialism.

Incentives, material or moral

The ultimate or ideal goal of the fully Communist state, according to Marx, is that people contributing according to their ability should be rewarded "each according to his need". But nowhere in the world has that goal so far been reached and such a distant goal can only be reached by stages. The present stage—the "socialist" stage—is one in which people are rewarded "each according to his work or output": the harder one works or the better one is qualified, the higher the reward. This at once involves the question of incentives. Chairman Mao believed that "incentives" are the focus for the understanding of the means and the ends of society. The revolution must be followed by a struggle to create a new collectivist order in which the people's outlook is transformed and their values changed. In the new collective life, personal interests would be inextricably linked with the common progress and people would work to serve the interests of all the people and not merely those of themselves individually. The Marxist aim is to socialise incentives and to transform society as a reflection of transformed minds and wills. But Chairman Mao recognised that the problem of transforming the incentives mechanism would be difficult to solve. He saw the progress from the old incentives to the new as proceeding in a dialectical line, with both material and moral incentives operating together at first, then, as material conditions improved, to be followed by a greater stress on the new non-material incentives.

Any incentive system has both external and internal elements. Marxists believe that society must move from the external to the internal incentive. Maoists claim that China did make progress in this direction during the first twenty-five years of the People's Republic of China. The motive of personal gain was being replaced by the identity of self-interest and group interest. Despite such claims, the points system for agricultural workers and the eight grades of pay in factories mean that the most highly skilled workers can earn three times more than the unskilled. Bonuses are awarded for piece work and special awards are made for inventions and innovations. At the same time non-material incentives tied to individual or group performance also operate. Every effort is made to encourage the collective spirit. Individuals must be prepared to go where they are most needed, to work for the collective cause. They must learn to view their work and personal life as part of the process of contributing to the larger collective life. This obviously demands overcoming an array of "bourgeois" values and selfish attitudes hitherto based on advancement, enrichment and intellectual élitism. Such things are supposed to be anathema to the true socialist as they were to Chairman Mao. Instead of material incentives ("according to his work") it is necessary to develop non-material and social incentives. Finally, in a fully Communist society everyone (or, perhaps, nearly everyone!) will be entirely internally or morally motivated and there will be no further desire for personal gain—only a sense of personal identity with the group interest. The slogan, familiar to everyone in China, is *"ta kung, wu sze!"* or "everything for the public, nothing for the private!" The Little Red Book says, "At no time and in no circumstances should a Communist place his personal interests first: he should subordinate them to the interests of the nation and the masses. Hence selfishness, slacking, corruption, seeking the limelight and so on are most contemptible, while selflessness, working with all one's energy, wholehearted devotion to public duty and quiet hard work will command respect." Another quotation says: "We must all learn the spirit of absolute selflessness from him (Dr. Norman Bethune). With this spirit . . . a man is noble-minded and pure, a man of moral integrity and above vulgar interests, a man who is a value to the people."

Changing people

Sentiments of this kind have been expressed ever since the early Communist writer Feuerbach recognised that no progress can be made toward changing society until man is changed. Che Guevara once said, "If our revolution does not have the goal of changing men it doesn't interest me." Hans Böckler, the German Trades Unionist once said, "If men are to be free from the old and outmoded, it can only happen as they set themselves a new goal and place humanity and moral values first. When men change, the structure of society changes and when the structure of society changes, men change. Both go together and both are necessary." The evolution of the new Communist man was Mao's own goal. He was willing to pursue the goal of transforming man even though it was temporarily at the expense of economic growth. He believed that, in the long run, the achievement of selflessness and unity of purpose would release huge reservoirs of enthusiasm, energy and creativeness. The two models of such achievement are Tachai in Shansi for agriculture and Taching, the Manchurian oil field, for industry. Both success stories were the result of almost superhuman effort against enormous physical difficulties. These achievements were, the Maoists claim, the direct result of being ideologically motivated, of correct political consciousness or, in short, of being "red".

The means and the mechanism

In order to enforce and expand this collective spirit, three things are necessary: first, group criticism and self-criticism as a regular practice. Frankness at such meetings is a high virtue. If a person is selfish he will resent criticism and will probably become bureaucratic or élitist. If men become selfless there will be discipline and unity of will. Secondly, serving others demands comradeship which replaces the "bourgeois" concept of friendship; as comrades, all are equal —teachers and students, doctors and ward-maids, managers and workers, cadres and peasants. The third necessity is that of self-reliance, a way of working, not as competing individuals, but as comrades in social groups working to improve the common lot by their own efforts and inventiveness.

Chairman Mao once wrote: "The outstanding thing about the masses of China is that they are poor and blank. On a blank sheet the freshest and most beautiful characters can be written, the freshest and most beautiful pictures can be painted." The characters Mao wanted to write and the picture he wanted to paint were of a totally selfless, socialist individual with a proletarian world outlook.

In practice, the mechanism of promoting the idea of non-material incentives, while still retaining the existing industrial and agricultural differentials in wages, involved greater emphasis on group performance, competition between groups, and rewards in the shape of group participation at national conferences dealing with common problems. The group reward for outstanding success might also be an honorific title or even a personal meeting with Chairman Mao himself.

Red or expert

All this sounds and is very idealistic and scarcely accords with the traditional pragmatic character of the Chinese people who, down through the centuries, have been a nation of strong individualists. They may have paid lip service to the idea of the *"ta t'ung"* (Great Unity) theory of the Book of Rites, but the Chinese are basically pragmatists rather than idealists. Thus, in contrast to Chairman Mao's "red" line, there have been those Communists who, while not rejecting orthodox Marxist ideals, which can in any case only be attained in some distant Utopia, were more immediately concerned to promote and speed up the material progress of China now and thereby create the kind of environment in which the selfless, socialist person can develop. This "line" placed the emphasis on improving expertise and adopting modern technology. Total self-reliance in the world of today, they believe, is out of the question and China must be prepared to learn from foreign expertise and technology to supplement her own. "Expert" was therefore the watchword of the pragmatists. From these different viewpoints arose the continuing debate between the two "lines"; is it better for China to be "red" or to be "expert"? What will best promote the country's material progress—ideological orthodoxy or a pragmatic programme? Both "lines" essentially seek the same goal—a prosperous modern China free from foreign domination. But they differ as to the best road to follow in order to reach that goal.

A Christian comment

The Christian observer of this debate detects an interesting parallel with Christian doctrine. Christians too recognise the dominance of self-interest in man and that society is bedevilled by man's selfishness and self-centredness. As with the Marxist, so with the Christian, the ideal is to be so freed from self-interest that one gladly and spontaneously lives a life of service for others. But whereas the Marxist can only offer regimentation, brain-washing, the power of public opinion and social engineering to effect this change, the Christian is offered the abundant grace of God to enable him to triumph over self and to live a selfless life. The Christian's inner motivation is the implanted love of God and the power of the Holy Spirit. Moreover, for the Christian, selflessness itself is "gain" and earns the reward of pleasing the Saviour whose pleasure is known in fellowship with Him.

Rightists and material incentives

As we have noted, Mao's ideal for the communes was that of an inner-motivated community willingly serving one another. The pragmatists, however, are more concerned with the practical economic and social development of Chinese society, though still within Maoist political lines. When the first communes failed, Liu Shao-ch'i introduced the principle of material incentives and every family was given a private plot of land to cultivate for its own benefit. During the early sixties, therefore, Mao saw his ideals being rejected and an entrenched bureaucracy denying them in practice. His reply was an anti-rightist crusade which continued all through the early sixties and affected many groups adversely, not least the Christians. Liu Shao-ch'i and the Central Committee controlled the superstructure, the labour unions, the Party Schools, the Communist Youth League, the millions of Party cadres and bureaucrats—all in Mao's name. But, from Mao's point of view, they "tend to put economics before men, encourage effort by material incentives first and zeal second, push production without class struggle, boost technology by relying on experts, put economics in command of politics to serve technology and favour the city over the countryside. They want expansion of state credit rather than Great Leaps Forward and ideological faith in building capital by hard collective labour." [1] Such were the allegations that produced the Cultural Revolution.

[1] Edgar Snow: *China's Long Revolution*. 1971.

"Economism"

During that revolution, the flagrant offer of greater material incentives ("economism") allegedly to "bribe" factory workers in Shanghai, the main stage on which the Cultural Revolution was played out, was seen as a weapon designed against Mao and it infuriated his supporters. In the end, the Maoists or Radicals won the day against those whom they denounced as "rightists", "revisionists" and "capitalist roaders", i.e. the Moderates. The old Party apparatus was smashed and Liu Shao-ch'i, the so-called "Chinese Kruschev" and "capitalist roader" was expelled from the Party to live in obscurity. Teng Hsiao-p'ing, Secretary of the Party, together with a large number of other officials who supported the "rightist" line, were denounced as "monsters" and "ghosts", hounded out of office and replaced by loyal Maoists. The three Shanghai men who had masterminded the Maoist cause in Shanghai—Wang Hung-wen, aged thirty-five, the young whizz-kid and a polished polemicist, Yao Wen-yuan, the publicist whose article in November 1965, criticising Wu Han the Peking deputy mayor's veiled literary attack on Mao's policies, heralded the Cultural Revolution and Chang Ch'un-ch'iao, the hero of the "January Storm"—all rose to immediate prominence. Wang Hung-wen was promoted to the Vice-chairmanship of the Party, second only to Mao; Chang Ch'un-ch'iao became Vice-premier and Army propaganda chief, while Yao Wen-yuan gained monopoly control over the press and radio and so, for ten years, was able to indoctrinate the nation with pure Maoism. Chiang Ch'ing, Chairman Mao's wife, strictly controlled the arts and used them to promote orthodox Maoism while exercising considerable influence as the wife of the ailing Chairman. These four would one day be denounced as the evil "gang of four", but for the next ten years they played a large part in the control of the course of events in China. Mao himself, the middle-of-the-road leader, was greatly distressed at the "left extremism" of the Red Guards during the Cultural Revolution and these eventually suffered rustication for their excesses. But the Cultural Revolution was, in the end, a resounding victory for the Mao "red" line and for pure Maoism, a victory for the Shanghai-based Radicals over the Peking-based Moderates, of whom Chou En-lai, the Premier and Chairman Mao's strong, wise right-hand man, was one. Lin P'iao was able to state at the Ninth Party Congress in 1969, "Whoever opposes Chairman Mao's Thought at any time or under any circumstances will be condemned and punished by the whole Party and the whole country."

Chou En-lai

This is perhaps the place to make a larger reference to Chou En-lai and his role in the history of the Chinese Revolution. He was born in 1898 in Kiangsu into a well-to-do family of gentry. He began his political career in 1919 as an activist in Tientsin and, as a student, went on a "work and study" project to France in 1920. He stayed in France until 1924, joining both the CCP and the KMT while there. Returning to Canton, Dr. Sun Yat-sen's political base, in 1924 he became a colleague of Chiang Kai-shek in the Whampoa Military Academy where he was the Political Director. He took part in the Northern Expedition and proceeded to Shanghai to join the Communist Party Centre. He was a prime leader of the workers' armed uprising there on 21st March 1927 and barely escaped with his life in Chiang Kai-shek's bloody suppression. A few months later Chou figured as a key person in the Nanchang Uprising and so was recognised as a founder of the Red Army. He became a member of the Central Committee in 1927 and enjoyed uninterrupted membership of the Politburo from 1928 on. He survived the Long March only because he was carried on a stretcher for the last part of the journey.

For a time Chou was stationed in Hankow as leader of an "anti-bandit" campaign and during 1930 he and his wife regularly attended worship at the Methodist Church in that city. He became a warm friend of Bishop Roots and Mme. Chou once publicly expressed her opinion that "Christianity is the only hope for the world and for China!" Many years later Chou En-lai, in 1973, issued a personal invitation to Bishop Root's daughter to visit China and the scenes of her childhood as his personal guest. Her tour included the lovely mountain resort of Kuling, now normally reserved for top

Government officials. In Nanking she met Dr. Wu Yi-fang, former President of the Christian Ginling University, only to find that she had become a convert to Communism.

Chou was not always an ardent supporter of Mao's policies and was one of those who sought to curb Mao's authority in 1931 in both the Party and Government. Mao's authority in the Army passed to Chou who, in 1933, was appointed the political commander of the entire Army. In contrast to Mao, he strongly supported the "Twenty-eight Bolsheviks" (the name given to a group of returned students from Moscow) and their orthodox Marxism. But after the Tsunyi Conference Chou wholeheartedly accepted Mao's leadership.

During the war with Japan Chou En-lai lived in Chungking as the official representative of the Communists in Yenan. There he is said to have remarked: "We have nothing against religion, much less the Christian religion, with which we have so much in common." When Mao proclaimed the People's Republic of China in 1949 Chou En-lai was his firm choice as the first Prime Minister, a post he held with loyalty and distinction until his death in 1976. He also held the post of Foreign Minister until 1968. It is of great interest to know that the classified documents in the U.S. State Department include a secret letter from Chou En-lai written in 1949 asking the U.S.A. to help China steer an independent course between the West and the Soviet Union. He represented a "liberal group" as distinct from a "radical group" which sought a closer alliance with Moscow. But the overture was not pursued. A year or two later it was at Chou En-lai's invitation that some Protestant church leaders held a three-day conference in Peking about the future of the Church.

At the Geneva Conference on Indo-China in 1954 Chou made a strong impression on the outside world and revealed himself as an urbane and skilful diplomat. The following year he attended the Afro-Asian Conference at Bandung in Indonesia and announced China's three principles of peaceful coexistence. He also appeared side by side with Nehru as one of the two primary representatives of the non-European world. He followed this with a visit to Africa where he declared: "Africa is ripe for revolution!"

In the Cultural Revolution Chou En-lai managed to support the revolution and at the same time to preserve the country's economy from total collapse. At one point his offices were besieged by a hundred thousand slogan-shouting Red Guards who denounced him as "the rotten boss of the bourgeoisie". In the post-Cultural Revolution period Chou was the architect of China's full-fledged membership in the international community when China entered the United Nations and was largely instrumental in normalising U.S.–China relations. A true revolutionary to the end of his days he was always the typical Chinese pragmatist, the level-headed statesman whose task it became to keep Mao's feet firmly on the ground and to modify his more extreme ventures. His wisdom and leadership alone saved China from civil war and greater disaster in the Cultural Revolution. Again, according to the *People's Daily*, he personally took control of the Chinese armed forces in 1971 during the attempted coup d'état by Lin P'iao. He promptly grounded all military and civil aircraft and they remained grounded for five days during which time Chou lived in the Defence Ministry. Only when he believed the plot well and truly foiled did he hand over to the General Staff. The event paved the way for Chou's further political ascendancy, to the chagrin of the Radicals who attempted to make both Lin and Chou targets in the abortive anti-Confucian campaign.

Chou sponsored the 1966 plan for industrial growth which was pushed aside by the Radicals. Again, in 1975, at his last public appearance, he outlined the ambitious national blue-print for economic development—"the four modernisations" —designed to enable China to catch up with the rest of the world by the end of the century. For the second time this failed to meet with the approval of the Radicals, who suspected a swing towards capitalism. But it is plain that Chou was the perfect example of one who was both "red" and "expert"—a fusion of the two "lines".

Chou's death in 1976 was a severe loss to China. His popularity was undoubtedly great, perhaps greater than that of Chairman Mao. His flair for administration and diplomacy, his extensive knowledge of world affairs and his boundless energy made him "indispensable". China is still finding it difficult to replace a man of such towering stature in the post of Premier. The "Age of Mao" might with equal justice be called the "Age of Chou".

Radical power

For ten years after the Cultural Revolution exploded in 1966 the Radicals enjoyed considerable power and influence in China and they clearly looked forward to supreme power just as soon as Chairman Mao might die. But they did not have everything their own way. In particular they failed to diminish the authority and prestige of Chou En-lai. Moreover they gradually lost the incentives battle and the Cultural Revolution tendency was reversed; income differentials became general. There was a retreat from "leftism".

The Lin P'iao affair

The Defence Minister and Chairman Mao's closest comrade in arms and his heir designate (the first was Liu Shao-ch'i) was a national hero as a victorious general in several wars. He had gained in stature with the PLA during the Cultural Revolution and appeared to be a loyal Maoist radical. Then, in September 1971, a dramatic event occurred, the details of which are still unknown or unverified in the outside world. The story goes that Lin P'iao engineered a plot to blow up a train in which Chairman Mao was travelling. When the assassination attempt failed he secured a plane in which to escape together with his staff and family. En route to an air base in Russia, the plane crashed in Outer Mongolia killing all the passengers and crew. However, Russian attempts to identify Lin P'iao's body among the dead failed. Was Lin P'iao therefore arrested and secretly executed in China while his family only attempted to escape? The facts are still a closely kept political secret in China.

But what were Lin P'iao's motives if the story of his attempt to assassinate Chairman Mao is true? Among the crimes of which he is accused by the Radicals was that of trying to disorganise the Maoist socialist mode of production by advocating the restoration of material incentives instead of political or moral incentives. Thus he was guilty of "apparently-extreme-leftist-but-in-fact-rightist" error, i.e. a seeming left deviation which is actually right sabotage. He was thus a secret ally of Liu Shao-ch'i!

So a campaign called the "anti-Confucian" campaign was mounted against Lin P'iao and (it is clear) against Chou En-lai, another "rightist". As usual the campaign was accompanied by accusations, arrests and executions. But it never succeeded in its aims. The masses were certainly not prepared to criticise Chou En-lai and they had excusable queries about the Lin P'iao affair. The whole thing bore the marks of a radical plot to strengthen their own position. Nevertheless Chou En-lai took the precaution of shuffling all the provincial generals and so loosening them from their potential power bases. Perhaps, under Lin P'iao, the PLA had become too powerful.

The power struggle

Both Mao and Chou were aging and ill. The inevitable power struggle for the succession was warming up. The political infighting was tearing great gaps in China's social fabric and causing the most severe upheavals since the Cultural Revolution. The Chinese press constantly reported "sabotage activities", absenteeism in the factories, arson, rape, bank robberies, and murder—things unheard of in China for many years. Everything was weighted in favour of the "leftist" or Maoist Radicals. Skirmishes on the Soviet–Chinese border led to a growing and genuine fear of Russia and probably precipitated a new entente with the U.S.A., symbolised by the state visit of President Nixon in 1972. The Radicals viewed this move coldly. It was, too, a year of poor harvests due to floods and drought—ten million metric tons down on 1971. At the Tenth Party Congress in 1973 there was another swing to the left, and the values of the Cultural Revolution were re-asserted. Wang Hung-wen became the third in rank in the Politburo after Mao and Chou. In Wang's speech he repeated Mao's theme that cultural revolutions were "to be carried out many times in the future" and that a true Communist must "dare to go against the tide". Radical Maoists clearly retained a dominant position in the Party.

The often-postponed Fourth National Congress finally

took place in January 1975 when Chou En-lai made his last appearance. Mao did not appear at all. The revised Constitution (among other things legalising the highly controversial plots for peasants in the communes!) was authorised and Chou En-lai unfolded the fifteen-year plan for comprehensive industrialisation in order to "catch up with the rest of the world by the year 2000". The Leftists were again far from enthusiastic. Suspecting a reactionary move towards capitalism, they launched a fresh attack on the incentive system in the daily press, but without achieving the desired effect. The "dictatorship of the proletariat" campaign opposing material incentives produced a down-turn in industrial production. At mid-year a central directive dampened down the campaign. In spite of this, labour unrest at major iron and steel works disrupted production, so that industrial production fell in early 1976 from ten per cent to seven per cent. Much of the unrest was due to dissatisfaction with low wages. Basically the Radicals were unwilling to operate a "two-stage revolution" which was necessary for an industrially backward nation. Only a prosperous economy can afford the luxury of progress by moral incentives alone.

On 8th January 1976 Premier Chou En-lai finally succumbed to his long illness. He was deeply and sincerely mourned. Before his death he nominated the brilliant but disgraced "rightist" Teng Hsiao-p'ing as his successor in the Premiership. He also restored many other disgraced "rightists" to positions of power. The pendulum was now swinging strongly in the direction of the Moderates. The enraged Radicals now only awaited the death of Mao Tse-tung to stage their coup d'état.

Spring Festival Riot

At the Spring Festival on 5th April admirers of Chou En-lai placed memorial wreaths on the Monument to the People's Heroes in the Great Square of the People. But these were removed overnight by order of the Radicals who were jealous for their Chairman's supreme honour. The result was totally unexpected. A huge and genuinely spontaneous protest and demonstration by the people of Peking ended in serious rioting by a hundred thousand people. Damage to public buildings and some loss of life occurred when the security forces tried to interfere with the demonstration. There were hundreds of arrests. The demonstration was denounced as "counter-revolutionary". Teng Hsiao-p'ing was immediately made the scapegoat for this event and for the second time in his life found himself dismissed from all his posts, both inside and outside the Party, banished into obscurity and made the object of nation-wide vilification at the hands of the Maoists. Wu Teh, the mayor of Peking and Hua Kuo-feng, the Minister of Public Security, joined in the public condemnation of Teng who was described as a "big poisonous weed which pins its hopes on foreign countries for the development of production" and "an unrepentant capitalist roader". An obviously stage-managed but unenthusiastic counter-demonstration organised by the Radicals followed a day or two later. Hua Kuo-feng was appointed Premier of the State Council in place of Teng and Chairman of the Central Committee of the CCP. Mao is supposed to have sent Hua a message, "With you in command I can be at peace". But the repercussions of the unprecedented public outburst were still being felt in late 1978. Wu Teh was dismissed in October and wall posters in late 1978 demanded that the criticism of the demonstration as "counter-revolutionary" should be withdrawn.

On July 6th "Marshal" Chu Teh, founder of the Red Army, another giant figure in the history of the Revolution, died. He had virtually been the titular Head of State, though little more than a figurehead. That summer the Yellow River overflowed its banks repeatedly and caused the worst floods since 1958. A violent earthquake struck Tangshan, a coal and steel producing town, causing vast destruction and the loss of possibly seven hundred thousand lives. Tremors also caused damage in Peking and Tientsin. Many people camped out of doors for months until the authorities gave the all-clear to return to their homes. But China, in the spirit of self-reliance, refused all outside aid. Hua Kuo-feng's energetic leadership in the crisis proved to be a turning-point in the fortunes of the new regime.

Death of Chairman Mao

Amid all these disasters and losses, Mao Tse-tung died on 9th September. The whole nation went into deep mourning.

At the state funeral the atmosphere among the masses was highly emotional and very tense among the top officials. Wang Hung-wen nervously delivered the funeral oration. If the Radicals were to succeed in seizing power, as they were planning to do, now was the time. But they did not enjoy the necessary support from the Army. Instead Hua Kuo-feng grasped the opportunity and with the support of the Army and the knowledge that most of the people of China, in spite of ten years of leftist indoctrination, were favourable to the Moderate line, ordered the arrest of the so-called "gang of four". This was a sensation indeed. For the "gang" included the widow of the Chairman whose recent death was still being mourned. The "crimes" of the "gang of four" were given wide publicity, not least in Shanghai where in the Cultural Revolution they had risen to power and been hailed as heroes. Now their effigies were publicly burned. The crimes of Mme. Mao included luxurious living, bringing in two hundred Hollywood films for her private viewing and the accusation that she aspired to be a modern "empress" in succession to her husband. Allowing for some exaggeration, it is clear that she was both ambitious, arrogant and hypocritical. All four were promptly and ignominiously expelled from the Party and now live in obscurity. Hua Kuo-feng was elected by the Politburo to be the new Chairman of the Party.

For the present, Moderate policies prevail. Teng Hsiao-p'ing, back in power, pursues the pragmatic policies advocated by Chou En-lai. Maoists have been largely repudiated. The country is once more pursuing what Teng's enemies would call a "right deviationist" policy and "following the capitalist road". Yet early Mao statements are carefully quoted in support of this policy for it is still necessary for national policies to have the stamp of Maoist orthodoxy.

The policy debate is by no means settled. Teng Hsiao-p'ing and his supporters apparently want to proceed with full-scale de-Maoisation, while Hua Kuo-feng and his friends are less eager to take that course. Teng urges the "rightist" policy of modernisation, while the "leftists", now silent, doubtless still hold to their rigid socialist principles. In late November 1978 a new poster flurry in Peking openly criticised Mao Tse-tung and even Hua Kuo-feng in a less open

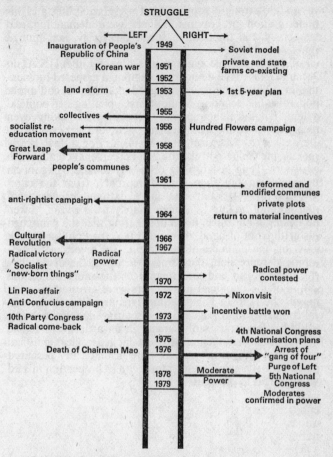

STRUGGLE

←—LEFT   RIGHT—→

	1949	
Inauguration of People's Republic of China		→ Soviet model
Korean war	1951	private and state farms co-existing
	1952	
land reform ←	1953	→ 1st 5-year plan
	1955	
collectives ←		
socialist re-education movement ←	1956	Hundred Flowers campaign
Great Leap Forward	1958	
people's communes		
	1961	→ reformed and modified communes
anti-rightist campaign ←		private plots
	1964	return to material incentives
Cultural Revolution ←	1966	
Radical victory Radical power	1967	
Socialist "new-born things"		Radical power contested
	1970	→
Lin Piao affair ←	1972	→ Nixon visit
Anti Confucius campaign		
		→ incentive battle won
10th Party Congress ←	1973	
Radical come-back		
	1975	4th National Congress Modernisation plans
Death of Chairman Mao	1976	Arrest of "gang of four"
		Purge of Left
	1978	→ 5th National Congress
	1979	Moderate Power
		Moderates confirmed in power

1949–52	Private and state farms co-existing	
1953–57	1st five-year plan on Soviet model	R
1958–60	Great Leap Forward incentives	L
1961–65	Return to incentives and private plots	R
1966–68	Focus on incentives played down	L
1969–76	Struggle	
1976–78	Return to material incentives	R

way, while strongly supporting Teng Hsiao-p'ing and his modernisation programme. Others were demanding real democracy, the freedom to speak out freely, and human rights.

Following the recognition of China by the U.S.A. in December 1978, the democracy campaign gathered momentum in 1979. Wall posters argued that China could not modernise her economy without first updating her political system. Unofficial newspapers circulating in Peking even openly criticised the Communist system and were exploring alternatives to Marxism and Maoism. For a few heady weeks some Chinese broke the ban on personal contact with foreigners. Teng Hsiao-p'ing originally looked benignly on the campaign but then earned reproach from the campaigners for restricting the more extreme criticisms of Maoism and the late Chairman Mao. At the end of March the Peking authorities, no doubt fearing that the campaign was getting out of hand, demanded that the Politburo crack down on the democracy movement. So, reverting to old-fashioned repression, the "free speech" of the democracy wall came to an end and several of the more outspoken editors of the unofficial newspapers were arrested. For the present the Human Rights campaigns are silenced. Unofficial contacts with foreigners are discouraged, and the young would-be democrats sadly lament in an article sent to the foreign press that their movement lacked a clear political programme and its supporters were insufficiently prepared for "secret struggle" under repression. The pendulum had swung too far to the right.

CHAPTER IX

The Cultural Revolution

The Great Proletarian Cultural Revolution which was such a landmark in the chequered development of modern China followed a very stormy path. Much that has been written about this lurid happening, even by the experts, looks rather foolish in the light of greater knowledge and subsequent events. Some of the causes of the Cultural Revolution have already been described. By late 1964 China had recovered economically from the Great Leap Forward errors. Food was again relatively plentiful and consumer essentials and services were more widely available. But during the early sixties the "rightists" or pragmatists were everywhere in power, a situation which Mao believed would lead to Soviet-style "revisionism" and therefore to a departure from Marxist orthodoxy. He saw no alternative to a radical purge of the Party and its re-creation in his own image. The deterioration of revolutionary idealism within the Party bureaucracy and Mao's intense desire to carry socialism into the social superstructure and to root out all remnants of "bourgeois" tendencies and life style among "intellectuals" led in 1966 to the Cultural Revolution. Mao's aim was to restore the Yenan spirit of self-reliance, austerity, self-sacrifice and revolutionary zeal.

The course of events

In November 1965 Mao left Peking for Shanghai where he gave his support to the future Party rebels, three of whom would one day be a part of the notorious "gang of four". The following May the Cultural Revolution was unleashed. The walls of the nation were soon to turn red under a rash of big character posters denouncing "demons", "monsters" and "capitalist-roaders". Mao returned to Peking in triumph in July after his dramatic swim in the Yangtze River at Wuhan. He immediately called a meeting of the Central Committee. The Committee met in August and drew up the guidelines for the Revolution in the Sixteen Points of the Socialist Education Movement.

On 1st June a girl student at Peking University fired the opening shot of the Revolution when she wrote the "first big Marxist–Leninist poster". This was an attack on Lu Ping, the president of the university. The Great Debate had begun. Liu Shao-ch'i, the National President, and Teng Hsiao-p'ing, First Secretary of the Party, (later to be denounced as "revisionists") and the mayor and First Secretary in Shanghai (both opposed to Chairman Mao's policies), feared the consequences of the attack on the Party apparatus and tried to curb the young rebels. Whereupon Chairman Mao wrote his own famous poster: "Bombard the Headquarters!" Here was the Chairman of the Party actually inciting rebellion against the administration—in fact against Liu Shao-ch'i, the Head of State. He also told the youth of the nation that "to rebel is justified!" And rebel they did, violating nearly every rule of the 1956 Constitution in five years of madness, violence, confusion and anarchy—"the most gigantic frenzy China had ever known since the Taiping rebellion".[1]

"Perpetual revolution", as Mao interpreted it, means giving every new generation an opportunity to experience for itself what their fathers had once experienced in the original revolutionary upheaval—its process and fervour. After all, the future was in the hands of China's youth and so they must be educated in a revolutionary manner. The Cultural Revolution, therefore, according to Mao, should be repeated again and again, perhaps every seven or eight years.

The Red Guards

On 13th July 1966 all schools throughout China were closed. On 18th August the Red Guard organisation which had first been formed in Tsinghua University in May was

[1] *Chinese Shadows*, by Simon Leys (Penguin Books).

formally inaugurated. Chairman Mao himself donned one of the famous armbands. One or two million youths, released from school and college made their long pilgrimage to Peking where, on August 18th, the Chairman reviewed a mass rally of Red Guards. A few privileged Red Guard leaders proudly met their Great Leader in person. All were issued with free passes to travel anywhere in China to "make revolution" and to spread the Mao "gospel". Accommodation and food were free. Little control was exercised from the top and the limits of the Sixteen Points were frequently exceeded. The Red Guards were often argumentative, ill-disciplined and ambitious. First of all they were commissioned to attack all power-holders, regardless of rank: high Government officials as well as countless lower-ranking cadres were humiliated, made to wear dunce's hats, were paraded along the streets of the cities and in many ways caused to suffer public scorn and disapproval.

The Red Guards were also commissioned to destroy the "four olds"; old ideas, old customs, old cultures and old habits. They interpreted this as licence to engage in an orgy of savage vandalism. They wrecked many of China's historical and cultural treasures in Canton, Hangchow, Sian, Hofei etc. Only the PLA, on orders from above, prevented this mindless iconoclasm from destroying the monuments of Peking's ancient culture and some of Hangchow's treasures. Loyang also miraculously escaped. Their aim was to gain control of all cultural institutions. This clearly included all religious institutions. They carried out their instructions in this respect with great enthusiasm and thoroughness. Christian leaders suffered similar indignities to their non-Christian "comrades", and were often physically assaulted. Not a few Christians were killed and some committed suicide. All church buildings were expropriated. Bibles and Christian books were systematically destroyed.

The Little Red Book

Early in the Revolution Lin P'iao, the Defence Minister, published the Little Red Book of "Quotations" from Chairman Mao's speeches on a wide range of subjects. It helped to raise the cult of Mao Tse-tung to fever pitch. Literally hundreds of millions of copies rolled off the presses and eventually appeared in many languages of the world. Its circulation rivalled that of the Bible. First the Army, then everyone else, carried a personal copy of the book. They read it, memorised it, discussed it in groups and applied the quotations to all kinds of practical affairs—surgical operations, athletic competitions and the solution of any and every problem: a quotation might even excuse an air-hostess, for example, from wearing a seat-belt on take-off. Thanks to the magical and miraculous quality of the Thoughts of Mao Tse-tung anything seemed possible.

A visitor to Canton at the height of the Cultural Revolution compared the atmosphere to a Christian revival. Everyone was studying the "book", sharing revolutionary experiences and was consumed with a love for their Great Teacher, Great Leader, Great Supreme Commander and Great Helmsman. No-one would appear in public without the Mao badge. The streets of China resounded from morning to night with the strains of "The East is Red!"

Factional rivalry

As time went on factional disputes broke out among the Red Guards who emulated one another in loyalty to Chairman Mao and who also argued the finer points of Mao theology to the point where fighting occurred between scores of rival factions—"Moderates" and "Radicals", "reds" and "blacks" and a variety of other colourful labels. Many fell into the error of "left extremism", exceeded Mao's own directions and lived to regret their excesses when millions of them were later deported for life to remote and often inhospitable regions of China.

Radical victory

Shanghai was the central focus of the Cultural Revolution and there the struggle was at its fiercest. Gradually the "radicals" gained the upper hand and in 1967 the "January Storm" finally signalled a great victory. But elsewhere in the country the rising tide of anarchy reached a peak that summer and delayed the formation of the new revolutionary committees or "great three-way alliances". These consisted of the revolutionary organisations (i.e. Red Guards), the revolutionary cadres (i.e. loyal old Party members) and the PLA whose role was now predominant. The "revolutionary committees" took the place of the old Party apparatus which had been effectively smashed. The aim was to set up such committees at every level — local, city, county, province etc., to replace the old Party organisation.

It was evident to everyone after January 1967 that the Cultural Revolution was not proceeding as planned. In Shanghai, the Revolutionary Committee, assisted by the local militia, attempted to seize power. This forced Mao, reluctantly, to order the Army under Lin P'iao to restore order throughout the country while at the same time it was told to support the Left. It was not a popular move. The Army and the revolutionary masses, Mao's two chief supporters, were soon at loggerheads. But gradually, as the violence died down, the nationwide "revolutionary committees" were one by one completed. Then on 1st October 1967, the National Day, the end of the Cultural Revolution was declared. In 1968, however, violence broke out again between the hopelessly faction-ridden rebel groups and Red Guards. Mao decided that enough was enough and in August the Red Guards were disbanded, and the Cultural Revolution entered a new phase of "struggle-criticism-transformation". In October Liu Shao-ch'i was dismissed both from his presidential position and from the Party. In flagrant disobedience to their leader, factions in many parts of the country continued to cause disorder well into 1969.

Socialist new-born things

The Chinese press, once it was firmly under the control of the Radical publicist Yao Wen-yuan, presented an assessment of the "socialist new-born things" to which the Radicals claimed the Cultural Revolution had given birth. These were listed as a revolution in education, a revolution in public health, a revolution in the arts and literature, a revolution in science and technology and a revolution in management. The article also stated that the rustication scheme ("up to the hills and down to the country-side"), whereby as many as fifteen million youth were sent to the rural areas to work on the farms, had had a revolutionary effect on the rural areas as a whole. The 7th May schools of 1968-9 also enabled cadres of every rank, including all kinds of "intellectuals", to engage in productive labour as farmers and so to learn from the peasants. Mao believed that this was the only way to reform "bourgeois" thinking and habits, to create a better understanding between intellectual and manual workers and to narrow the gap between the urban and rural areas. Much good has undoubtedly come of this practice in a country where intellectuals once despised working with their hands. But the rustication of youth has also produced much discontent, friction between peasants and city folk and hardships for young people suddenly faced with the end of their educational prospects and separation from their own families. Rustication was undoubtedly the most unpopular aspect of the Cultural Revolution. It drove thousands to attempt a dangerous escape from China to Hong Kong where they hoped—as it proved, in vain—to continue the education which had been so ruthlessly terminated.

On the other hand, Edgar Snow affirms that by rustication revolutionary successors were trained—"a one-class generation of many-sided, well-educated youths inspired by ideals of service to the people, at home and abroad, contemptuous of personal wealth and dedicated to a world outlook anticipating the final liberation of man from hunger, greed, ignorance, war and capitalism".[1] Fine words, but far removed from reality. If there *is* any truth in the claim, then these "extreme leftists" may still constitute a threat to China's growing stability. More probably, fifteen million disillusioned ex-Red Guards are a potential focus of discontent.

The cost

Whatever gains may be claimed for the Cultural Revolution, the cost of the enormous upheaval was high: national

[1] *China's Long Revolution*, by Edgar Snow.

unity was endangered, as the distinction between the "two lines" threatened to divide the country into two opposing factions, and civil war was only barely avoided; the Maoist leaders had again sacrificed economics to revolution, so that production, distribution and trade were seriously disrupted. Twice in twenty years the Chinese leaders allowed political campaigns to disrupt the economy just at a time when the situation was otherwise favourable for economic growth. Only the PLA intervention in 1967 averted complete economic dislocation. Premier Chou En-lai said in 1968 that China was "six months behind in production". Industry was hit harder than agriculture because most of the violence occurred in the chief industrial centres. But, worst of all, the Cultural Revolution, with its hatred and violence, has left deep scars on the minds and memories of the Chinese people. They dread a repetition!

Examining the "new-born things"

But did the gains outweigh the losses? This question now requires a closer examination. The first "new-born" thing was:

1. The revolution in education

Education has always been the critical sector in the history of the People's Republic of China—a battleground between those who believe that political indoctrination must not interfere with academic education and those who insist that education divorced from ideology is worthless.

In 1949 the new Government inherited a traditional educational system which undoubtedly favoured the more privileged classes. But the modified system merely followed a Soviet pattern and geared all education to training a class of technocrats for industry. By 1956 the drive for universal education found the country with totally inadequate facilities and teachers. This resulted in quite general hooliganism. In the "Hundred Flowers" campaign of 1957 both students, teachers and college lecturers joined in bitter criticism of the management of education since "liberation", and suffered the miserable consequences of their protest.

A conference on education in April 1958 emphasised the principle of "walking on two legs": i.e. "part work, part study" education. The emphasis was now placed on political education and students were expected to be "red" rather than "expert". The failure of the Great Leap Forward was followed by new plans for educational reform, but real standards continued to fall alarmingly as more and more time was devoted to political and ideological training.

Then came the Cultural Revolution, which began with an attack on the educational system and a claim that Liu Shao-ch'i had sabotaged the 1958 reforms. The Red Guards attacked the enrolment system, the curriculum and the examination system, all of which were said to discriminate against the children of workers and peasants. For the present, however, all universities and secondary schools were closed. In February 1967 the Red Guards were ordered back to their desks, but, after months of footloose freedom when the youth of China had enjoyed not a little power and adulation, they were most unwilling to obey. Actually, secondary schools stayed closed for nearly four years. Many universities opened again in 1970 but with a small hand-picked enrolment. Only two hundred or so institutions of higher learning out of five hundred before the Cultural Revolution were functioning in 1972 and the return to normality was slow and haphazard.

The Sixteen Points drawn up by the Central Committee in 1966 had established the guiding principle for educational reform, namely: "All education must serve proletarian politics (i.e. political policy) and be combined with productive labour so as to enable the young to develop morally, intellectually and physically and to become labourers with social consciences and culture." In the place of the millions of "privileged" students who had been ordered into the countryside to work in the communes, "proletarian" children of peasants, workers and soldiers now filled the colleges. The "Sixteen Points" required the abolition of college entrance exams and students to be selected largely on political grounds following two or more years on a farm or in a factory. Youth with a "wrong" class background or "label" (including Christians) were disqualified from higher education. Both secondary and tertiary courses were shortened by a year each, fewer subjects were to be taught and the "part work, part study" principle was to be implemented.

The Cultural Revolution thus claimed to be fulfilling the hopes of the 1958 reforms and to be setting China on the path of a truly socialist education system. Lecture rooms became factories for making radio components, matches, soap and other commodities. "Open book" exams were to replace the old examination system, and the standard textbooks were scrapped in favour of new ones heavily overloaded with Mao Tse-tung Thought, whatever the subject. Mao also decreed that, because the working class is the main driving force of the Revolution, "worker-soldier propaganda teams" were to be permanently deployed on every college campus to restore discipline and to ensure ideological purity. The constant insistence was on the need to learn Chairman Mao's philosophy and so to make dialectical materialism the power weapon to change the world. Education became the tool of politics ("politics in command"). It was more important to be ideologically motivated than to be technologically efficient: i.e. better to be "red" than "expert".

Since teachers had been severely criticised and even physically assaulted in the Cultural Revolution, many of them found it difficult to resume their teaching with any degree of self-confidence. Some were clearly frightened by the new breed of pupils, whose average age was twenty-four. Some "ultra-leftists" among the students, arguing that since one learns by practice alone, believed that they could do without teachers altogether!

Secondary schools

In the secondary schools, every school had a full-time political cadre on the staff whose task it was to supervise school discipline, advise on political training and be available for consultation. This cadre, together with the local Party committee, had the power to hand out jobs and recommend students for further education. But everything depended on the student's degree of "redness" or "political consciousness". Consequently, in order to get on or to have any hope of further education, it was essential for a student to demonstrate his political consciousness by enthusiastically supporting each successive political campaign. To win favour with the political cadre it became common practice for the "progressives" to report on their more "backward" fellow-students, with the result that these "backward" or politically disinterested students became very bitter against the "progressive elements".

Disastrous consequences

Mao's so-called "revolution in education" was really only a return to measures tried and abandoned as impracticable in 1960. Although the new pattern may have helped to spread the benefits of education more widely to all social levels, it also involved the denigration of excellence and imposed egalitarianism. Men are only equal as human beings before God, but in every other respect they are far from equal. Egalitarian attempts to level everybody down are, therefore, disastrous for education in its highest sense. The new type of college student was hopelessly out of his depth, in spite of a preliminary course of six months to give him a start, and university studies became devalued in the eyes of the people. Real education at every level and indeed all intellectual activity suffered a serious setback. The anti-intellectualism and political dogmatism encouraged by Mao, who always held intellectuals in contempt, lowered the quality of graduates and probably deprived the country of a million engineers, doctors and teachers, a loss China will not quickly make up—the so-called "ten year gap". Mao's educational shortcut may have pleased the ideologists, but it was disastrous in the eyes of the educationists.

By 1972 some of the more extreme excesses were being corrected. But the President of Tsinghua University said that the Cultural Revolution was "a fine lesson in waste of time and money". The Minister for Education from 1975–6 was Chou Jung-hsin, a long-time Party member with wide educational experience. He was among those attacked as a "capitalist roader" in 1967, but re-appeared as a leading member of the resurrected Academy of Science. In 1975, as Minister, he made a number of speeches lamenting the lack of any real culture in current education and said that it was "not worth a fag end!" He complained that "practice . . . practice . . . practice . . ." had taken the place of theory. Consequently standards everywhere were low and no-one bothered with excellence any more. He also criticised "open schooling" for the way it was conducted and the intrusion of politics into all aspects of the curriculum. He was, in the educational sphere, what Teng Hsiao-p'ing is in the fields of industrial and scientific development. All this was too much for the Radicals who were then counter-attacking after earlier setbacks. So they fabricated charges against Chou and hounded him, already a sick man, to an early grave. But, on 28th August 1977, a solemn meeting was held in Peking to honour his memory, to which the highest officials in the land sent wreaths. Posthumously, Chou Jung-hsin was thus rehabilitated and his views given official approval.

2. The revolution in public health

Doctors in China were for a long time members of an élitist profession. They tended to stay in the cities enjoying the good life with little concern for the needs of the rural areas. Early in the revolution, however, Christian doctors were the first to go and serve in the rural areas. Even before the Cultural Revolution, on 26th June 1965, Mao had given his directive: "In medical and health work, put stress on rural areas." As a result, the "co-operative medical service system" was set up in a majority of the communes and brigades and "bare-foot doctors" were already everywhere in action. By 1975 China had one million three hundred thousand "bare-foots". So, to claim this innovation as a fruit of the Cultural Revolution is to falsify the facts.

Medical training was adversely affected by the new post-Cultural Revolution directives: a full medical university course was reduced to three years and the emphasis was laid on clinical experience at the expense of theoretical knowledge in keeping with Mao's beliefs. The idea of a medical élite was to be eliminated and the practice of both Western and Chinese medicine was encouraged. Changes in hospital management were introduced by which all the staff was required to take part in manual labour. The structure which thus emerged amounted to little more than a support system for the bare-foot doctors and the rural clinics: a clinic manned by "bare-foots" cared for a thousand people; the commune hospital, where both "bare-foots" and fully trained doctors worked together, for twenty-five thousand people;

the district hospital for two hundred thousand people and finally the teaching hospitals treated serious illness of every kind.

A short-sighted policy

It was understandable that, in the light of China's enormous population and the need to train many more doctors quickly, another short-cut should be attempted by reducing the medical course to three years. But the emphasis on clinical experience at the expense of theoretical knowledge produced mixed results and certainly failed to raise the standard of medical practice. It is clear that the so-called "revolution in medicine" was a short-sighted policy from which medical standards will take a long time to recover. The claims on behalf of the "bare-foot" doctors, who are really just untrained district nurses, are now accepted as grossly inflated. China's enormous environmental and health problems can only be solved by producing many more well-qualified doctors, nurses and auxiliary medical personnel, and providing them with far better facilities and more medicines. University medical courses, therefore, have been restored to the normal length and are being upgraded. The *Chinese Medical Journal*, which ceased publication in 1967, is again in circulation.

3. The revolution in the arts and literature

The Cultural Revolution may be said to have begun with skirmishes in the field of culture, particularly over the new and the traditional operas. Chiang Ch'ing (Mme. Mao) was in the midst of this controversy. A play called "Hai Rui dismissed from Office" written by Wu Han, the vice-mayor of Peking, an opponent of Chairman Mao's policies, was an indirect defence of P'eng Teh-huai who had been dismissed from his post as Defence Minister in 1959 after disagreeing with Mao over the Great Leap Forward. Chang Ch'un-ch'iao and Yao Wen-yuan, two of the clique later known as the "gang of four", published a hostile critique of the play with the approval of Chairman and Mme. Mao. The incident raised the curtain on the Cultural Revolution.

Mme. Mao assumed the censorship of all plays, films and art. Almost everything that was produced in the pre-Cultural

Revolution period was banned and only such works as promoted the Maoist line could be seen at the ballet or on the stage. For years the public could attend only Mme. Mao's six Revolutionary Model Operas. The Cultural Revolution brought cultural activity in China to a standstill that lasted for several years. Intellectuals were dismissed, pilloried and deported to the countryside. Scientific, artistic, literary and cultural periodicals, with the exception of those for foreign consumption, ceased publication. Museums were closed pending re-arrangement. All books published prior to the Cultural Revolution were removed from the shops, so depriving the people of the magnificent and varied literature of China. Only the works of Mao Tse-tung remained on the shelves. A good number of writers, artists and intellectuals committed suicide, including Wu Han and Lao She, China's greatest and most universally respected modern novelist.

A cultural tragedy

The Cultural Revolution, disastrous as it was for the cultivation of intellectual life of every kind, merely revived Mao Tse-tung's own prejudices expressed in Yenan in 1942 in his "Talk on Arts and Letters". That talk sounded the death knell of Chinese intellectual life and expressed Mao's intention to destroy all critical intelligence. This intention was followed up in the "rectification movement" of 1951–2, the Hu Feng purge of 1955 (the other name sharing the headlines was that of Wang Ming-tao, the great Peking preacher who was also arrested that year), the repression following the Hundred Flowers episode in 1957 and finally in the massive purges of the Cultural Revolution. The consequence was the almost total extinction of Chinese intellectuals as such. The so-called "revolution in the arts and literature" had, as its sole aim, brainwashing or indoctrination on a nation-wide scale.

4. The revolution in science and technology

Like other intellectuals and so-called "bourgeois" class enemies, scientists were among the chief targets of the Cultural Revolution. After 1967 the higher institutions of science, including the prestigious Academy of Science, were closed down on ideological grounds as expressions of élitism.

Many of China's greatest scientists and scholars were consequently denied the opportunity to pursue their various lines of research. The Radicals even sabotaged the nuclear research programme upon which China's defence against Russia may depend. Scientific research was thus a major casualty of the Cultural Revolution.

5. The revolution in management

By this one understands that every effort was made to end the previously existing system of wage differentials, incentives, bonuses and even the eight-tier wage structure in industry. All these were held to be symptoms of incipient capitalism. The "radicals" insisted that factories and communes must be so managed as to achieve high productivity without material incentives and by the inspiration of inner motivation alone—serving the community without thought for self. An attempt was made to reduce the number of wage scales to three. The Cultural Revolution slogan expressed in the Sixteen Points was "Grasp revolution and promote production!" Furthermore the Radicals advocated "centralism" in management after the Russian pattern rather than local autonomy.

But the post-Cultural Revolution years in no way bore out the truth of the claim that production can be promoted by revolutionary motives alone. "Pure Maoism", or the emphasis on political consciousness, in practice meant that peasant workers were afraid of accepting material incentives and workers' differentials were narrowed. This led to discontent with the level of wages and widespread strikes and go-slows. The programme for industrialisation announced by Chou En-lai in 1965 was scuttled by the Left and their ideological insistence led to widespread industrial sabotage. Workers were intimidated from working too hard lest they be accused of following the theory of "productive forces" and of being "capitalist-roaders". In Szechwan, factories were paralysed, workers could not go to work, schools could not teach and shops could not open. The province came close to civil war. Wuhan, the industrial heart of China, suffered equally badly and a well-publicised crisis occurred in Hangchow. Some experts believe that the turmoil in industry through a breakdown in management cost China three years of economic growth. Farms were unproductive, factories were inefficient, railways were frequently paralysed and the work ethic undermined. 1976 was the year when the economy almost collapsed.

The news cover-up

All this time, due to the manipulation of the propaganda organs by the Radicals, the people of China and the gullible world at large, fed on glossy periodicals like *China Reconstructs* and *China Pictorial*, were criminally deceived as to the true conditions prevailing in China. Yao Wen-yuan exercised total control of radio broadcasting and television as well as the press for ten years after 1966. Public speeches and publications were subject to his censorship. Consequently, every paper and every radio broadcast spoke with a single voice—the voice of Maoist radicalism. The "socialist new-born things" were perpetually praised and no voice of criticism was ever heard. "Rightists", "revisionists" and "capitalist-roaders" were interminably castigated as "demons" and "monsters". Even the prestigious *People's Daily*, which corresponds to the London *Times* and has a readership of forty to fifty million, was described as "stereotyped and repetitive" and its pages were said to be "filled with endless long and smelly clichés". It has now been accused of "hoodwinking the masses". Certainly nothing resembling freedom of the press was permitted for a whole decade.

Bureaucratic confusion

The Cultural Revolution did not follow the course that Mao Tse-tung intended. At times it alarmed him and certainly did not achieve all that he hoped. Even he is reported to have assessed it as only seventy per cent positive and thirty per cent negative in its results. Others might estimate less favourably. Nevertheless Mao's own personal prestige seems to have been relatively unaffected up to the time of his death. Even if, from the Marxist point of view, there were some positive gains, yet a look at the balance sheet reveals far greater losses. The self-inflicted wounds will take a long time to heal. For ten years the Chinese people endured the oppression of the Radicals and their policies. During this time the shifting winds of ideology blew China off-course. No-one knew from one day to the next what new wind might be blowing— "black wind" of reaction, deep "red wind"' of Maoist ortho- doxy or "pink wind" of pragmatism. Maoist bureaucrats faced an impossible task, avoiding "leftism" on the one hand and "rightism" on the other. Even the traditional Chinese "middle way" was fraught with danger to their survival. Obeying the Great Leader was always problematical because his instructions were often contradictory and changing. So, for cadres whose careers and livelihood depended on up- holding the banner of Mao Tse-tung Thought, life was very difficult. Survival depended on carefully scrutinising the *People's Daily* editorials and even reading between the lines. The *Liberation Army Daily* in 1978 referred to three groups of cadres still fighting to survive the purge of "leftists": the "Wind Party" which trims its sails to the prevailing breeze, the "Slippery Party" which clings to office despite political change and the "Earthquake Party" which remains hidden in order to stir up political trouble.

The interminable and confusing arguments and political manoeuvrings of the post-Cultural Revolution years eventu- ally left the Chinese masses cynical and frustrated. One Christian doctor reports that not only have the Chinese people lost faith in their earlier political dreams but they are suffering from a lack of close relationships and mutual res- pect, both destroyed by years of uncertainty and mistrust resulting from the ever-changing winds of ideology.

The voice of dissent

The presence of political dissent has never been far be- neath the surface throughout the thirty years of China's Communist revolution. Large numbers have in the past and still do protest with their feet and make their escape to Hong Kong from the tyranny of a totalitarian bureaucratic society in which the Communist Party has never doubted its right to dictate the nation's policies. Between 1972 and 1978 nearly two hundred thousand Chinese crossed the border to Hong Kong legally and perhaps eighty thousand illegally. The pea- sants were deeply dissatisfied when, following the land distribution of the early fifties, their newly acquired land was taken back again to become "cooperative" farm land. Only the conceding of private plots has kept them contented. The outburst of criticism by the intellectuals in 1956, on the other hand, revealed the depth and extent of the opposition of China's intelligentsia. But restrictions on political expression are tighter in China than almost anywhere else on earth and so such expression is more hazardous.

It required great courage, therefore, for the thirty-year-old former Red Guard Li Cheng-tien and his two collaborators to unfurl in Canton a wall poster that was "both physically and intellectually staggering". This was in November 1974. No doubt they had the support either of their work unit, the local police or of a high-placed official: otherwise the poster could never have appeared, especially as the same trio had already, in the spring, written a well-publicised wall poster which had shocked the whole province. This new poster was more than one hundred yards long, covered sixty-seven sheets of newsprint and contained twenty thousand Chinese characters. The title read "On setting up a socialist democracy and legal system". It was a scholarly argument embracing the realities of political and economic thought. It complained that the Cultural Revolution had fallen short of success because the masses had failed to achieve a democratic dictatorship. It expressed opposition to all special privileges and élitism, urged the setting up of social democracy and the reform of the legal system, which had broken down in the 1950s and never been restored. The poster also protested against the alleged slaughter of forty thousand revolutionaries and cadres and the jailing of a million people following the Cultural Revolution under the "Lin P'iao system". In short, the "Li-i-che poster" voiced a protest against the denial of democratic rights and called for an electoral reform process whereby cadres could be voted out of office. It also demanded freedom of speech and of association. These sentiments were, and are, undoubtedly representative of the views of many educated and thoughtful people all over China, as the late 1978 poster campaign in Peking confirmed.

But this was not the only such protest. The first "big character poster" in Peking since the Cultural Revolution had already appeared in June 1974. It criticised the city leaders and the Peking Revolutionary Committee which included a certain almost unknown person called Hua Kuo-feng. That same June there was violence and bloodshed in Nanking and nine other provinces and posters announced the massacre in recent years of seven hundred people in Kiangsi province.

The "Li-i-che poster" was reported to Peking and Li Hsien-nien denounced it as "reactionary" and "a poisonous weed". A local paper then added its criticism. But, in February 1975, the Government instituted the "Study the Theory of Proletarian Dictatorship" campaign which possibly reflected the views of the notorious trio. Li Cheng-tien brilliantly defended his views in the face of opposition and won considerable support, but he was eventually silenced, sent to work in a coal mine and finally sentenced to imprisonment in a labour camp as a "counter-revolutionary".

All three men were released and reinstated on 1st January 1979. They were the forerunners of the 1978–9 Human Rights campaigners.

Extraordinary as it now appears, this whole post-Cultural Revolution scenario was the subject of never-ending eulogies from university dons and intellectuals in the West, most of whom seem to have been pro-Maoist, and from hypnotised (or bewitched) Christian theologians alike. The works of Han Su-yin, the supposed authority on China, contain no hint of criticism of pre-1976 China. The bemused admirers of Chairman Mao and the Radicals actually suggested a comparison between the China described in this chapter and the Kingdom of God. One Cambridge don pronounced China to be "the most Christian country in the world today"! They might have been describing the Reformation instead of a revolution! The bitter truth was altogether different. The people of China themselves had become nauseated with the political manipulation they had endured and the young generation was suffering from a great sense of disillusionment with the Cultural Revolution and all that it brought in its train. The "gang of four" was fraudulent and its policies anarchical. And yet, according to the theologians, here was China experiencing the salvation of God!

The "second liberation"

After ten years of "chaos" the arrest of the "gang of four" on 26th October 1976 was hailed by the entire nation with an almost audible sigh of relief. For days the streets of Peking resounded with martial music and the explosion of fire crackers as gleeful and spontaneous anti-radical parades provided an atmosphere of carnival. A controlled and one-sided press, a drastic censorship of the arts and their use to promote leftist policies, the havoc created in the educational system, the brake on industrial productivity, the ruthless treatment of large numbers of cadres of all ranks who, as "rightists", had displeased the powerful "gang" and the universal fear on the part of the masses of saying anything or taking any action which might be interpreted as favouring "rightist" or "revisionary" policies or of "taking the capitalist road"—these things had become intolerable. The dramatic event was actually described as a "second liberation". After all, it was an end to another form of despotism: the first had been a liberation from feudalism in 1949. The analogy is striking. The arrest of the "gang" marked a resounding victory—this time for the Moderates or "rightists" and a defeat for the Radicals or "leftists". There were even whispers about the "gang of five", because everyone knows perfectly well that the "radical four" enjoyed the full support of Mao Tse-tung—except for Mme. Mao in the last year or two of her husband's life, when the two were estranged.

The end of the Cultural Revolution

At the Communist Party Congress in 1977 the Cultural Revolution was for the second time declared officially at an end. The political *volte face* was now complete. The Politburo immediately underwent considerable changes in personnel, "leftists" being excluded. The process of de-Maoisation began.

Mao Tse-tung will always be honoured in China as the man who led the Chinese Communist Revolution to a successful conclusion. The new leaders lost no time in erecting a huge mausoleum to his memory in the Great Square of the People, astride the route once taken by the emperors on their way to worship and sacrifice at the Temple of Heaven. A fifth volume was added to the Selected Works of Mao on 17th April 1977 and in the first ten days twenty-eight million copies were sold. Readers will find the word "selected" appropriate; most of the matter selected dates back to the Yenan and pre-Cultural Revolution period and is designed to support the "revisionist" policies now being officially followed.

Mao's later and more radical "thoughts", however, have been discredited in the eyes of the majority of the people of China and are unlikely ever again to become the guide-lines for China's progress into the twenty-first century. Even the Little Red Book is now condemned as being a misleading collection of quotations taken out of context. Its use to prove anything, just because Mao said it, has likewise been criticised. People are being urged, as Mao once advised, to "think for yourselves". This is by no means easy after years of being discouraged from doing any such thing. Mao speeches which prove that he did not consider himself infallible and in which he confessed to many mistakes have been reprinted in the press. Mao quotations which once appeared prominently in the daily papers have disappeared. Simon Leys, while agreeing that many of Mao's Thoughts may have been valid at some earlier stage in China's revolution, thinks that they "have lost their relevance, become anomalous, incompatible and incongruous in the changing situation". Many Maoist policies were idealistic or unworkable and some just wrong or contradictory; and that is true of Marxism in general. The doctrine of class struggle is quite foreign to the Chinese mind which prefers the ideal of harmony and compromise, while "perpetual revolution" will never have any appeal to the Chinese people.

What they are now seeking, as the 1978–9 poster campaign shows, is stability, unity, democracy, higher living standards, peace and freedom. They deserve something better than endless "struggle", and the suppression of art, culture and religion. They need above all else strong and imaginative leadership and skilful planning, unimpeded by futile political upheavals and extremist actions. Christians will pray that their hopes will not be disappointed.

CHAPTER X

The Dream Is Over

Revolutionary violence

"A revolution is not a dinner party," remarked Mao Tse-tung in 1927 in a masterpiece of understatement, "or writing an essay, or painting a picture or doing embroidery; it cannot be so refined, so leisurely, and gentle. A revolution is an insurrection, an act of violence by which one class overthrows another." Every Marxist-inspired revolution has been violent and bloody. "Force," said Marx, "is the midwife of every old age giving birth to the new." Victims both in Russia and China were numbered in many millions. Eastern Europe also suffered heavily. No-one knows the total of dead in Vietnam's twenty-odd years of revolutionary war or that in Laos her neighbour. Cambodian revolutionaries have indulged in a welter of massacres amounting to genocide of the most brutal kind. The Marxist victories in Mozambique and Angola were very costly too while the atrocities associated with the Marxist revolution in Ethiopia do not suggest that there or anywhere revolution is in any sense a light-hearted thing like a dinner party. It is a terrible and tragic waste of human life.

Disillusionment with Soviet Russia

But every revolutionary believes that out of the fires of revolution there will arise a new age, a new society, a new humanity and an ultimate socialist utopia. Perhaps sixty years since the first Communist revolution in Russia is too short a time to prove anything either way. But Marxist regimes have so far nowhere succeeded in creating any semblance of utopia. Change, yes! some evils done away with, some injustices corrected, some socialist programmes implemented, but always at the cost of new injustices, lost personal freedom, the denial of human rights, the encouragement of mass hatred, an all-pervading fear of the secret police and at every level a lust for power, a lust to possess and a lust to dominate. Russia, even to many Marxists and Communists all over the world, is a disappointment—an all-powerful bureaucracy operating "state capitalism" rather than a socialist "dictatorship of the proletariat", an imperialist power seeking self-aggrandisement. The disillusioned experiment with even greater extremes on the one hand and modified versions of Marxism like Euro-Communism on the other. Where could true Marxism–Leninism be found operating today as its founders expected? Where should the revolutionaries look for guidance and inspiration as they work towards their socialist utopia?

China—the real hope?

The answer to those questions seems to have been—China! There, surely, was something different, something unique. There was a leader who had succeeded where other leaders had failed. China had, many believed, achieved a new kind of society and was witnessing the evolution of a new kind of human being. Was not China's "liberation" a spectacular one? And so, after 1972, an endless flow of excited admirers from all over the world began to go, like the Queen of Sheba, to pay their deep respects to the modern Solomon in Peking and to see for themselves the reality of the "new China". It was a re-run of a similar pilgrimage to Moscow in the thirties about which Malcolm Muggeridge, then a Moscow correspondent, reminisced when addressing the Congress of Laity in February 1978: "People believed that a phase of history was coming to an end, that Man, struggling to be free with rights pertaining to his individual status, was going to give place to Man as a part of a collectivity, a tiny digit in a huge total . . . whereas, in point of fact, a new serfdom was taking place. This view was approved by the truly extraordinary antics of visiting European and American intellectuals for whom Moscow in the thirties was a place of pilgrimage, as Peking is today to their heirs and successors. They arrived there, an unending procession ranging from the famous superman Bernard Shaw and Julian Huxley, an André Gide, a Joseph Steffans, to crazed clergymen who could not keep away from the anti-God museums, drivelling dons, an occasional eccentric millionaire, actual or aspiring intelligentsia of every sort and condition . . . The credulity with which they accepted whatever their guides handed out to them provided a spectacle of rare comedy . . ." So history repeats itself! After 1972 a trickle of Christian visitors to China joined the growing volume of delegations of experts in industry, agriculture, medicine, social welfare, etc., at first mostly from the U.S.A. The reports of Christians were usually glowing in praise of the "New China" which they had glimpsed in a very limited way as shown by guides and interpreters trained in skilful propaganda. What they saw and heard was undoubtedly impressive, but it was always a deceptive sample. A life-long resident of China with a many-sided experience of life there up until 1972 described the report of an early group of visitors—so-called "concerned American scholars"—as "too naïve for words!"

Here and there in the world, groups of Marxists, disillusioned with the Soviet model, began to call themselves Maoists. The cult became world-wide. China had become the bright hope of the "developing" or "emerging" nations of the Third World and indeed for many Marxists the world over. Had she not succeeded in feeding her hungry millions, increasing industrial production, providing universal medical care, eliminating diseases long endemic, emancipating women, reducing crime to unbelievably low levels, vastly reducing illiteracy, creating a sexually puritan society without prostitution or promiscuity and fostering a collective spirit of selfless service for the community? These, to the extent in which they were true, were no mean achievements. Glossy full-colour illustrated magazines beautifully produced in Peking in many languages and having a world-wide circulation—*China Pictorial* and *China Reconstructs,* etc. were visually very impressive. The text was a translation from the original Chinese papers for home consumption. China began to look like some kind of paradise—an actual preview of the future society of mankind.

Meanwhile, Latin American theologians were elaborating a "theology of liberation" which equated "salvation" with social and political revolutionary change. The World Council of Churches meeting at Uppsala in 1968 was primarily concerned with injustice and social need and they adopted what was virtually a Marxist programme for the world, while the resolutions showed little concern for the two-thirds of the world's population which had never yet heard the name of Christ. Slight emendations were reluctantly made to the resolutions to meet the wishes of those who would give priority to world evangelisation as a prime task of the Church.

China Studies Programme

In 1974 the Lutheran World Federation joined with the Catholic Pro Mundi Vita Institute to launch the "Ecumenical China Studies Programme". From the first the programme has been conducted by scholars on a scholarly level and all available sources of information in China, including a constant stream of books by experts, were consulted. The initial meeting was held at Bastad in Sweden to consider "The Theological Implications of the New China". Papers were read which were later to be distributed among the churches of the West for further discussion. A Chinese contributor, Dr. Choan Seng-song from Taiwan, quoted Mao Tse-tung approvingly when he prophesied that "the Chinese revolution is a part of the world revolution" and that China would make a tremendous contribution to humanity. Therefore, Dr. Song argued, there must be a theological critique of the New China to answer the question "Do we have in New China a viable alternative to the Gospel of salvation interpreted, developed and propagated by Western Christianity? . . . Is the 'salvation' we have seen in New China going to be the norm determining the shape and content of man's search for happiness? Is New China going to be the main instrument in the appearance of a new world order in which the salvation of man is to have its fulfilment?" These were said to be "sober theological questions". The writer was prepared to make out a case for China playing the part in future world history which Israel had played in past millennia. And since "salvation history" is present in the history of the New China where the Chinese Communist Party is endeavouring to transform man and his society, the old concept of Christian mission as the extension of Western Christianity is completely nullified. China, we are asked to believe, is a telling example of how men can do without a hypothesis called God. The writer then made even bolder claims that there is now in China a pattern and shape of life which proposes to offer the ultimate to the truth for which man searches. While agreeing that New China is not the realised Kingdom of God, yet Song regards China's liberation from poverty, starvation and exploitation as acts of God in China.[1]

Dr. Joseph Needham, one of the world's foremost sinologues and historians of Chinese culture, an eminent scientist, the Master of Caius College, Cambridge, and a self-confessed "Christian Marxist", in a learned article which appeared in *China Notes* in 1974 made a statement of conviction that Chinese society as he had seen it was further on the way to the true society of mankind, or the Kingdom of God, than our own in Britain. In the same article Dr. Needham expressed the belief that China is "the only truly Christian country in the world today, in spite of its absolute rejection of all religions. Where is Christ to be found? Where the good are and where good things are done." Elsewhere Dr. Needham has also expressed the view that "the China which broke the hearts of the missionaries has accepted the Spirit of Christ from another source, namely Marxism. . . . If the Chinese have indeed created a society with more faith, more hope and more love than the 'Christian' West, they deserve not only attention but allegiance. As apostles of Christ we must follow where the spirit blows." [2]

When a small group of British scholars and China specialists met in London in March 1974 to consider one aspect of the Bastad papers, "The New Man in China", no consensus of opinion could be reached. Some questioned whether China had any special theological significance and noted that the expression "the new man" is not used in China at all. Professor John Fleming of St. Andrews University warned against the blurring of the "distinction between the spiritual

[1] Bastad Papers 1974. "New China and Salvation History", by Choan Seng-song.
[2] *Christian China*, Logos. Colombo 1967.

and the political, between the historical/immanent and the eschatological/transcendent and between salvation and humanism". Ralph Wang, the Chinese already referred to, urged the conference to distinguish carefully between the Chinese model and the reality. From his own life-long observation he suggested that there was more myth than reality about the "new man" in China. The report of this small conference spotlighted the issues seen to be most important, but the overall discussion which represented a variety and even a contradiction of viewpoints, was inconclusive. No agreed statement was possible.

The Louvain colloquium

These regional conferences were followed by another conference at Frankfurt, Germany (Arnoldsheim), before the major Consultation or Colloquium on China held at Louvain in Belgium in 1974. This was attended by eighty-eight eminent Protestant and Catholic scholars from several European countries, the U.S.A. and the Far East—both Chinese and Japanese. Most of the time was spent in five workshops, each occupied with one of the following topics: "The New Man in China", "Faith and Ideology in the context of the New China", "Revolutionary Antagonism and Christian Love", "The New China and the History of Salvation" and "The Implications of the New China for the Self-understanding of the Church". The main issue seems to have concerned "Mao and the Lord of History". Were the spectacular changes and achievements of the Maoist regime really the acts of God in salvation history? Is "salvation" equivalent to "liberation" in a political and economic sense? No, they agreed, it is something more, but political liberation is not excluded from our understanding of the salvation process. "The liberation movement in China led by Mao Tse-tung is not excluded therefore from an understanding of God's saving work in history." Much of the discussion seems to have centred on "the cosmic Christ". The thesis that Christ is found everywhere in all religions and faiths as the omnipresent but anonymous Christ leads some to adopt the extraordinary view that even Mao Tse-tung is a manifestation of "the Christ", as was Jesus.

Another quotation from the document reads : "We believe that God is present in the process of painful struggle, wrestling and agonising with the people of China to bring their efforts ultimately under the fulfilment of His saving love for all mankind."

While we may assent in some degree to the latter statement, the question must be asked : "Why China in particular?" Is not a sovereign God equally active in all nations with the same ultimate purpose? And as for the other propositions, they are insecurely based on a mistaken view of what has actually happened in China, especially since the Cultural Revolution. The theologians have surely been seeing a mirage. The Chinese revolution has so far clearly followed a course no different from other Communist revolutions; brutality and violence in the initial stages, power struggles among the leaders, the steady attrition of freedom among the masses, the effective thought control of the brainwashed millions and long days of hard toil without adequate reward such as no Western trade union would tolerate—and all for the goal of a material progress which so far is severely limited in its scope. China remains a backward and poor country compared with the other large nations of the world and even her Asian neighbours. Mao's achievements may be good so far as they go but they fall far short of providing a standard of living and a quality of life such as any nation is entitled to enjoy towards the end of the twentieth century.

The ultimate absurdity is found in a quotation from J. Pullen in the Louvain papers: "Mao's China is certainly a place where during the last four decades God has been at work to liberate nearly a fifth of the human race from the clutches of sin." To which Charles West of Princeton Theological Seminary replies: "So it doesn't really matter that the Church is stifled in China and the Gospel is not proclaimed. The transformation of China by Communist Party leadership is itself the redeeming work of Christ! Mao's Thoughts are covert Christianity . . . There is only one thing wrong with this; it is idolatry not theology!"[1] No truer word was ever pronounced, for the statement simply implies that Mao takes the place of Christ.

And yet the Louvain theologians were urging the Christian

[1] *China Notes.* Vol. XIV, No. 4.

churches of the West to accept the challenge of the Chinese experience in terms of self-understanding. "What challenge? What experience?" we must ask.

Follow-up consultations

Louvain was followed by regional meetings at Glion (July 1976), and Aarhus (April 1977), when the consultations were concerned with "The Encounter of the Church with Marxism in various cultural contexts". Catholics met in Manila in August 1976 and in Singapore in September 1976. In the U.S.A. consultations were held in St. Paul, Minnesota, in May–June 1976 and in July 1977 at the University of Notre Dame in the U.S.A., and yet another consultation was held in Hong Kong in September.

At the Notre Dame conference the Rev. Raymond Whitehead read a paper entitled "Christ, Salvation and Maoism".[1] In it he put forward six propositions:

1. Faith, hope, love, struggle, and sacrifice are not absent among the Chinese, even though they (almost universally) are not Christians.
2. Maoist atheism does not exclude the spiritual dimension of life.
3. The professed atheism of Maoism should not exercise us unduly.
4. Christians from the West should resist the urge to evangelise China.
5. Salvation is not complete in Maoism, nor in the Church, and therefore Maoist–Christian dialogue is useful.
6. The Churches of the West should make a statement of repentance for their involvement in structures of imperialism in China prior to "Liberation".

In the United Kingdom a theological consultation on China was held at Ely in June 1977. At all these gatherings papers by scholars of international repute were read and discussed, largely laudatory of the "new China". So much so that one German evangelical scholar described the ecumeni-

[1] *China Notes.* Vol. XV, No. 4.

cal theologians as "bewitched" or "mesmerised" by the "new China". Perhaps the Roman Catholics were more cautious than the Protestants and at the Catholic conference in Manila, one Jesuit priest pointed out the danger of a near assimilation of the "new China" to an advent of the Kingdom of God, though even he thought that China's "liberation from the sin of selfishness"(!) should be understood as an action of the Spirit in the Chinese people.

Shock waves

The arrest of the "gang of four" in 1976 sent shock waves reverberating through all these theological circles. For the post-Cultural Revolution China, the oppressive and obstructive regime of the orthodox Maoists with all the bitterness of an internal struggle for power, was precisely the China which the theologians and others had so highly praised and even described in "Christian" terms. What were they to do? Persist in their mistaken "assessment" (a term used repeatedly by Raymond Whitehead in his article) or join the new regime in its condemnation of the China of the radical Maoists? They were on the horns of a dilemma. It is time to look the facts in the face. Is China the Marxist model that many Western "leftists" have depicted?

The "new man"

In the previous chapter we have examined the pros and cons of the "socialist new-born things" of the Cultural Revolution. We must now turn our attention to the most publicised "revolution" of all — the revolution in human conduct, the much heralded "new man". A chorus of voices has acclaimed China as a Puritan society where there is a remarkably low crime rate, little corruption, little sexual irregularity and a total absence of prostitution. In normal times these claims have apparently had considerable justification because political and moral discipline are inseparable. As in most Communist countries criminal activity is ascribed to faulty political thinking and to "class enemies". But community sanctions in China are very strong and, in a closely-knit, collective society in which all life is lacking in privacy and where everyone is involved in regular criticism and self-criticism exercises, it is almost impossible to get away with even the smallest moral peccadilloes, while such things as bank robberies are almost unthinkable! Whatever would the robbers do with their ill-gotten gains? It is community sanctions, the fear of stepping out of line and the total lack of personal freedom which account for the low crime rate and make the apparently high standards of conduct possible. Only a completely regimented society could possibly achieve such a state of affairs. In a "free" society neither public opinion nor the force of the law can fundamentally alter human conduct. So China's admittedly remarkable achievements are no proof that there has been any fundamental change in human nature in China.

Indeed, during every time of upheaval in China when law and order have broken down or been relaxed, crime has suddenly increased. It was so during the Cultural Revolution. Crimes of every kind were committed, and the law was flouted. As young people, freed from school and from all social restraints, roamed the country together, the birth rate rose sharply. So much for the puritanism of the young generation! One notable effect of the rustication of tens of millions of young people since the Cultural Revolution has been the secret return to the cities of a small proportion of them who could not endure the rough life of the peasants. Not having food coupons for their rations, girls turned to prostitution and boys to mugging and petty theft to keep alive. Cases of rape, ticket-touting and hooliganism are also attributed to these "fugitive" youth from rural areas. Following the Tangshan earthquake, the Chinese press reported large scale looting—another example of the ugly face of unregenerate man once the restrictions are removed. Theft is by no means uncommon. Two Italian Marxists who had just arrived in Shanghai to join the staff of the Foreign Languages Institute went out on their bicycles to explore the city. They had heard of the honesty of the Chinese today and innocently believed stories that you could not lose anything without the article being returned. So, as they stopped to go into a shop they happily left their bicycles outside. It was a long walk home when they came out to find their bicycles had been stolen! Everywhere, in the cities, bicycles are carefully chained and guarded in the bicycle parking places.

The Cultural Revolution emphasis on "going against the tide" also encouraged the spirit of lawlessness. Indeed the Radicals gloated over the "great chaos" that spread all over the country. The province of Szechwan became notorious for its factional feuds and ideological struggles over the ten year period after the Cultural Revolution. Recently (July 1978) China reported the arrest of two leaders of a Szechwan gang which, under Mme. Mao's instructions, was responsible for the deaths of thousands of people. Now, as in the rest of the country, Hua Kuo-feng declares that "great order" is succeeding "great chaos". But even at the Fifth National Congress in 1978 Yeh Chien-ying, the Chairman, referred to "those newly-emerged elements who resist socialist reconstruction, gravely undermine socialist public ownership, appropriate social property and violate the criminal law". He added that "not a few of the embezzlers, thieves, speculators, swindlers, murderers, arsonists, gangsters, smash-and-grabbers and other evil doers have also committed serious crimes and offences against the law and discipline, and disrupted public order in our society, and belong to this category". Quite a catalogue! The expression "new man" is not used in China. It is only used by the idealists outside China who thought that they had discovered the emergence of the "new man in China". China's own leaders have no such illusions.

In 1977 begging and other anti-social activities were reported from many parts of China—yes, and even armed bank raids in Chekiang and Honan, in one of which a bank manager was killed. The Chekiang Communist Party Standing Committee met in late 1976 and called for action against "embezzlers, swindlers, murderers, arsonists, criminal gangs and bad elements who seriously sabotage public order". Theft, profiteering and private trading were also condemned. The post-Cultural Revolution political upheaval understandably made possible an increase in crime. Consequently a wave of death sentences was reported from at least eleven provinces, mostly of youth in their early twenties. The Government was determined to restore public order.

"Serving the people"

For Christians, the concept of the community is very old. The Israel of the Old Testament enshrined many collective principles. Certainly the Church of the New Testament conceived of as a Body is basically collectivist. Church history is full of examples of collectivist communities—the monasteries in particular. C. P. Fitzgerald claims that Marxism borrowed its collective ideas from Christianity. In our own time Christian communities or communes have multiplied, all attempting to implement the ideal of "body life" and mutual service for the good of all. Thus Christians must feel considerable sympathy for the collectivist idea and attempts to popularise and practise it among nine hundred and fifty million people. But, in the context of a collective society, the well-worn slogan about serving the people is not so much a recipe for individual action, as we saw in the last chapter, as working for the community or for the state without seeking any material reward for oneself. It is in fact the Communist "work ethic". And it is plain that this work ethic does not in itself prove that the Chinese people have been "liberated from the sin of selfishness".

On the positive side it is also essential to ask why the notion of a supposed selfless humanity—a sort of test-tube creation with pre-determined genes—has come about. Is there any truth in the claim of "China's liberation from the sin of selfishness"? Again let us listen to one who knows China only too well from life-long experience. According to Marxist theory there can be no Communism without adequate material wealth. And here is where "serving the people" comes into the picture. Where a person is conscious of his role, the Communists say, he has a place in the onward march of history. According to Lenin and Mao's ideas on "democratic centralism" (see Chapter VI) "serving the people" is inseparable from loyalty to the Party which is representative of "the people". The one without the other would land a person in a reform centre. Since no institution is privately owned, everything that one does is a contribution to socialism and therefore an act of "serving the people". With the allocation of private plots to every family in the commune and the restoration of motives of private gain, now legitimised in the 1975 Constitution, this statement clearly needs modification. No longer does everything one does have this altruistic motive. Mr. Wang says, "Despite the Lei Feng legend, I seldom saw people going out of their way to help others." Socialist "serving" is therefore very different from the Christian concept of love-motivated service to others. The Maoist ideal of "serving the people" can only operate in a collective society through a system of regimentation. Moreover, who are "the people" whom one serves? Not *all* the people! There are also class enemies of the people. While Christians are bidden to love their enemies, Maoists regard kindness to class enemies as cruelty to the people. Only ruthlessness to one's class enemies is kindness to the people!

The real China of Maoism

The overall picture of China under the Radicals' dominance, now that the strict censorship they imposed has been removed and the truth is known, is not a pretty one. Oppression, denial of human rights, ruthless suppression of religion, a great leap backward in education, lawlessness, the deliberate retarding of industrial progress—and all in the name of ideological purity—are a severe condemnation of the era of the Maoist Radicals. Ask the former Red Guards who won the struggle for Maoist orthodoxy but who have since risked life and limb in attempting to escape to Hong Kong. They feel deceived, manipulated and shocked at the deception of the Chinese Communist Party and even of Mao Tsetung himself. Formerly enthusiastic French Maoists, after two or three years' work in China with the Peking Foreign Language Press, expressed a bitter disappointment which has completely reversed their attitude to China. Simon Leys, a China scholar, a socialist and a former Maophile, is so sadly disillusioned with the "new China" that in his book *Chinese Shadows* (written in 1973), true as it is to the facts, he has allowed himself to be, in his own words, too "negative" and to write in the tone of "sterile sarcasm".

The questions now being raised about the late Chairman echo similar queries raised about Stalin who also encouraged a personality cult, even though to do so was un-Marxist.

Articles in the *People's Daily* have dared to recall "some historical figures who were deified who were beyond criticism", i.e. Emperor Ch'in Shih-huang. The emperor is analogous to Mao. Marxists are not supposed to believe in supermen but only in the role of the masses in the making of history. The former de-Stalinisation debate in Russia is being echoed today by a de-Maoisation debate. Mao, like Lenin, preached the doctrine of perpetual revolution; the Cultural Revolution was to be only the first of many. But the Chinese people are still haunted by the memory of that Revolution and its horrors. They fear any repetition that would again halt the onward march of progress. The press, therefore, is conducting an all-out campaign to warn the rising generation against any repetition of the Cultural Revolution. Officially the Great Proletarian Cultural Revolution is still a "good thing" but by describing Lin P'iao and the "gang of four" as saboteurs, reactionaries and revisionists the leader writers are including all the "leftists" who in the Cultural Revolution achieved their desired goals. The Peking University philosophy student whose poster was described by Mao as "the first Marxist–Leninist big character poster" and was broadcast all over the country was arrested in April 1978 at the same time as the most famous "Red Guard" of all, notorious for his violent leadership of university students. Meanwhile the "wrong targets" against which the Red Guards rebelled are now the men in power. The fact is that historians are finding it difficult to assess a man whose words and actions were so ambivalent. Simon Leys says, "In a way, Mao has finally become as irrelevant to China's needs as Nixon to Americans." He speaks of the robotisation of the Chinese people in these terms: ". . . this gigantic enterprise of cretinising the most intelligent people on earth is animated, beneath the grotesque exterior, by frightening rigorous and coherent intention. The aim is to anaesthetise critical intelligence. . ." On the people of China, Leys comments: "The leaders manipulate the people cynically, but the people are still the country's only capital."

And yet this was the China of which it was said at Louvain: "Post-Liberation China has come to exert some particular impacts on our understanding and experience of God's saving love. The social and political transformations brought about in China through the application of Mao Tse-tung Thought have unified and consolidated a quarter of the world's population into a form of society and life-style at once pointing to some of the basic characteristics of the Kingdom of God . . ." Raymond Whitehead talks of the "spiritual values China has discovered". We are bound to ask "What spiritual values?" or "What does Mr. Whitehead mean by 'spiritual'?" He continues, "It is difficult to see what would be added to Chinese life by formal religion at this time." "Formal religion"—agreed! But the supreme need of the Chinese people is for dynamic religion to fill the spiritual vacuum left by the collapse of Maoism. There is no substitute for the truth of God's revelation in the in-carnate Jesus of Nazareth, His life, His death, His resurrec-tion, His ascension, His sovereignty and His return as ob-jective realities, not just "myths".

The China of yesterday was a lovely dream, a beautiful mirage. But now the dream is over and the mirage seen for what it is—an optical illusion. Or is it? As a further con-sultation in London in September 1977 a few Bastad and Louvain theologians were not at all prepared to "reverse their verdicts". Despite a first-hand report of the "second liberation"—this time from the tyranny of the Radicals—they still clung to their illusions about the Maoist era. It was left to scholars and China experts at a London University seminar a few months later to admit that the process of de-Maoisation in China was likely to continue and that the post-Cultural Revolution decade was being quietly written off as a disastrous interlude in China's struggle to catch up with the rest of the world.

CHAPTER XI

The Folly of the Wise

One of the tragic and fatal effects of modern liberal theology is the debasing of the coinage of words. Great Biblical terms have been emptied of their original meaning, diluted or even transmuted to mean something quite different. Such glorious themes as "Salvation", "the Kingdom of God", "the New Man", "Christian", and even the title "Christ" itself, have, in the jargon of the day—and not least that used in speaking about China—become unrecognisable.

Definition of terms

Take the word "Christian", for example. When Dr. Joseph Needham describes China as "the most Christian country in the world today", what does he mean? (Actually Lord Soper once used the same sort of language about Russia not so many years ago. But no longer!) Can anything be truly "Christian" unless it is Christ-centred? Neither Russian nor Chinese society is that! If, in any beneficial social changes in either nation there is a pale shadow of certain Christian ideals and ethics, does this warrant the use of the adjective "Christian" to describe them? Communists would angrily repudiate the suggestion. And so do Christians. Humanism is not Christianity and humanistic "progress" does not warrant the use of the term "Christian". That China is the most humane country in the world today is seriously open to question, but it is absurd to describe China as "Christian" in any sense of the word.

Similarly, the "Kingdom of God" is precisely the Kingdom of *God*, not the kingdom of man which Marxism or any other political system seeks to bring in. It stands in contrast to the kingdom of this world out of which men must be translated into the kingdom of our God and of His Christ. It is a God-centred kingdom where the risen and glorified Christ reigns, not a system which exalts man to the centre of the universe. The principles of the two kingdoms are as different as chalk from cheese. Christ's kingdom is "not of this world" in the sense of being upheld by politics and weapons of war. Precisely because it was not of this world it did not need the backing of physical force, as capitalism, socialism or communism do. The kingdom of Marxism is of this world only, on the Marxist's own admission. It concerns itself with food and drink, whereas the kingdom of God is not primarily concerned with food and drink but with "righteousness and peace and joy in the Holy Spirit". The characteristics of the members of God's kingdom are stated in Matthew 5: "The kingdom of heaven belongs to the poor in spirit, those who mourn over their sins, the meek, those who hunger and thirst for righteousness, the merciful, the pure in heart, the peacemakers and those who are persecuted for righteousness' sake." In no way does the life style of China's Communists point to any of these basic characteristics. There is neither love for God nor love for one's neighbour in the sense in which Christ interpreted it. Communism, whether in China or elsewhere, teaches hatred of class enemies not love; breeds envy not comradeship; leads to slavery not freedom; creates fear not peace; gives promise for this life but rules out the life to come. If there is "faith", as Dr. Needham asserts, it is not Christian faith, for Marxism has no transcendent Christ. If there is hope it is not Christian hope because it is limited to a finite passing world. And if there is love it is certainly not Christian love, which reflects God's love endlessly out-poured on the ungrateful and unlovely. In contrast to the ephemeral mirage ecumenical theologians are observing, the hope of the Christian lies beyond time. While Communism does its worst in deriding religion as superstition and in persecuting the Church, Christians have their eyes fixed on a glorious objective which no persecution can remove. Their hope, unlike the Marxist mirage, is a living hope which nerves them through suffering and enables them to die triumphantly.

Salvation today

It would need a Hans Küng to grapple with the current fashions of the theologians who, like the philosophers of ancient Athens, "spend their time in nothing except telling or hearing something new" (Acts 7. 21 RSV). Liberation theology, originating in Latin America, is one of these new things which has become a popular theme with many theologians today. Jurgen Moltman understands God as immanental in history rather than transcendental over history. Thus his interpretation of mission is of political and social liberation rather than the call to a faith committal to Jesus Christ. At Bangkok in 1973 the World Council of Churches discussed "Salvation Today" and took a long look over its shoulder at China, which then seemed so full of socialist promise. Now it is the turn of the Louvain theologians to talk of China as actually experiencing salvation. By this they mean liberation from feudalism, imperialism, hunger, illiteracy, etc. Isaiah 61. 1–3 is the Biblical text. "The Spirit of the Lord God is upon me, because the Lord has anointed me to bring good tidings to the afflicted, he has sent me to bind up the broken-hearted, to proclaim liberty to the captives, and the opening of the prison to those who are bound . . ." Jonas Jonson of Lutheran World Federation writes, "Acknowledging that salvation history is world history and that God fulfils His promises also through secular means . . . there should be no problem talking about what has happened to the Chinese people as God's mighty work in the world through Mao Tse-tung and the Chinese Communist Party": viz. social justice promoted, the poor and oppressed elevated, the hungry fed and the homeless given shelter. But what shall we say about the rest of the list—millions "liquidated" in the fifties, the continuing oppression of over forty million "class enemies", the severe discrimination against "intellectuals", the arrest, sentence without trial and execution of thousands after every political change of direction, the limitation of freedom in movement, in education, in the choice of job, the withholding for twenty years of justly deserved wage rises for workers and not least the repression of religion—are these, too, the mighty works of God? How selective can we be? Where do we draw the line between God's mighty works in China and man's evil works? How do we determine what is ultimately "good for the masses of the Chinese people" and what is "perversion"?

Missions and salvation

In proclaiming a Christ-centred message of salvation throughout a century of China's modern history Christian missions witnessed the power of God at work in China transforming individual lives, influencing society, meeting the needs of the sick, the poor, the orphans and the outcast, and building up the Church. We can readily admit that missionaries made mistakes but those mistakes, serious as they may have been, were far outweighed by the positive contribution Christian missions made to China. The Chinese Church, too, fell short of God's purposes and yet, though small, it often proved itself to be a faithful and heroic minority in the first-century tradition. With hindsight, there are many sober lessons to be learned, as *Christian Missions and the Judgment of God* by David Paton helped us to see. But while the Communist revolution was certainly a Divine discipline for both Church and Missions we need not conclude that it was a "judgment" on either. For both Missions and Church were God's own instruments. There is obviously a case for deep regret for the mistakes made but what is the "sin" for which repentance is demanded? Any association with imperialism" was an accident of history, a burden missions have had to bear, and certainly not a deliberate sin for which missionaries could be held responsible, because the association could not have been avoided.

Biblical salvation

Salvation in the full Old Testament and New Testament sense, while obviously inclusive of the liberation of which Isaiah prophesied, is not exclusively identified with it. Salvation, whether in the Gospels, the Acts or the Epistles, primarily concerns a salvation from sin and its consequences, which the Lord Jesus Christ came into the world to achieve. Isaiah was significantly quoted by Jesus at the outset of His earthly ministry, which was to be a clear fulfilment of the prophetic terms. "Today," said Jesus, "this Scripture *has been fulfilled* in your hearing." (Luke 4. 16–21). The atoning death of Christ, foreshadowed in the Exodus deliverance, by which believing sinners can be put right with God, is the heart of Christian salvation. Nowhere in the New Testament is salvation related to liberation from Roman imperialism or slavery, nor to social conditions which it required revolutionary action to change. Jesus Christ Himself spoke some strong words about social justice but repudiated the offer to make Him a revolutionary leader, even though there were Zealots among the twelve disciples. He actually commended loyalty to Caesar, while at the same time demanding that the claims of God must be paramount. Only a gross misrepresentation of "salvation" as taught in the New Testament can possibly restrict it to political and economic liberation. To suggest then that the history of the past thirty years in China is, in any specific way, a continuation of God's salvation history is to be misled and to mislead others.

In his BBC Reith lectures (1978), Dr. Edward Norman, Dean of Peterhouse, Cambridge, justifiably accused many leading churches and theologians of politicising the Gospel, i.e. transforming the Christian faith in such a way that it is defined in terms of political values and becomes essentially concerned with social morality. "The temporal supersedes the spiritual." This tendency, Dr. Norman says, starts from a belief that the churches in the past have been too concerned with spirituality. These contemporary churchmen pay less attention to personal sin and the need for reconciliation with God than to the "collective sins of racism, economic or cultural exploitation, class division, the denial of human rights and so forth". The result, Dr. Norman argues, is that "the Christian religion has lost the power and also the confidence to define the areas of public debate, even in moral questions. Not only so but the Western churches continue to distribute the causes of their own sickness—the politicisation of religion—to their healthy offspring in the developing world." This exactly describes the China theologians. It is time therefore to recover a Biblical theology of salvation and to assert the priority of the spiritual over the temporal. At the same time we can agree that whatever justice is seen to be done, wherever the hungry are fed, the naked are clothed and the homeless housed, there the gracious hand of God is to be seen. These benefits, however, are not to be confused with God's saving grace in putting men right with Himself through the sacrificial death of Christ. This is where the distinctively Christian good news must start.

Divine sovereignty in history

Turning now to the matter of the Divine sovereignty in history, the Christian firmly believes in a transcendent God exercising sovereign power and wisdom in His rule over the nations. Bible history is an example of that sovereignty in the destiny of nations and their rulers. God has at no time left Himself without witness among the nations, nor does He cease to be sovereign Lord, even where He is not acknowledged as such, as in China. The Pharaohs in Joseph's time and the various kings of Daniel's time had to bow in the end to the only God. Isaiah said of the all-wise and all-powerful God, "Behold the nations are like a drop from a bucket and are accounted as the dust on the scales. . . . All the nations are as nothing before Him. They are accounted as less than nothing and emptiness. . . . He brings princes to naught and makes the rulers of the earth as nothing." As God was sovereign in the rise and fall of Egypt, Israel, Assyria, Babylon, Persia, Greece and Rome in the ancient world, so He has been sovereign in the entire history of the world right up to the present. Great world empires like those of Spain, Portugal, Holland, Germany, Italy and the British Empire have prospered, served God's purpose and then fallen. So with the U.S.A.—all God-fearing at the beginning but subsequently coming under the righteous judgment of God. Indeed the whole world is hastening towards the day when God will consummate history in the Second Advent of Christ. Then the kingdoms of this world—Russia and China included—will be seen to be subject to God's judgment and rule.

The servant theme

Some China theologians have equated Chairman Mao with Nebuchadnezzar whom God called His servant, or more correctly "slave" (Jeremiah 25. 9; 27. 6) and with Cyrus whom God called "my shepherd" or "king" (Isaiah 44. 28) and His "anointed" (Isaiah 45. 1). They seem to be saying that, in a way not true of Russia, America or any other nation, God has been uniquely active in Chinese history under its Communist leaders. We must therefore ask in what sense was Nebuchadnezzar God's servant and Cyrus God's anointed? Clearly because they unwittingly fulfilled the Lord's intentions; Nebuchadnezzar took Judah into captivity, so fulfilling the prophetic prediction and disciplining God's people, while Cyrus sets them free again to return to make a fresh start. There is no suggestion that Antiochus Epiphanes, for example, was God's servant: and in his idolatrous defiling of the Temple is there not a parallel with Mao Tse-tung in his persecution of the Church? Nor were Pompey or Nero, both of whom had a political viewpoint to be imposed on God's people, called His servants or shepherds. The "pax Romana" is often heralded as one of the providential conditions for the spread of Christianity in the first century, but no Roman emperor is called God's "servant" or "shepherd". Nebuchadnezzar, it must be remembered, though called God's "servant", did not escape God's judgment for his pride and arrogance. Mao Tse-tung is dead, but has not Mme. Mao been "driven from among men", if not, perhaps, made to "eat grass like an ox", for comparable arrogance? No, to talk of Mao as God's servant is a misuse of biblical phraseology and totally inadmissible. And what, incidentally would Chinese Christians think of such a suggestion? We know that Bishop K. T. Ting, the Government spokesman for the Christian Church in China, has virtually repudiated the Louvain talk.

The new man in China

Finally we return again to the theme of the "new man" in China. The claim to have produced a new type of humanity —the selfless person devoted to the service of others—is nothing new in the history of Communism. Communists know as well as Christians that unless human conduct (Christians would say more fundamentally human nature) can be changed, it will be impossible to change society. Feuerbach,

Böckler and Che Guevara have all said the same thing. *"Pi-tou-kai!"* the post-Cultural Revolution slogan, meaning "Criticise, struggle, change!" defines a progress aimed at fundamental change, but one which can only succeed in producing external conformity to Party policies not a fundamental character change. The Chinese slogans are there: "Fight self-interest, serve the people!" but reform by slogan is not on. The Chinese have always, long before the arrival of Mao, been clever at inventing high-sounding and colourful slogans with which to plaster the walls of their cities. The one about "serving the people" is, of course, the most publicised. A whole "theology" has been built by their foreign admirers on the myth of the Chinese selfless service for others. What shall we say about the claim from a Christian point of view?

A century ago James Froude wrote, "To deny the freedom of the will is to make morality impossible." In other words a morality imposed and sustained by social sanctions is not morality. Atheistic morality in any case is a delusion for it has no permanent code of conduct. In the interests of revolution even evil can be good. As Lenin said, "All morality taken from superhuman or non-class conceptions is a deception, a swindle, a fraud. We must be ready to employ trickery, deceit, lawbreaking, concealing of truth, etc . . ." Lenin's followers have followed his advice ever since. To read Lenin's works is to discover volume after volume filled with intense hatred. Paul Kaufmann of Asian Outreach writes, "Divorcing morality from God is like divorcing the tree from the root and morality divorced from the Christian faith becomes a thing of custom—changeable, transient and optional." The post-Cultural Revolution period has fully borne out this truth. The "new man" in China does not exist. The Maoist "law code" may be there but "all have fallen short" of even Mao's ethical standards; how much more of the standards of a God who requires truth, not only externally, but in the heart and in the very springs of human nature? Archbishop Ramsey once said, "Man can never haul himself up to such heights of unselfishness, only Christ can lift him up."

What, therefore, the Chinese and humanists everywhere are attempting to achieve by education, by indoctrination, by persuasion, by slogans, by special pressures and by fear is doomed to certain failure. No political idealism, no power of the mass media, no pressures of public opinion and no social manipulation can ever possibly give birth to the "new man", the totally selfless individual. The post-Cultural Revolution decade has abundantly demonstrated that even the Radical leaders and their massive following, far from being selfless individuals, were consumed with a lust for personal power, a hatred of their "class enemies" and rivals and a total lack of anything akin to the Christian love which loves not only friends but enemies. Mao Tse-tung himself, great leader though he was, was also surely one of the most egocentric and paranoid of men. He was quite unable to tolerate any opposition to his own ideas and repeatedly swept aside those who opposed him. And is it not pure self-interest that has kept China's cadres ever with an eye on the political weathercock to see which way the ideological winds were blowing? Their choice has always been between hypocrisy and opportunism; after all their livelihood depended on it.

Alexander Solzenytsin in his novel *Cancer Ward* put these words into the mouth of Shelub: "We thought it was enough to change the mode of production and immediately people would change as well. But did they change? The hell they did! They did not change a bit!" And that strikes at the very heart of Marxism, the mirage of the twentieth century. The restraints of conscience, law, convention or public opinion can only moderate human conduct, not change it fundamentally. In facing the realities of human nature in China one is certainly not denigrating what is being attempted nor making unfavourable comparisons with Western man. Human nature is the same everywhere in the world—basically selfish and selfcentred and capable of every kind of evil. And, although the Christian Church proclaims the truth of redemption and regeneration of man, it does not follow that the Church itself is free from inborn corruption. The Church is only true to itself when it takes the place of the publican rather than the Pharisee in Jesus' well-known parable. "God be merciful to me a sinner!"

Ultimately it is the Eternal God, the Creator, who is the source of all righteousness. He makes on man unchanging moral demands and will on the Last Day be the judge of the living and the dead. The morality that God demands is totally opposed to the opportunism of Communist "morality".

Marxism—a delusion

In brief, Communism is a system of beliefs or theoretical principles which form an absolutely indispensable basis for action—namely Marxism–Leninism. Chairman Mao called them "the most complete, progressive, revolutionary and rational system in human history". That is why the Chinese Communists spend so much time attempting to teach the people dry theory, for it is theory that gives their actions any legitimacy they possess. Communist theory, admittedly, has a strange fascination about it which David Aikman of *Time* magazine compares to the study of poisonous spiders— beautiful but deadly. Communism is a sort of alternative religion offered to a world that has turned away from religion. Professor Arnold Toynbee defines Communism as "the worship of the collective power of man in place of the worship of God". But, as an alternative religion it cannot be considered. Indeed Communism is actually a subtle counterfeit of God's eternal programme. This fact alone adequately accounts for the apparent good in Marxism, enough to deceive the unwary, the ignorant and even "the elect" (Matthew 24. 24). In this sense it represents the spirit of antiChrist, the "strong delusion" which makes people "believe what is false" (II Thessalonians 2. 11 RSV). Communism is a masterpiece of the Great Enemy of whom the Bible says, "That ancient serpent, who is called the Devil and Satan, the deceiver of the whole world . . ." It is Satan's most successful "con" trick perpetrated on mankind, a humanist fraud, a diabolical parody of the Christian faith. In Maoist China this parody can be seen in the emphasis on "sin", "repentance", "confession" and the "new birth".

Are Marxism and Christianity compatible?

"Much has been made of the so-called Christian–Marxist dialogue," says David Lyon of Ilkley College, West Yorkshire, "and it is in this interchange that there is perhaps more fuzziness and confusion than in any other aspect of the relationship. . . . Each side seems to have accepted a caricature of their positions as fair representation of what they claim to stand for; in other words, as the Christian minimises the character of God and the fallenness of man and the Marxist minimises the need for revolution and the eventual abolition of religion, so each is forsaking what others would consider essential elements of their belief for the purpose of conversation." But there is no intellectually honest means of building a bridge between Marxist materialism and Christianity. The denial of the morality of personal choice, the reduction of history to a pre-determined conflict between the classes wholly shaped (as Marxists contend) by their role in the economic process—these are an outright denial of the Christian faith.

In terms of Christian theology the cardinal error of Marxism lies in its doctrine of God—or rather the systematic denial of the Christian concept of God as the ultimate sanction for moral conduct. But error about God at once leads to error about man. Nicholas Berdyaev writes: "Where there is no God there is no man." [1] The Marxist emphasis on the importance of society rather than the individual inevitably leads to a low estimate of the individual as such and the denial of moral values, as Lenin himself confessed. In Marxism–Leninism moral values are dictated by the State and serve the welfare of the State, not that of the individual. Man becomes merely an amoral, expendable instrument to be manipulated and exploited in the interest of some ultimate social utopia. Moreover, if God is ruled out man must take the place of God. Human autonomy becomes the rule and the norm. And that leads to disaster. No, neither Marxism nor Maoism are the answer to China's or the world's problems. D. R. Davies, the former Communist, said, "Marx without knowing or intending it, revealed the ultimate bankruptcy of mere humanistic thinking at its best."

Needed—a life-line!

The "liberation" that China, like all other nations, needs supremely is liberation from human error, self-will and pride. China's hopes for salvation lie not in Mao Tse-tung

[1] *The Evil of our Time* (Sheed and Ward), p. 40.

Thought but in the Truth—God's Truth, the Truth that alone sets men free. Tragically this is the very Truth which her leaders deny and which the people are not permitted to hear. The Christian Church, said the Apostle Paul, is the "pillar and ground of the truth" and that includes the Church in China, small and weak though it may be. The Chinese people need a life-line to rescue them from godlessness and eternal ruin. The despised and rejected Christian Church in their midst in its witness to the living Christ is that life-line.

Folly of the wise

Unless their yardstick is the authoritative Word of God in the Bible and not the speculative theologies of the day, even learned scholars can fall into foolish error. Is it not folly to regard China as an example of the way Marxism can provide a salvation which makes Christianity superfluous or redundant? Chinese Communism is neither worse than other Communist regimes nor is it demonstrably better or more successful. Like every other Communist nation, China is totally committed to the denial of all religious or supernatural truth and to the ultimate destruction of religion of every kind. It is therefore almost incredible that anyone can equate life in China in any way with Christianity or regard the "new China" as a preview of the future society of mankind. The Apostle Paul offers the only explanation. "Where is the wise man? Where is the scribe? Where is the debater of this age? Has not God made foolish the wisdom of the world? For the foolishness of God is wiser than men and the weakness of God is stronger than men." (II Corinthians, 1, 18–25).

God's purposes

God's purposes for China will ultimately be achieved, but not through Communism. Victor Hayward wrote in *Chinese Christians*: "If the ends in any particular case are identical, or even consonant, with those of Christian mission, will not true faith acknowledge the works of God . . . ?" [1] But the materialist "ends" of a Communist power, whether in China or elsewhere, are certainly not identical with nor are they

[1] *Chinese Christians*, by V. Hayward, p. 108.

even consonant with those of the mission of the Church. The suggestion must be totally refuted. The mission of the Church has always been primarily that of proclaiming the Apostolic Gospel worldwide so that God may call out from the nations a redeemed people to become the Body of Christ on earth. China's rulers, in spite of their achievements on a material level, far from fulfilling God's sovereign purposes for that land, have actually opposed them and they continue to do so. But in vain! Have not those leaders who commissioned the destruction of the Church by the Red Guards in 1966 already been judged? Have they not been "brought to nothing" (Isaiah 40. 23), that is, overthrown by the powers that be and ultimately by a sovereign God? Others like Mao Tse-tung and Chu Teh have gone to "meet their God" in judgment. And, so long as China's rulers continue to exalt themselves against God and to thwart His saving purposes for the Chinese people, they can expect further judgment — famines, earthquakes, floods and economic distress, of which China has recently had her fair share! Do not such calamities serve as divine warnings leading the people of China and indeed of other lands to repent and turn to the only true and living God and to seek His mercy?

"Be still and know that I am God. I am exalted among the nations. I am exalted in the earth." Psalm 46.10.

"All authority in heaven and on earth has been given to Me," declares the One who has been exalted "far above all rule and power and dominion and above every name that is named ..."

CHAPTER XII

China's Life-line

The social needs of China's masses have always been over-whelming: widespread poverty and starvation in times of famine, the lack of health care and devastating epidemics, general insecurity amid lawlessness, inadequate housing and the constant threat of flooding in certain regions, opium addiction and the dire social consequences of superstition, ignorance and idolatry. The early missionaries were appalled at what they found.

Missionary social work

Consequently, numerous Christian doctors—long before Dr. Norman Bethune, the lone Canadian folk-hero of the Chinese Communists—served the Chinese people sacrifici-ally and pioneered modern medical services throughout China. They set up hospitals everywhere, established the first medical schools and trained the first doctors and nurses. Leprosy was treated and the leprosy patients were lovingly cared for in institutions. Many Christian doctors laid down their lives in the service of the Chinese people over the past one hundred years.

Poverty and natural disaster left many orphans and these too became the concern of missionaries, as well as the blind, the deaf and the dumb. It is to the shame of the Communists that they are perpetuating a gross libel against Roman Catholics in Shanghai where an illustrated booklet distribu-ted among schoolchildren alleges their cruel treatment of orphans in that city and their responsibility for many deaths. The fact is that many more would have died of starvation but for the compassion of the Roman Catholic sisters.

It was missionaries who opened the first schools and pioneered education for girls. The sixteen Christian universities, two hundred and nineteen hospitals and four hundred and nineteen middle schools were institutions of which no country in the world would have been ashamed. These were never allowed to be institutions for indoctrinating students or patients with Christianity, but were places where the Gospel was explained, Christian ethics were taught and high moral standards demonstrated by the Christian staff. In the 1930s fully one third of all leading Chinese received their education in a Christian institution. Not a few of the early Communist leaders were educated in such schools. Social reforms are the sole responsibility of governments. Foreign missions could do no more than sow the seeds of social justice in the minds of students.

And all this was the fruit of a sacrificial outpouring of money and a dedication of talent entirely for the benefit of the Chinese people, without ulterior motives of any kind. Missionaries were not, either consciously or unconsciously, the "tools of imperialism". The history of a century of Christian activity in China shows that the missionary movement and the Christian Church did, in a large degree, fulfil their social obligations to the Chinese people.

The primacy of the Gospel

But Christians see man as infinitely more than a product of matter to be utilised and subjected to manipulation of every kind by his fellow-men for ideological purposes. Man is a Divine creation, not merely an instrument of society. "What matters, therefore, is not the utilisation of man," says Helmut Thielecke "but rather the infinite value of the human soul." If a man's value depends on his ability to function, then, like a machine that no longer works, he can be liquidated, as in the Communist world. In spite of Marxism's original concern for man, it essentially makes a man a thing whose sole function is to try to control nature and to produce. He must be utilised and manipulated to these ends. For when man rejects a belief in God and in man as made in the image of God, the consequence is a low view of man himself. It is no longer as an individual but as a social being that man is regarded. Thus Christianity and Marxism, while they may have something in common in the sphere of economic theory, take opposing metaphysical viewpoints. Marxism is atheistic, materialistic, and concerned primarily with society, not the individual. Christianity, on the other hand, believes that God exists, spirit is primary and man has a personality that needs to be redeemed. Thus, in addition to its responsibilities for society, the primary task of the Church is to proclaim the Gospel of Christ reconciling man, alienated as he is by sin, to God. This is the overriding topic of the whole Bible and particularly of the Gospels and the Epistles. The example of Our Lord and His teaching in certain parables bears out the teaching of many Old Testament prophets that man's physical and social needs are important. The Epistles reinforce this truth. But overwhelmingly the New Testament writers and Our Lord Himself are concerned with how sinful man can be put right with and be reconciled to a holy God and be brought into a personal and living relationship with Him. The Gospel certainly has its social implications, but basically the Gospel is the Good News of salvation from sin and judgment, of eternal life beginning now and the certainty of heaven and immortality.

The difficult years (1842–1900)

The early missionaries, and their successors too, made their mistakes. But they were the products of their age and we should not, with the benefit of hindsight and in the light of present-day thinking, pass judgment on them. They acted by the highest standards they knew, although by present-day standards their attitudes and methods were certainly open to criticism. Missionaries were at times aggressive and tactless, especially in relation to the Chinese gentry whom they thus alienated. Although the Gospel originated in Asia and the Bible is Asian in its cultural background, to the Chinese mind the Christian religion, unlike Buddhism, always appeared as something "foreign". Missionaries sometimes made the mistake of assuming that converts should accept Western culture with Christianity. In doing so they offended the susceptibilities, both of the intelligentsia and the peasants alike. Eventually, missionaries came to realise their mistakes. They learned to appreciate the exquisite ancient culture of China and to welcome indigenous expressions of the Christian faith. And not a moment too early! For, no sooner was Christianity beginning to root itself in the soil of China, than the social upheaval of the twenties and thirties began, leading eventually to the departure of the missionaries in the early fifties.

The first Protestant missionaries gained access to China only as the result of the Opium War and the Treaty of Nanking in 1842. This was a disastrous start to the missionary enterprise and, although missionaries were never in the employ of foreign governments or in any way their agents, Christianity has ever since, in Chinese eyes, been tarred with the brush of imperialist aggression. Naturally, therefore, the early years of missionary endeavour were exceedingly difficult. The hatred of foreigners caused by the "Unequal Treaties" was universal and missionaries shared this opprobrium. They also faced physical dangers as well as insanitary conditions in days when there were no prophylactics against typhoid, cholera, typhus and the plague. The death rate among missionaries and their children was very high. In 1900, anti-foreign agitation finally exploded in the Boxer Uprising when thirty thousand Christian converts and about two hundred missionaries and their children died in a terrible massacre ordered by the ruling Empress Dowager.

Years of opportunity and change (1901–1911)

Those difficult years were followed by ten years of opportunity when the climate of opinion changed and large numbers of Chinese received the Gospel and crowded into the Church. Even Confucian scholars like Pastor Hsi, the former drug addict, confessed Christ. Pastor Hsi himself planted a dozen or so churches in Shansi which were the foundation of a very vigorous Church in that province.

But 1911 was the year of the Nationalist Revolution, spearheaded by the Christian Sun Yat-sen. It brought with it a fresh wave of patriotism and anti-foreign sentiment. At a time when theological liberalism was undermining the basic truths of the Gospel and so cutting the nerve of evangelism, many missionary societies changed their policies and gave priority to education, believing that the only way to reach the heart of China was by winning the children of the gentry for Christ. Bishop Stephen Neill sums up the consequences thus: "These students were little interested in the quest for personal salvation. How can China live anew? was the big question. Those who were baptised had almost no interest in the Church though they were loyal to Christ as far as they understood it. The Gospel was presented to the Chinese people less as a Gospel of personal salvation than as a means of political and social salvation." So these were *the political years (1911–1921)* of Revolution, World War One and its fateful consequences for China and the first appearance of Communism in that land.

The years of growth (1921–1951)

The Communist Party of China was formed in 1921 and the first Communist-inspired anti-foreign and anti-Christian movement took place in 1925, driving most missionaries to the coast and three thousand of them out of China altogether. The writing was on the wall and mission leaders realised that the churches must be taught the necessity of standing on their own feet, independently of the missionaries, if they were to survive at all in the dangerous times ahead. The "Three Self" slogan was then first coined—"self-supporting, self-governing, self-propagating". The National Christian Council of China was established in 1922 and some fifteen denominational groups united in the Church of Christ in China in 1927. These were significant moves to transfer leadership from the missionaries to the Chinese. Anglican and Lutheran groups formed united Anglican and Lutheran federations. Indigenous church movements also sprang up under Chinese leadership—a form of protest against missionary domination as well as an expression of the new life springing up within the churches.

The message of revival, so greatly needed, was carried with powerful results to every province of China by both Chinese and missionary evangelists. Membership of the churches reached new records. But the dark clouds of civil war between the Nationalists and the Communists and the aggression of Japan were hanging heavily over China and the

Church. Christians, both missionaries and Chinese, had already suffered at the hands of the Communists. Now, in the war between China and Japan which broke out in 1937, they were to suffer at the hands of the Japanese. Amid the suffering, however, the churches prospered and grew both in "occupied China" (the east) and in "free China" (the west). The war ended in 1945 and was followed by a positive explosion of spiritual life and activity. The indigenous movement led by Watchman Nee had a vision of evangelising unreached areas by migration. Instead of sending one or two individuals as missionaries, groups of Shanghai and Foochow Christians sold houses and property and moved to devastated areas of Kiangsi to establish agricultural settlements and ready-made churches. Jesus Family groups similarly migrated from Shantung to Shensi. But the time was already too late and these inspired plans never fully matured. In the universities and among the students of China, too, there was a great awakening and a spirit of revival. As the Communist armies swept over China thousands in all the universities found Christ and dedicated their lives to Him, come what may. In 1949 the Nationalist leaders took refuge in Taiwan. The missionaries did not long outstay them and in 1951 the great exodus began. But looking back it is clear that the years 1921–1951 were outstandingly the years of growth for the Church in China.

The years of persecution (1951–   )

They were followed by the years of persecution under the Communist regime. It is not generally known that the Christian Church in China, in spite of all the labours and sacrifices of Chinese and missionaries alike over a century of time, never had a following of more than a tiny percentage of the Chinese people. In 1949, when Chairman Mao began his rule over five hundred million Chinese, only three million belonged to the Roman Catholic Church, with its longer history, and less than one million to the Protestant Church. So, combined, the four million represented only about one per cent of the whole population. In contrast, the number of Christians in the African continent was approaching one hundred million.

And yet the words of Our Lord have been fulfilled in the case of China: "I will build My Church." Through the years the Risen Christ has been building His Church—not the man-made building of institutional Christianity which was anything but indestructible and has in fact been largely swept away, but that against which the gates of hell will never prevail—the spiritual temple, the living stones, the members of His Own Body, the Invisible Church in the sense that it consists of the born-again men, women and children whose life is hidden with Christ in God. The visible Church in China was, like churches elsewhere, mixed. There was both the institutionalised and the living church, both those who followed a liberal theology and those loyal to the Holy Scriptures, both the imported main-line denominations of the West and the independent and indigenous church fellowships of the latter years. Despite all the wood, hay and stubble of much missionary effort, God used missionaries to plant and to nurture that which was becoming a true expression of the Holy Spirit's activity—the Living Church of the Living God. *This* is China's life-line!

CHAPTER XIII

Built on the Rock

The Church in 1949

In 1949, according to statistics given by Allen J. Swanton,[1] there was an estimated total of baptised Protestants (including infants) of 1,811,700 of whom 823,506 were communicants. They included 2,155 ordained ministers, 8,508 evangelists and 2,396 women workers. There were 19,497 Protestant places of worship, 270 high schools and universities, and 262 hospitals. 40 Christian periodicals were in circulation. 110 Protestant missions were working in China. The affiliation of the largest groups of Christians was as follows:

Church of Christ in China (Methodists, Congregationalists, Baptists, Lutherans, etc.)	166,660
China Inland Mission	89,665
True Jesus Church	80,000
Southern Baptist Convention	70,346
Assembly Hall (Watchman Nee assemblies)	70,000

I am unable to speak for the "main-line" churches represented in the Church of Christ in China and the Anglican Church. The reports in this chapter, with a few exceptions, do not describe the activities of those churches. But it is true to say that many churches of China, though numerically small, were spiritually alive and exercised an influence out of all proportion to their size. They had experienced the cleansing and renewing fires of revival in each of the first five decades of this century. The independent church move-

[1] "Taiwan: Mainline versus Independent Churches" (William Carey Library, U.S.A.).

ments were born in revival. Consequently the churches were characterised by a devotion to the Bible as the Word of God, a spirit of prayerfulness, a lively fellowship and a willingness to endure hardness for Christ's sake. These characteristics did not, of course, mark all professing Christians but were seen in the lives of very many, especially in the years immediately before the Communist victory. Even where missionaries of a more liberal theological trend took the places of older missionaries, the "main-line" Chinese churches themselves generally retained their evangelical faith and convictions. But the churches were, on the whole, neither intellectually nor organisationally prepared to meet the challenge of Marxism–Leninism–Mao Tse-tung Thought. They were at first too easily deceived and too fearful and so became the ready victims of the subtle policies of the new Government. Only a few students and pastors had any understanding of Marxism–Leninism and the churches certainly had no united policy. Thus a divided church too easily fell into the hands of its self-appointed Marxist leaders, who later attempted to reconcile Marxism and Christianity and to establish a link with the churches in other Communist countries. Personal exchanges actually took place.

Land reform period

As the Communist armies advanced, People's Liberation Army posters in every city promised religious freedom. Christian fears were further allayed when Chou En-lai, the Prime Minister, paid the Christian Church the unprecedented compliment of inviting some of its leaders to Peking for a three-day conference. Out of this conference came the Christian Manifesto which sounded the death knell of the foreign missionary movement in China and pledged the Church to total submission to the Communist Party. Late in 1949 a group of eleven Chinese leaders sent a long message to missionary societies abroad expressing their appreciation of the work of missions on behalf of China. But they made it clear that a new era was opening when the old relationship between the Chinese Church and Christian missions must undergo a change. They also expressed their hope of continuing the witness of the Church within the new society of

Communist China. *Tien Feng* (Heavenly Wind), an official church publication, became the voice of the Communist-dominated Church. It welcomed the Communist victory and claimed to see a kind of "kingdom of heaven" in the coming new society. The Student Christian Movement in Peking, as elsewhere, saw in the new society the fulfilment of their hopes for China and voluntarily disbanded. The SCM was an organisation long associated with the politically orientated YMCA under the leadership of the Marxist Wu Yao-tsung, who also became the head of the new Three Self Reformed Church. The evangelical students of Peking and other cities, on the other hand, continued their faithful Christian witness until forced to disband in 1955.

Tien Feng rationalised about the campaigns of the Three Self Movement, comparing the "accusation campaign", for instance, with Jesus' denunciation of the Pharisees. Accusation, confession, public testimony and rebirth were the stages by which individuals and congregations were redeemed from their previous "bondage to imperialism" and accepted into the new Christian community: a blatant counterfeit of Christian experience. For many true believers it was a harrowing and soul-searching process. The few who bravely refused to confess their "wrong stand", suffered prison and even death. In the countryside, most rural churches were forced to close in 1950 for the duration of the land reform programme and church activities came to a temporary end. In the terror and turmoil when landlords were accused (often justly) of sins against the peasants—oppression and exploitation—it must have been very hard for peasant Christians to "love their enemies", when the masses were demanding their death or other punishment.

But there was also good news. In the mountains of south-west China six to seven thousand Lisu Christians celebrated the harvest festival in 1951 while Chinese missionaries to Tibet reported the first Tibetan converts in a border monastery town. In Kiangsi, where Chairman Mao set up the first Chinese "soviet" in 1932, and where Christians had suffered so greatly, the Holy Spirit was now powerfully at work everywhere. Membership in one church increased by fifty per cent in the following years. One wrote: "I have never seen so many waiting to be saved." In the province of Kweichow, at

Tsunyi, where Chairman Mao held his historic conference during the Long March in 1934, thirty-seven believers were baptised. At Wenchow on the Chekiang coast, a large work pioneered by the China Inland Mission, three hundred converts were baptised. These were no "rice" Christians. They had nothing to gain and everything to lose by their stand. Under the changed circumstances it required courage to identify oneself openly with the Christian Church. Meanwhile students in Bible schools and theological colleges in Peking, Chungking, Shanghai, Hangchow, Wuhu etc. calmly continued their studies.

In May 1950 the Christian Manifesto was issued and eventually signed by about four hundred thousand Protestants. It required the churches to implement the "Three Self" principle by the total severance of all ties with foreign imperialism and to accept no further financial aid from abroad. Very soon after this missionary societies reluctantly advised the withdrawal of their missionaries. The C.I.M. was the last to take this decision. The Government required the deeds of all mission properties to be handed over to them before the missionaries were allowed to leave.

An encouraging visit

As the C.I.M. missionaries prepared to leave Shanghai God graciously gave them rich encouragement by sending an earnest group of Christians from a region of Hopei where C.I.M. missionaries had long been active. Hearing that their friends were soon to leave China they made the long journey from the north to say goodbye. They represented churches which had been without missionary help for over ten years— a very troubled ten years of war, Japanese occupation, catastrophic floods, famine and finally the change-over to a Communist Government. But what a marvellous story these tried and tested Christian warriors had to tell! Between them they had endured privation, imprisonment, persecution and faced death for Christ's sake. But quite obviously their faith was the stronger for their experiences. And the Church had not faded away when deprived of missionary support. When the use of the city church was denied to the Christians they conducted worship in a dozen local places of worship instead. Several leaders formed a team for pastoral visitation. They also started an industrial Bible school in which the students learned a trade by day and studied the Bible in the evenings in order to become "tent-making missionaries". Moreover, these faithful shepherds had seen signs following the preaching of the Word—demons exorcised, a paralysed man restored to normal activity to the chagrin of scoffing atheists, lives transformed, public baptisms and a growing Church. Clearly, as Elisha once said: "They that are for us are more than they that are against us!" The invisible armies of God give Chinese Christians a superiority over the forces of the enemy, whatever the outward appearances may at present be. And, for the Mission that was about to withdraw from China after eighty-five years of service, it was as though God was sending a special message to say, "Your labour is not in vain in the Lord!"

Reign of terror

The departure of the missionaries coincided with a reign of terror during the campaign against spies, counter-revolutionaries, landlords and capitalists. Public executions took place almost daily and many—including some Christians—were driven to suicide. The Korean war further assisted the subjugation of the churches, for patriotism demanded that they place the love of country above the love of their church. "Love country, love church!" was the slogan. Tentative moves were also made at this time to unify the Protestant churches and to unite Roman Catholics and Protestants. The accusation campaign was a tragic chapter in the history of the Christian Church. Congregations were made to accuse their pastors and in organisations like the Christian Literature Society the staff was required to accuse their executives. Many prominent Christians, including a President of the World Council of Churches, were also denounced by their colleagues and associates. This practice was a stage in the political education of Christians and was designed to highlight their alleged submission to imperialism.

In 1952 Nee To-sheng (Watchman Nee), the leader of the indigenous "assemblies" movement ("Little Flock") was arrested in Shanghai, accused of "counter-revolutionary" activities and other "crimes" and sentenced to fifteen years imprisonment. Other leaders of the movement were arrested later. A Roman Catholic bishop was sentenced to twenty years imprisonment. In 1951 the "Jesus Family" community-farming organisation was forcibly disbanded. In 1952 over two hundred Chinese priests died in prison or labour camps and in 1954 another four or five hundred. In spite of the threats and dangers, Wang Ming-tao, pastor of a large and flourishing local church in Peking, continued to preach courageously and to refute the claims of the Three Self Movement that missionaries had perverted the Gospel. He also continued to produce his outspoken magazine which had a nationwide circulation. In eloquent language and with clear Biblical teaching he urged Christians to stand their ground, without compromising, against error of every kind. He himself refused to have anything to do with the official Three Self Reformed Church and its activities. In 1955 he conducted what was possibly the largest and most fruitful evangelistic campaign of his life in the heart of the capital of the "new China". But even as the campaign was in progress a torrent of violent abuse was mounting against him in the national press. The Christian students in Peking valiantly and publicly defended him, but in vain. Mr. Wang was arrested and given a life sentence for "counter-revolutionary activities". The Three Self Movement could now congratulate itself that "the counter-revolutionary rings headed by Nee and Wang had been smashed!" When the People's Political Consultative Conference first met in 1954, Protestant leaders were invited to attend. So Christians were, under the terms of the New Democracy, given a place in the New China, provided that they toed the government line.

Still Christianity flourished. Even in Shanghai, travellers reported that the churches were in a healthier spiritual condition than those in Hong Kong, in spite of heavy pressures. At the other extremity of China, in Sinkiang (Chinese Turkestan) where C.I.M. pioneers like Hunter, Mather and the Misses Cable and French had laboriously sown the seed of God's Word without living to see a harvest, every city now had a church and Christians were numbered in their hundreds. In Tihwa a converted Muslim who spoke Arabic and the Wei dialect, as well as Chinese, was teaching in a half-day

Bible school and holding nightly evangelistic meetings. (Yet another Muslim who heard the Gospel first in the C.I.M. church in Lanchow was later converted in Taiwan, trained in the American College in Beirut and finally became a missionary in Turkey.) One church was operating a Christian book-shop using stock supplied by Miss Helen Willis in Shanghai. In a town largely populated by Mongols many were turning to Christ. In 1954 Chinese missionary organisations continued to report their activities in Inner Mongolia, Sinkiang and Tibet. At Wenchow on the coast a further forty families turned to Christ in nine months and over six hundred were baptised in 1955–6. The church buildings had to be enlarged. In the neighbouring county of Wenling where the C.I.M. had founded fifty-nine country churches, twenty thousand Christians were awaiting permission for these churches to reopen after land reform. In this same province of Chekiang, Kiangshan registered many baptisms at this time and hundreds were converted at Shaohsing, the wine-producing county, where revival conditions prevailed. Communist observers were totally mystified by the inexplicable joy of the congregations. But the most sensational church growth was in once "dark Anhwei" where, between 1951 and 1955, the Hwochiu church membership increased from two thousand to four thousand and in Honan, where membership increased from three hundred in 1951 to three thousand in 1956 despite the arrest of some of the leaders. Christmas 1957 saw many baptisms in Central China. Between 1953 and 1956 membership within the Chekiang synod of the Church of Christ in China increased by eighteen per cent, the Shantung Synod by twenty-two per cent and the Kiangsi Synod by thirty per cent. As baptisms had to be registered with the Government these figures indicate great Christian courage. In one area, a group of women went into the mountains to pray for a whole month before special meetings. Is it surprising that God added many to the church in consequence? In one city near Peking a hundred and seventy people were baptised. A White Russian released from a Peking gaol reported meeting many Christians there whose faith held firm. Another White Russian from Harbin in Manchuria met a missionary in Hong Kong and told him that the churches there were all closed but that the Christians were standing firm. In some big cities of China evangelistic campaigns were being held annually with numerous conversions. Christians everywhere evidenced a deep and wonderful spirit of simple faith in spite of the hardships. In south-west China the tribal Christians of Yunnan and Kweichow zealously witnessed for Christ and were seeing hundreds baptised. Four Christians were invited by two men who had believed twelve years previously to visit their home. There they found that the whole village had turned to Christ. In three days they baptised four hundred and thirty-three believers. From Kwangtung came news of hundreds of baptisms in the Tung tribe and the ordination of thirteen deacons.

Bibles and literature

One result of this healthy growth was seen in the continued sale of Bibles. The China Bible Society continued to print Bibles in Shanghai and between 1949 and 1955 sold 171,278 Bibles, 170,493 New Testaments and three million posters. The Society also produced forty-three new editions of the Scriptures. Twelve Bible depots continued to operate. Copies of the recently completed Mongolian Bible were also reaching the Mongolian oases from Hong Kong. In 1956 a commission was set up to produce a new translation of the Bible. It was a severe blow, therefore, when the fifty-six Christian publishers were forced to combine in one joint state-private enterprise and eighty per cent of their stock was destroyed. But Miss Helen Willis was somehow allowed to continue her independent Christian Book Room in Shanghai from which she met the requests for Christian literature in many languages from all parts of China. 167 pounds of tracts and 11,678 books, of which *The Existence of God* was most in demand, were despatched by parcel post. Miss Willis reported a great hunger for the things of God. One woman who visited the Book Room told her how she had started thirty-six house meetings, one of which had an attendance of two hundred. Miss Willis was finally forced to leave China in 1961. The Chinese Sunday School Union and the China Baptist Publishing House of Shanghai jointly produced "Gospel Light Lessons" for Sunday Schools which, in some areas, continued to be well attended. But eventually *Tien Feng* launched an attack on Sunday Schools on the ground that they were putting out reactionary propaganda.

In 1956 a party of Australian clergy, including Archbishop Mowll, formerly of the West China diocese, visited China. In Szechwan the archbishop found the churches he knew carrying on normally and discovered new churches under the leadership of Bishop Ts'ai Fu-ch'u. Ordination of clergy continued. However, by 1958, due to mergers and closures, only six theological and Bible colleges remained open, with a total of about five hundred students. In 1960, even the Peking Theological College closed its doors.

Christ in the universities

But, most surprising of all, was the persistent activity of Christian students in the universities. The original Peking group was forcibly disbanded in 1955 but their successors obtained permission to meet again in 1957—a large group which, like its predecessors, spent much time in prayer, even half-nights of prayer, as well as maintaining a clear witness to the Gospel of Jesus Christ. In 1957 a student conference in Swatow was attended by representatives from universities in Peking, Tientsin, Shanghai, Wuhan, Nanking, Kweilin, Nanning and Canton. In most universities Christian students continued to enjoy liberty to hold their meetings. But that was not everywhere the case. A lone Christian in a college of 1,700 who persisted in giving thanks at meals for his food, sometimes found his rice bowl removed as he closed his eyes and he went hungry: he was the constant butt of criticism for not thanking Chairman Mao for his food. In the summer of 1957 many conferences for young people were held in different parts of China. Over a thousand attended a student rally in Wenchow.

The "Hundred Flowers" period

In 1957 the Assembly Hall (Little Flock) also called a conference in Shanghai to plan for the consolidation of their work. Delegates came from all parts of China. Chekiang was their chief stronghold with 362 places of worship and about thirty-nine thousand members. Perhaps it was this challenge that marked a turning-point in the experience of the Christian Church. At the end of the year the Three Self organisation replied by intensifying the campaign of "re-education" for church leaders. These leaders had already been subjected to political indoctrination at different periods since 1949. Now they were required to attend all-day sessions for months on end. The comparative freedom which the churches had hitherto enjoyed suddenly became restricted. Christians were told: "Surrender your hearts to the Party!" The two hundred places of worship in Shanghai were reduced to twenty and one of the largest Shanghai congregations was disbanded. In Peking the sixty-five churches were reduced to four. All over China churches were forced to close down and more Christians faced accusation meetings. Two Shanghai pastors were forbidden to continue their ministry. Hundreds of leaders throughout China were similarly denounced as "rightists" and silenced. It is estimated that eighty per cent of Christian ministers became redundant and went to work on Three Self farms or in factories. Discrimination against Christians was intensified: a promising young physicist, the son of a scientific worker, was banished to Tibet to work as a carpenter: Christian doctors faced the possible end of their careers. The Christian unions in the universities were one by one disbanded and the open Christian witness stamped out. The authorities exercised stricter control over church activities and Christians were forbidden to hold "unauthorised meetings" outside the officially designated buildings. Infringement of these regulations was punishable by imprisonment or a term in a labour camp. In the cities, church pulpits became little more than platforms for Marxist–Leninist–Mao Tse-tung Thought.

The situation was now so bad that, at the first session of the People's Political Consultative Conference held in 1957, the Rev. Marcus Cheng Ch'ung-kwei, one of the Christian delegates and hitherto a warm supporter of the "new China", was driven to make a fiery speech indicting the Government for its failure to fulfil its promises about religious freedom. And when, in the same year, widespread disillusionment with the Government and with the Party was loudly expressed in the "Let a Hundred Flowers bloom . . ." episode, who knows how many Christians expressed their dissatisfaction and, like thousands of others, were silenced and disgraced? The techniques of deception were by now plain for all, except the wilfully blind, to see—the exploitation of nationalism, patriotism and progress to persuade and finally to dragoon Christians to support the policies of the Government. A feigned tolerance and a show of patronage covered up a determination to destroy Christianity by a long process of re-education. The promised freedom was steadily attenuated until the churches were finally reduced to impotence, and forced to wear the oppressive mantle of atheism. All this time the press kept up its vicious attacks on religion.

The Great Leap Forward period

1958 was the year of the Great Leap Forward and the start of the ill-fated commune experiment. So tight were the work schedules and so long the working day (sixteen hours) that all normal church activities ceased and only irregular family gatherings were possible. As 1959 drew to a close the promised freedom for Christians ceased to have any reality. Government persecution of the churches was open and universal. So harsh was the lot of the Lisu church in Yunnan that twenty thousand Christians in bitter weather secretly crossed the fifteen-thousand-feet-high passes to escape into Burma. There the Lisu church is growing apace and enjoying for the first time the possession of the whole Bible in their own language. But the once flourishing churches in the Salween valley were effectively eliminated. Those who could not escape were either dead or in prison. All over China the arrest of Christians and their denunciation as "rightists" were now commonplace. Some suffered the penalty of death. At the second session of the People's Political Consultative Conference in 1960 missionaries were viciously denounced in their absence and Chinese Christians were urged to reform themselves even more radically.

But the tragedy of China's premature and disastrous attempt at communisation continued to unfold in 1959–60. Natural disaster compounded the mismanagement. In August 1960 a hundred and fifty million acres of farmland—half of the total area under cultivation in China—were devastated by drought and pests. Famine spread and hunger gripped the millions. The anguish of the hardworking masses was terrible. Refugees from China poured into Hong Kong. Relatives in Hong Kong swamped the Post Office with food parcels for the more fortunate. Shortages and reduced rations, even in the cities, continued well on into 1961 and 1962. No wonder the thousands of Chinese repatriated at this time from Indonesia to China were soon disillusioned about the paradise they had been led to expect. The letters of Christians to friends back in Java told a sad story and urged them to make the most of the liberty they enjoyed there. They also confirmed the stories of false accusations, arrests, prison sentences, labour-camp terms and discrimination against Christians, but reported that a living witness for Christ was continuing. The whole nation was disillusioned with the Government for its failure to live up to its promises and because of the prevailing hatred and wrong-doing. The Government knew this and was struggling to regain the lost confidence of the people. One Christian from Java wrote sadly in 1964 of the spiritual failure of half the Christians who had returned to China, but said that a small group remained strong and brave and continued to walk with the Lord.

The anti-rightist period

Another Three Self conference, held in early 1960, appointed five delegates to accuse the missionaries of being a "reactionary force within the church". The fierce anti-Christian pressures were maintained. But, in the midst of the tragedy and the growing opposition to the Church, news of the churches in Chekiang, Hunan (Chairman Mao's province) and Shansi was encouraging. In Shansi young people were especially active for Christ, according to a visiting Honan Christian who had just been released from prison.

After three successive years of crop failures and low food rations the autumn crop in 1962 was better and the food situation continued to improve through 1963 and 1964. Changsha, the capital of Hunan, the last province to open to the Gospel, was closely associated with the Communist revolution. But a letter from that province, written on 9th June 1962 by a well-known old pastor, came as a shaft of

light in the darkness: "I am exceedingly glad to receive your
letter. We are separated physically, yet we never forget
fellowship in the Spirit. I have never ceased to do my church
work through the past years. Preachers in other places have
also been as they were and services continue normally. I am
now 77 but still able to do all kinds of work. I know how to
be abased and how to abound, to be full and to be empty, to
abound and to suffer need. I truly thank God for being content in whatsoever state I am. Indeed the barrel of meal
wasted not, neither did the cruse of oil fail and in Christ all
needs are fully met. May God's grace be upon you all . . ."
Elsewhere in Hunan, a farmer and a tailor, on fire for Christ,
were used to open three new preaching centres where sixty
or seventy people met in each place and where a hundred
and seventy people were earnestly studying the truth and
awaiting baptism. Hunan Christians generally were standing
firm.

During the early sixties the anti-rightist campaign continued inexorably. Inevitably it affected church life. But in
Honan and Shansi the country churches seemed to grow ever
stronger and healthier. In Shantung, the scene of revivals in
the thirties, the Holy Spirit was again at work renewing the
Christians. A report in the *Hong Kong Standard* said:
"While the visible and formal churches in China are dying
out, the invisible, formless, non-political and true churches
are growing . . . Genuine and devout Christian men and
women, living under trying conditions and having survived
Communist persecution, have become all the more faithful
and dedicated to their faith."

The stubborn persistence of religious activity, the progressive nature of the Church and the numerous baptisms
in all parts of China prompted the *Liberation Daily* to protest on 13th June 1963: "We are Marxists and the most
fundamental atheists. Not only do we not believe in any religion, but we believe that religious superstition is uncon-
scious, ignorant and blind. Therefore we cannot avoid paying attention to superstitious thought and action among the
masses and we must actively preach atheism and promote
scientific universal education." Fresh attacks on Christianity
and the Bible followed. The religious aspect of the Socialist
Education Movement was the Atheist Education Campaign.

A debate on religion in the press continued from 1963–65 entirely concerned with how to eradicate religion of every kind. Edgar Snow once spoke of Mao's "revolutionary opposition to religion". This opposition was now no longer disguised. It was out in the open though the official policy was not yet outright extinction, but one of restriction, reformation and utilisation with total control as the end in view. In March 1964 further attacks on religion appeared in the Chinese press with special reference to Islam and Lamaistic Buddhism.

A March 1964 letter from three sisters in the southwestern province of Yunnan—an administrator, a doctor and a school teacher—assured the recipient that all three were faithfully going on with the Lord. Another letter from a girl in the same province described a simple Christmas celebration and testified to the comfort of hearing familiar hymns on her radio. She found strength in the faithful witness of a neighbouring Christian family. Externally there was less and less evidence of the Church's presence. So many churches were closed that an Indian Christian visitor to the Ganefo Games in 1965 wrote: "The Church in Communist China appears to have no future!" How deceptive appearances can be!

The Cultural Revolution period

But now the Church was about to pass through an even darker valley—the valley of the shadow of death. In order to regain his lost control of the Chinese Communist Party and to ensure the continuation of Maoist ideological orthodoxy, Chairman Mao plunged the nation into the chaos of the Cultural Revolution. Millions of youthful Red Guards were given the experience of making revolution. In the process of eliminating the "four olds", religion was a major target, and especially "foreign religion". Unquestionably they did a thorough job. All churches were closed, sealed and confiscated. Church leaders, like many political personalities, were humiliated and sometimes physically assaulted, including leading figures in the Government-sponsored Three Self Movement. Some Christians are known to have been killed by the youthful zealots. They also sacked Christian homes in their search for Bibles which, with all Christian literature, were systematically destroyed. The Christian Church became a Church without buildings and without Bibles. 1966 was the first year since 1842 that Christmas was not publicly cele- brated in China. A spate of letters from listeners to the FEBC [1] during the lawless period of the following years told of suffering, but also of the strong faith of believers. China has the unenviable distinction of being the only Communist nation in the world, with Albania, to have driven the entire Christian Church underground. With the liquidation of the organised Church in 1967 the living Church became de- institutionalised—"an unstructured fellowship of the re- deemed". A curtain of total silence fell and for years foreign visitors were unable to detect any signs of Christian activity. Their enquiries were met with the bland answer "Religion no longer exists in China!" The world was left to wonder and to speculate.

[1] Far East Broadcasting Company—a Christian radio organisation.

CHAPTER XIV

After the Silence

Good news

Six years after the Cultural Revolution started the silence was broken. From the southern coastal provinces news of the most exciting kind began to reach the praying world outside China. Faith was confirmed that the Church in China was still living and thriving in the tradition of the first century—a church in the catacombs. Scepticism and unbelief were rebuked. The first surprise was that in 1973 in Foochow a Christian community numbering from a thousand to one thousand five hundred had grown up over the previous four years. A work of the Holy Spirit had led to many conversions including at least one atheistic cadre. The Christians met clandestinely in three different locations. The authorities were at first perplexed, then in 1974 they acted to ban large gatherings and arrested five leaders and paraded them in dunce hats through the city streets. After a term of imprisonment the same leaders, undeterred, continued their pastoral ministry. This news and much that follows was brought by refugees from the Mainland of China or by Chinese visitors to the Mainland, of whom there are many thousands at the time of the Spring and Autumn Festivals. Letters from China to relatives are usually cautious as to what they say, but they too are sources of factual information.

1972 marked a turning point in China's relations with the world. President Nixon of the U.S.A. accepted an invitation to visit Peking following earlier visits of American table-tennis players. Now journalists, diplomats, kings and queens, scientists, scholars, medical teams, demographers, social scientists, economists, university professors, technologists and traders, etc. from America and from all parts of the

world began to pour into China to see for themselves what
the "new China" was like. Most were impressed with what
they saw. Then China took her seat in the United Nations
and in the Security Council. A growing number of nations
exchanged ambassadors with the Government of Peking and
withdrew recognition from Taiwan. Largely for the benefit of
Peking's diplomatic corps the Chinese Government authorised the opening of one Roman Catholic church and one
Protestant chapel in 1973 for Sunday worship. A mosque
and Buddhist temple were also made available for overseas
visitors. These facilities were only provided in response to
foreign demand and they tell us nothing about the general
attitude of the Government to the Christian Church or religion in China. The churches throughout China which were
closed in 1966 in fact remain closed in 1979.

The Chinese Church today

Since the Cultural Revolution Bibles have been in very
short supply. The few copies retained are often shared or
their pages torn out and distributed. Some Bible teachers
duplicate passages for their classes and gradually sizeable
sections of Scripture are collected. Christians have also taken
advantage of listening to the Scriptures read at dictation
speed on the FEBC programmes and in this way have accumulated their own hand-written Bible manuscripts. But,
above all, the fabulous memories of the Chinese have enabled many Christians in the past to memorise large portions of Scripture and what is thus hidden in the heart cannot
be taken away. Furthermore, many portions of the Bible
were set to music and became a popular part of the Church's
musical repertoire, to be memorised and sung over and over
again. A modern translation of the Bible in the new simplified script is available in Hong Kong, but so far only a trickle
of copies is getting into China.

Two representatives of the FEBC travelled widely in
China during 1976 and heard the FEBC signals clearly
wherever they went. In eighteen places they met with Bible
study groups which use FEBC programmes to help them in
their study of the Word of God.

Reports from China as a whole

News of churches other than those in the south-east is scanty, but encouraging. A Canadian minister on a visit to Peking in 1978 met a pastor from Inner Mongolia who had been sent there from Honan for re-education. After his release he continued to work in Mongolia where, he reported, there is "a considerable number of small groups of Christians meeting together", but they lack Bibles. A Christian from Hopei in North China who reached Hong Kong said that, while some Christians have fallen away, others have been strengthened in their faith. Some, however, were still in prison and many lived in fear of arrest and under great psychological pressure. Now, he said, Christians meet in small numbers and many of them are zealous young people. One young convert memorised the whole New Testament in four months and the Psalms in one month! This was given as an example of the thirst there is in China for God's Word. Then from south-west China there is news of Bible "couriers" from Burma crossing the frontier into Yunnan to discover thousands of believers—probably tribal Christians—worshipping regularly in spite of severe persecution. In sixteen villages the courier reported that the entire population was Christian. For tourists in China, the Great Wall near Peking is inevitably and deservedly on the list of ancient monuments to be visited. Recently a tourist engaged a group of Chinese in conversation on the Wall. They asked him: "Are you a Christian?" "Why, yes," he replied, "I am a missionary!" "We too are Christians," came the happy response. And there are Christians in high places too, as a visiting American official discovered after he had given away a few New Testaments in the new script in the Great Hall of the People. "I, too, am a believer!" one of them quietly confessed.

Reports from the south-east

The windows, though not the doors, of China are opening to allow us a glimpse of the Church in China. It was on the coast of south China that the Church was first planted after 1842. The churches were, therefore, larger and more solidly established there than elsewhere. It is also from these provinces that most "overseas Chinese" come and with which they retain links. Naturally, therefore, it is from these provinces that most of our information comes.

Shanghai has many house churches, so have Chekiang and Fukien, both in the cities and in the villages. Attendances at these churches range from a few to a few hundred. In some cases a whole commune production team (i.e. a village) is Christian—perhaps thirty or forty families. In one county, pioneered by the Church Missionary Society and the China Inland Mission, in a population of four hundred thousand, Christians are now numbered in tens of thousands—many of them young people. Conversions are adding to the Church continually. Conditions vary and rural areas enjoy more freedom than the cities, but baptisms, weddings and funerals are often made the occasion of a powerful Christian witness. At one funeral attended by a thousand people, the Christians celebrated their belief in the Resurrection. Leaders devise means for exercising pastoral care and, in 1976, five hundred of them attended a retreat for leaders. One church in Fukien is known to hold retreats and training courses for young believers, in the near-by mountains. Instances of miraculous healing and exorcism are not infrequent. The power of believing prayer is fundamental to the Christian's belief and practice.

In 1976 Miss Mary Wang of the Chinese Church in London had the joy of fellowship with a Christian who had recently come out of China. She wrote: "The deep love for Jesus, firm faith in God and well-memorised Bible verses manifested in this Christian point to a Church which is very much alive. In fact, this Christian's home in China is a centre of Christian activities: prayer and Bible study meetings are held three evenings a week and fulltime itinerant Bible teachers come regularly to teach and baptise young believers. Moreover, as a result of the blameless life and conduct of Christians, others are drawn to accept Christ as their Saviour." Miss Wang also met a Christian in Holland who, for twenty-five years, had been living far away from God. Then he revisited his family in China and, to his surprise, found that half the population in his home village had become Christians. He returned to Holland renewed in his faith. In 1978 a Chinese Christian living in Paris revisited China and, during the six weeks that he was there, he regularly met with one or other of two groups of Christians with seventy to eighty in each—most of them young people. A member of the True Jesus Church, an indigenous denomination founded in 1917, recently reached Hong Kong. In an interview she reported that, in her area, from fifty to one hundred groups were meeting regularly without any prohibition from the authorities. In fact, they had never even received so much as a warning. Baptisms are held publicly, and, as the result of the miraculous healing of a child, a whole village is now Christian. "We envy you," she said, "not for your luxurious living, but for the freedom you enjoy to make Christ known."

Finally, another 1978 letter sums up the situation: "Over here our people are of the same Spirit and are even more revived, more progressive and becoming more perfect in Christ. We have greater freedom and are meeting quite openly now. Everything is so convenient compared to the past. Every week we have great meetings—very crowded and very warm in the Spirit. Many people have turned from their old superstitious ways and from their old beliefs. Also quite a number are coming back to us who were previously with us but because of the difficult situation left us. Therefore we are adding new members very rapidly. Great miracles and strange events with powerful manifestations are happening frequently. Not only are they more in quantity but also greater in quality. In the past few decades we have seen such wonderful things. Comparing now with the past we can expect even greater things from Him. He is really working among us. The time is ripe for Him to reveal His glory . . ."

Lessons to be learned

What has enabled the Church in China to survive in face of fierce persecution, unceasing discrimination against Christians and their families and an all-out attempt to destroy the Church? Unless that Church had been rooted in the Word of God and unless it had shared the essential experience of the new birth it could not have survived. In fact, those former adherents who had no "born again" experience have already dropped out. All that is merely of human origin and organisation is destructible. Mercifully, such has already been swept away. What remains is the Temple that Christ, through the Holy Spirit, has built of "living stones" related to Himself, the Living Stone. Or, to change the metaphor, only those who are spiritually incorporated in the living Body of Christ by the new birth of the Spirit are likely to survive amid the fires of persecution.

Indeed, this living Body of Christ that has been purified by suffering, that has experienced the miracle-working power of believing prayer, and to whom the Word of God is infinitely precious has much to teach us. Their corporate life is marked by loyalty and love to Christ and to one another. They have learned how to do without buildings and institutions and to centre their worship in the family and the home. Their witness, too, is personal where public preaching is impossible and by loving service to neighbours as well as words.

Christians in the West should learn from their Chinese brethren. Peter's first epistle, written to prepare the Church for imminent persecution, expounds the need to make sure of our foundations (chapter 1), to prepare ourselves for the fiery trial of suffering whenever it may come (chapter 4. 12ff), to master the differences between alien creeds and Christianity and so be able to give a rational defence of our beliefs (chapter 3. 15), to live such blameless lives that we refute and rebuke our critics (chapter 3. 16, 17; 4. 16), to adopt a correct and Biblical attitude towards authority and towards the society of which we are a part (chapter 2; 11–17) and to foster a warm and close fellowship among believers (chapter 3. 8, 9; 4. 7–12; 5. 2–5). These were the lessons urged upon the Church in China before the Communist take-over. Our turn may come! We should likewise be ready.

Former leaders

Is there news of former Christian leaders? Dr. Chia Yu-ming, the saintly octogenarian, died in April 1964. Pastor Eo-yang, a leading figure in the suffering church of Kiangsi, also died in 1964. Watchman Nee was released from prison in 1972 but died soon after his release. Mrs. Wang Ming-tao and a younger woman were both released from prison in

1975. (Of the latter her mother testified that she was still the same bright Christian at the end of fifteen years in a Communist gaol as at the beginning! Many prisoners have reported hearing other prisoners singing "songs in the night" for their mutual encouragement.) In May 1979, Mr Wang Ming-tao, aged 79, was finally released from a labour camp in Tatung, North Shansi, where he had been working as a male nurse. But, as the old and loved leaders pass to their reward, God is raising up a new generation of leaders, trained in warfare, for that new day of opportunity that awaits His inauguration.

The key to the future

The Church in China may be a contemptible minority, totally insignificant and powerless in the world's eyes. But so were Gideon's three hundred. And so has the true Church always been. It is, nevertheless, the Church of which Christ said, "I will build My Church . . ." He has built His Church in China in the past. He is still building it today. He will certainly continue to build it in the future.

Thirty years have passed since the last missionaries withdrew from China. Chinese Christians have surely in this time purged themselves of the stigma of being "running dogs of the imperialists"! Christians, for the most part, have shown themselves to be both loyal servants of Christ and also loyal citizens of their country. They have survived every onslaught on their faith and witness. They have done more—they have flourished under persecution and multiplied. As George Patterson wrote in *Christianity in Communist China*, "If the Church has survived the past quarter of a century in China, it can surely survive anywhere!"

During the Great Leap Forward Mao taught that by the power of the human will it is possible to modify natural conditions! Stalin once talked about man's ability to conquer nature by the power of the human will. The Chinese Government has at times urged the people to "fight against heaven and earth", claiming that "human beings will overcome nature"! At the reopening of the Central Committee's training school for cadres in 1977 one speaker described the tasks ahead as "carrying out deep-going social reforms, declaring war upon nature and developing the social production forces with high speed". But such romanticism has been exposed for the folly that it is. In China climatic conditions and earthquakes have laid bare the emptiness of such boasting and revealed the helplessness of puny man before the almighty, transcendent God. It is as if God through natural disasters is demanding that China bow her knee before the Creator and Sustainer of the universe. Jesus Christ alone showed His mastery over nature; the winds and the waves obeyed Him; the devils trembled; disease was done away and death itself conquered. Followers of Jesus Christ in China are demonstrating that their God does enable them too to conquer nature. He sends rain in drought and, in answer to prayer, provides protection amid floods and earthquake disaster, heals the sick and expels demons in the Name of Jesus, while, in the moment of death, He fills the believer with hope. Death has lost its terrors. God is manifesting His power in China today, perhaps as never before, and many are in fact repenting and coming to know the Lord. Christians do not accept Communism as the final answer for China. God's programme for China is not at an end. He has many yet to be called out from the masses to become members of His Church. God always has the last word as He had the first. The Resurrection is the victorious answer to the Cross. And in His Church in China God is preparing an instrument for His purposes, tempered in the fires of trial and persecution.

Open doors?

Since 1972 China has increasingly opened her doors to foreign visitors and would-be traders. Groups of sympathisers from the U.S.A. and Europe began to visit China for well-planned propaganda tours of factories, communes and schools in a few cities, though what they were shown was very limited and confined to what was exceptional rather than the normal, samples of what China hopes to become in the post-Mao era. By 1978 the volume of tourists was growing apace. Preparations were being made to receive even more tourists and the areas open for tours were expanding. But open though the doors into China might be for many categories of person, they remain firmly closed to all whose sole purpose is to be ambassadors for Christ. Christian Chinese can visit relatives and they do so. Foreign Christians can pay short visits as tourists. And both may take the opportunity to carry a few Bibles or New Testaments and to witness as they go. But no-one with "missionary" or "evangelist" plainly recorded in their passport would find a welcome. A few Christians have entered as employees of commercial firms. Others have spent longer periods as students or as teachers. And these opportunities point the way to the future. With the large exchange of students and the numerous technical personnel expected to go to China, surely there will be Christians among them. And we should pray that increasing numbers of Chinese Christians will hear God's call to pay visits to China or, better still, return to reside there in a professional capacity as witnesses for Jesus Christ.

CHAPTER XV

God Lives in China

There are unfortunately many sceptics who are not prepared to believe reports of Christian activity in China such as are recorded in the previous chapter; or, if they do, they tend to dismiss them as a pietistic irrelevance in the China of today. Should we not rather admit that in the midst of severe repression and persecution Chinese Christians have re-discovered the vital personal experience of fellowship with God which is the central theme of the Bible. To emphasise the fact that God is still calling men and women in China into fellowship with Himself the following case histories are reported in some detail by the individuals themselves.

A visit to Shanghai

A lady who visited her relatives in Shanghai in 1973 reported: "I found about thirty or forty Christians in a small room. Fellowships meet several times a week or just weekly, mostly in the afternoon. During the meeting someone keeps watch outside, doing chores to cover their activity. Their programmes include singing, Bible study, sharing and praying. Few have Bibles. These are sometimes torn up and circulated a chapter or two to each person in rotation. No-one dares carry a whole Bible. Most of the hymns are written by themselves but they also sing Bible portions set to folk melodies. A few records of hymns exist and are played secretly at Christmas. Prayer is mainly for their own faith, Christians in prison and overseas Christians. They long to be able to preach the Gospel freely, to have the Bible and other religious books to read and to teach their children. They testify to Christ by the joy in their lives. A new believer must be willing to suffer for the Lord before receiving Jesus as Saviour. Thus his conviction is very real. Baptisms take place quietly in a river. Two sisters and one brother have been imprisoned, one for reading a Bible and another for leading a secret Christian meeting. Healings of various kinds are experienced. Most of the members are retired and some were former members of the Bethel Church. I only met four or five younger Christians. One brother told me that the number of Christians is growing considerably."

This visitor also brought out a handwritten pamphlet outlining:

1. The ten main points for a Christian to know.
2. The seven points to remember every day.
3. Suggestions for prayer.

A student's story

"I grew up in a Christian family. I was converted in my teens, before the revolution in China, and was active in the university Christian fellowship when the Communists took over. At first the Party did not hinder our meetings, but suddenly, everything changed. The pastor and several deacons in our church were taken away and we knew that the Communists were hardening in their attitudes and that suffering lay ahead.

"In October 1951 Land Reform reached our area and all university students had to take part. I had lived a sheltered life hitherto and now I was to take part in this great movement. At first I enjoyed the work and was conscious that God was with me. I realised how much social injustice there was with great differences between the rich and the poor, while the land-owners frequently oppressed their workers. The Land Reform movement and the attack on the landlords seemed to me right and just. On the other hand the people had little time or thought for the Gospel. Many young people accepted Communist teaching and joined the Party. But as a Christian I neither believed in Communism nor joined the Party.

"To be a witnessing Christian in those days was not easy. People thought it strange that we were not willing to go along with Communist teaching. The Communist leaders knew which of us were Christians and set out to oppose our beliefs in every way possible. They took a very pragmatic approach—'Think of the future!' 'If you want to have good prospects give up Christianity and accept Communism!' 'If you are not one of us then you are against us!' I became very confused and prayed that God would deliver me from temptation.

"During the following year I had no opportunity to attend church, read the Bible or have fellowship with other Christians. I witnessed many landlords being accused and killed and I was very afraid. I cried to God, asking Him whether He saw or cared about these evils. Leader Ch'eng of our working group urged me not to be so sensitive. 'There is no point in being merciful and kind to our enemies,' he said, 'If we don't kill them they will kill us.' I could not bear to think about these things, and was afraid for my own future.

"The Land Reform project completed I returned to college only to discover that eighteen members of our Christian Fellowship had fallen away. Some had even become Communists. I knew that I had to make a choice—either turn my back on Communism and move into a country area where I could be a farm worker and an active Christian or give up Christianity and become a Communist.

"As this battle was going on, all my companions were Communists and I had only Communist books to read. So my resolution weakened and I decided to sacrifice myself for my country and the Communist Party. Consequently I was sent to a distant mountainous area as a business manager. There I was very satisfied as the boss in authority. At times I was aware that things were wrong in my life. Sometimes I prayed. Mostly I worked hard for the Party. After two years I was promoted. My reputation, position and authority increased. Finally, I gave up all pretence of being a Christian and joined the Party. As a Communist I now considered all Christians to be capitalists. I agreed with Marx that religion is the opium of the people. And as I studied the history of the Communist Party and of China I became convinced that the church and foreign missionaries had used religion to destroy China. The Party was right to oppose these enemies. But God still cared for me. My family wrote constantly urging me to pray and trust God, but I did not return home for many years, fearing that their pleas would turn me back to God.

"One day my father and uncle unexpectedly came to visit me. They brought photos of my baptism and of the choir. My father and I had a heated argument, as a result of which my father was forced to parade through the streets bearing a placard saying that he was 'superstitious'. The two elderly Christians remained very calm, singing praises to God. They felt glad to suffer for Christ and of the opportunity to witness for Him. This finally broke me down. I repented and returned to God, confessing His great love to me."

A revolutionary romance

What follows is the story of a former Red Guard: "If anyone had told me two years ago that today I would be a Christian and serving God I could not have believed it. I was born into a revolutionary family and brought up to accept Communist teaching. As a high school student I was an active leader in the Red Guards. Because of this I was chosen to go for nursing training. When notified of my first appointment as a qualified nurse, I was told that in the hospital there was an outstanding doctor who was a Christian. My task was to 'change his thoughts'. It was unacceptable that such an outstanding doctor should be a Christian. Dr. Shek was an extremely clever doctor and had been brought up in a Christian home. My whole life I had opposed and despised Christians. How could I persuade him to give up his faith? But had I not been a Red Guard and was I not pledged to serve the Party?

"The first step in the Communist strategy to change a person's thoughts is to get to know him. So I began to find out about Dr. Shek and his background. His mother was a widow with four children. I could find nothing wrong in Dr. Shek's family though theirs was a Christian home. Dr. Shek was a graduate of the Chung Shan University in Canton, where he had been an excellent student, worked hard, and got on well with his fellow-students. He had become a specialist while quite young. In the hospital he was always friendly and open and enjoyed good relations with his colleagues. His patients respected him for his ability and his care and concern when treating them. We often met and discussed many things. Our friendship progressed and before long I realised I was falling in love with the doctor. But I knew my responsibilities as a member of the Party and my duty not to let my feelings get the better of me.

"I was having an inward struggle; I both wanted Dr. Shek to renounce his Christian faith and I wanted him as my husband. Communists often use friendship and even marriage to influence people in the Communist cause. One thing about Dr. Shek perplexed me. Whenever he talked about the things he believed he had assurance and power and I was unable to stand up to him. I continually urged him for the sake of his career to give up his superstitious beliefs, join the Party and become 'red' and 'expert'. The doctor was unmoved. He was not opposed to being 'red' and 'expert' but maintained that Christianity is not superstition but the truth. He refused to renounce his faith. I was all the more confused. If Christianity was false as I had been taught, how was Dr. Shek so strong? Marx said that religion was only for the weak. In spite of my opposition to his beliefs he continued to be loving and caring towards me. Although his mother had been put in prison for preaching the Gospel he bore no grudge but just praised God. Moreover his mother in prison was not anxious nor afraid of death. How could this be?

"Dr. Shek continued to tell me of God's love and I began to read the Bible. When I read: 'The fool says in his heart "There is no God"', the Holy Spirit enlightened me and I recognised that I had been blind and opposed to God. I started to question Marxism. Marx and Engels spoke only of men and this life. Their teaching could not tell me how to get rid of pride, sin, selfishness and how to become patient and kind and good. I could see that the Communist's conception of caring for the welfare of the people was not in the same class as the Christian's love for them. Marxist teaching was atheistic, materialistic, and talked only of self-reliance. Lenin gave us the concept of Party authority—nothing else. But Jesus Christ came to bring me salvation, forgiveness and a new life. As I pondered on this I came to know Jesus Christ myself.

"So I, a Communist Party member, became a Christian

and a member of God's family. I thank God that He sent such a strong Christian to lead me into the truth. Dr. Shek and I were eventually married. As a result of my conversion I was expelled from the Communist Party. We were both sent 'down to the country' to work in a health clinic. But we see God's hand in this. Life is hard but we have many opportunities to serve the country people and to share the Lord Jesus with them."

Rural Christians maintain the faith

"My home town is in South China. On market day the peasants come to town to sell their farm produce and to buy daily necessities. So on market days the town is crowded and busy. It is an opportunity to exchange news, discuss marriage and just chat.

"During the Cultural Revolution Bibles were burnt, church premises closed and Christians were criticised and faced 'struggles'. But Christians have learnt to regard such attacks of Satan as training experiences; they stand firm and wait for God to give them victory. There is such a group of Christians in my home town, who gather round Chang Ma—a faithful servant of God—and take every opportunity to worship together and to grow spiritually. They lie low when things are difficult and resume activities as soon as the situation eases.

"Chang Ma is in her sixties now. She was converted in 1948 when working as servant for a foreign missionary. For more than twenty years she has remained faithful to God and borne a witness for Him. She is well-respected and everyone calls her 'Chang Ma' (Mother Chang). Chang Ma has always been busy visiting the Christians. If anyone is in difficulty she goes to comfort them and to share their burden. She is full of love and wholly devoted to the Lord. She teaches them to bring their problems to God in prayer. When persecution increased Chang Ma was quite prepared to be a martyr, but God had other plans. Her whole family moved out of the city to a small town. At a farewell party Chang Ma read Romans 8. 35 to the Christians. 'Brothers and sisters', she said, 'we should always remember . . . in all these things we are more than conquerors through Him who loved us.'

"Chang Ma came to live in our little town. At first, she knew no-one and the place was strange. But she prayed without ceasing and began to look for fellow-Christians. One day she went to a neighbour's house to borrow a knife and heard a middle-aged woman correcting her small son, saying, 'Who said that there is no love besides class love?' 'My teacher!' the boy replied. 'That is not true,' she went on patiently, 'there are many kinds of love. For example, there is your parents' love for you, your sister's love for you—' Chang Ma at this point interrupted saying, 'There's also a Book which tells us about God's great love for men.' 'Do you have that book?' asked the woman. 'Yes, do you want to read it?' Chang Ma replied. The woman said with joy, 'I have it too.' Just like that! God brought them into touch with one another. This sister introduced Chang Ma to two other sisters and two brothers in Christ who had not held worship services for three years.

"After much prayer and planning they decided to meet at Chang Ma's house because all her family were Christians. They chose market day as the best time for meetings, since it was easier to cover up their activities then. Chang Ma decided to provide stoves and cooking utensils in her home so that people coming to market could cook lunch for themselves, instead of trying to find seats in the crowded restaurants. She charged ten cents per person for firewood, etc. Her venture was a great success. Within two weeks peasants were flocking to her place so she increased the number of tables, and Chang Ma's house became just like a mini-market with the peasants chatting to each other as they cooked their meals. In this way Chang Ma got to know a good deal about the villages around, and the people, some of whom were open to the Gospel. Even more important, on those busy days, Christians were able to gather together for worship upstairs.

"On 3rd March 1974 I took part in one of their Sunday services. Eight other Christians were present. They put up a wooden cross, and a copy of the doxology was hung below it. The bread for Holy Communion and nine cups were placed on the table. While Chang Ma's daughter took charge of things downstairs the Sunday worship began. A brother led in prayer and Chang Ma spoke about the Christian's prayer life. She had never had any theological training, but, from her own experience she told us of the importance of prayer. 'Prayer,' she said, 'is just like the antenna of a radio. It can transmit our prayers to God and it can tune in to God's wave length to receive His word . . .'

" 'Mother! we have run out of salt!' This was the agreed warning signal from En-ping downstairs of possible danger. Chang Ma's talk was interrupted. Hurriedly she left the room, closing the door behind her. We kept silent until Chang Ma and En-ping came back. Then we sang hymns softly and Chang Ma presided at the Holy Communion. After the service I showed them how to tune in to the Gospel broadcasts from overseas. There were tears of joy in their eyes, as they thanked the Lord for His grace. Finally Chang Ma told us of those she felt were responsive to the Christian message and we discussed how best to help them. She also gave us news of Christians in other places."

A Christian wedding

"On the wedding day, after lunch, Ching-ping put on his wedding clothes and three of us went to fetch the bride, he and I by bus and his cousin by bicycle. The bride's relatives welcomed us. Photographs were taken and refreshments offered. Then Chao-yuen's mother called us all together with another Christian couple into the bride's bedroom. She indicated that it was time to pray but seemed uncertain whether I was to be trusted. Ching-ping explained, 'He is a keen Christian from Hong Kong. Won't you let him stay here to pray with us?' We formed a circle, bowed our heads and prayed, the bride's mother leading in prayer. She thanked God for His leading in the marriage, asked Him to bless the new family and to help them to love God more. Her prayer lasted only a few minutes. Then they sang the Doxology and recited the Lord's Prayer in classical Chinese. It was all very informal.

"Soon a 'mini-car' arrived, the bride and groom bade farewell to her relatives and, escorted by the best man and me, returned to the groom's house. Friends and relatives greeted us at the front door. Fire crackers were let off and after some excitement the bride and groom entered the house and served tea to the groom's parents and other relatives. The witnesses at the tea-serving ceremony were all Christians, except for the children, who had not been taught the Gospel because of fear stemming from the Cultural Revolution. Ching-ping's mother had prayer with the bride and groom before we all proceeded to the restaurant.

"At the restaurant reception there was no public prayer and no-one bowed his head to say grace before the meal. There was no trace of uneasiness at this suppression of their Christian profession. Two days later, at another feast in the groom's house, of the thirty or more people present, many had once been earnest members of the church. I was surprised that none of them dared to lead in a prayer to thank God for the meal. It was a shock to find that relatives living in the same house together should distrust each other so, and be so afraid of being accused of superstition."

A visitor to China

"It was early on a Monday morning. After prayer I checked over my simple baggage. I held the two Testaments in simplified Chinese script and meditated for a while. Then, excited and almost fearful, I set out for Canton. At Sumchum, Chinese Customs Officers spent fifteen minutes inspecting my bags. One of them picked up my Bible, read it for more than ten minutes, then asked me abruptly, 'Why do you read the Bible if you don't believe in religion?' But they let me take just one copy of the New Testament with me to Canton.

"Next morning I spent an hour in prayer. I asked the Lord, 'Please, Lord, let me witness to at least one person each day. I have only this one copy of your Word. I want to give it to someone who really and sincerely wishes to know You. Give me courage and faith, Lord, Amen.'

"I was strolling along the shore of a lake in Yuehsiu Park, looking for someone to talk to. A young Senior High School student had come with three school mates for a row on the lake, but they were only able to hire a three-man boat, so he was left behind. I invited him to come rowing with me. In the boat we chatted about his life and his school, gradually leading on to the life of the ancient Chinese poet and statesman Chue-yuan, of whom he had not heard. Then we talked of another historical figure, Jesus, of whom he had also not heard. As he seemed interested and wanted to hear more, I took out the Bible and shared the contents with him. Using Scripture, I explained to him that Jesus is God who loves everyone of us, and wishes us to have happier and more meaningful life.

"But we have sinned, and the greatest sin is unbelief. The result of sin is death, physical and spiritual. My companion said he believed that man has a soul and that Jesus is the only way by which we must be saved. I asked him whether he would accept this life from Jesus. He said he would be very willing to do so. He then followed me and prayed aloud, telling God of his willingness to accept Jesus as his own personal Saviour. After we had prayed I asked him if he would like to have the book. He said, 'Yes' and even offered to buy it from me! I refused and only asked him to show his thanks by reading it carefully.

"Then he volunteered to be my guide for the afternoon. We went to the Mausoleum of the Seventy-Two Martyrs at Huangkuakang. Because of a torrential downpour the crowd of tourists thinned out, so I had another chance to talk with him about Christ. I taught him how to pray and how to study the Bible, underlining some Scriptures for him. I also faced him with the cost of being a Christian and how he should prepare himself for what might lie ahead. Lastly I suggested to him that, as he found meaning in his new faith and in the Bible, he might share his discoveries with those whom he knew well and whom he could trust. He gladly promised me he would do this. My heart was full of joy, though I was sad that I would not be able to keep in touch with him in the future. Finally we parted at the bus station and he waved me goodbye. May God bless him!

"The Lord heard my prayer. He enabled me to witness to at least one person each day. I tried to use their vocabulary wherever possible. I presented the Gospel to them point by point, aiming to make it easy to understand and easy to remember. In this way they should be able to think about it again and again, allowing the Holy Spirit to continue working in their hearts. There were three people to whom I witnessed. One was a twenty-six-year-old university student from Szechwan province. He was in his third year studying marine engineering. Both his parents were well-educated. I had discussions with him on two evenings for about three hours. He received glimpses of the Gospel, but talked only of materialism, class struggle and dialectical theory. He found it difficult to accept what I said, and would not accept Jesus.

"Another was a fourteen-year-old junior high school student. He had never heard of Jesus before. I talked with him for an hour. He was willing to accept Christ as his personal Saviour. I urged him to pray to God every day. He said he would try to do so.

"On the morning I was to leave Canton, as I was on my way to the railway station I met a fourteen-year-old girl. She was begging and asked for ten cents to buy medicine for her father. She said they came to Canton from Shao-Shing a year ago. Their family were classified as a "black family" who had no family registration, no work and no food allotment. Back in the village they made only nine cents a day. Her father was suffering from an incurable disease. She was the eldest child and with her four younger brothers made a living by begging money from Hong Kong and Maçao tourists. I felt sorry for her and began to talk to her about Jesus. Beginning with the miracle of the 'five loaves and two fishes' I talked to her for more than ten minutes. I saw a lost look in her dark face. She told me she dared not pray because she was afraid she would say the wrong words. With a heavy heart I gave her two dollars and went on my way to the railway station.

"On board the train I looked at the misty fields outside the window. Apart from a slight chill due to the rain everything seemed as it was when I had come. But deep in my heart I now had more joy and more sadness. I was joyful for I had had opportunities to talk to my own people about Christ. I thanked God for the four who had had the chance to hear the Gospel. I was sad because of the unmet physical and spiritual needs of the nine hundred million people in China.

" 'O Lord! Please look after them the way you look after us. Please help us to show them your love by our words and our deeds.' "

Escape to Hong Kong

"I have lived the nineteen years of my life in Mainland China. My parents were dedicated Christians yet I did not learn the Gospel from them. In 1970, at the end of the Cultural Revolution, I had to drop out of the middle school and join the ranks of the so-called 'educated young people', though I was not compelled to work in the fields because I am the oldest son. However I could find no job in the city because my family as Christians belonged to the 'Black Seven', which means I had a bad family background. I was no longer able to study and there was nothing to do. A feeling of emptiness settled on me like a black cloud. I had to attend endless self-criticism meetings. I had no freedom of thought or belief. What was I to do?

"Many factors combined to make me consider escaping to Hong Kong—my personal emptiness, my bad family background and the reported success of 'freedom swimmers'. My parents and friends, too, encouraged me to plan my escape. I began preparations. Every day I exercised and swam in the Pearl River to strengthen my body. Finally, in August 1972, I made my first attempt. But I was caught and sent to the Chang Mu Tou prison. After hours of interrogation I was put in one of the six big prison wards with about two hundred other prisoners. Line-up for work started at six a.m. each day. Each person had to move heavy boulders from the hilltop to the plain for building purposes. After breakfast at half-past seven we were questioned again by the prison officer. Afternoons were given to self-criticism classes, study of China's newspapers and posters about Hong Kong, which was portrayed as a dirty, difficult place in which to live. At five p.m. we were given a bowl of rice with a bit of salted vegetable. Once while we were working a prisoner attempted to escape. The guards spotted him and beat him savagely. In the afternoon he was taken to the interrogation room where the guards tied the man's hands behind his back and tossed him up into the air and let him fall to the ground. This was repeated again and again. Finally they whipped him with chains and put him in the ward again. The next morning he was not to be seen.

"A week later I was transferred to the Canton prison.

How wonderful to find meat in the rice! But I became very ill due to the unclean water in the prison. For two days, I could not eat. No medical help was given to me. I asked the guard for medicine but all I got was a beating. Then I was released.

"The following winter I willingly left the city to work in a commune. Two kinds of 'educated young people' work in the rural areas, those who do as they are told, hoping for a chance to transfer to work in the city, and those who are on the lookout for an opportunity to escape to Hong Kong. I belonged to the second group. Commune life was hard and the wages poor. We even had to beg from others or overdraw from the production brigade.

"In the autumn of 1974 three of us, two boys and one girl, secretly left the commune and returned to Canton to prepare for our escape to Hong Kong. Our gear included inflatable bladders and twelve pounds of food for each person. This consisted of flour and sugar mixed with vegetable oil. A friend helped us to hide our supplies at Fu Tin village. Then we took a bus from Canton to Fu Tin, collected our equipment, slipped into the East River and swam across. On the first leg of our escape route across the Tung Woo plains our girl companion was lost and not seen again. As we reached the Nam Mien mountains a fierce typhoon struck and we couldn't move for two days. Later as we prepared to climb the Hung Fa mountain two farmers volunteered to help us and warned us that guards had been posted on the mountain. How glad we were for their help! To show our appreciation we gave them some old clothes. They were overjoyed. Ten days later our food ran out and we had to steal sweet potatoes and vegetables from the farms. On the fourteenth day we met Mr. Chang, another escapee who knew the countryside well as he had tried to escape several times before.

"Two days later we reached the sea but it was already one a.m. and we could not begin to swim across to Hong Kong because it would get light before we were across. So we hid among the rocks a little way back from the shore. We were still without food and were becoming very weak. Next evening, as we prepared to slip into the sea we spotted two patrol boats and heard gun fire. We all three jumped into the water and began to swim madly towards Kat O Chou in

Hong Kong territory. We passed about one hundred feet from the patrol boats but luckily they did not see us. Our limbs felt like lead. We were so exhausted and weak we could hardly lift our arms or kick our feet. I prayed to God for strength. Finally we struggled on to the Kat O beach and fainted. It was three a.m. A Hong Kong helicopter landed on the other side and picked up a bloody body. It was Mr. Chang who had been killed by sharks. Fishermen kindly took me to my uncle's home. At last we had reached the dream of our hearts—freedom."

A Youth League member converted

Recently in an interview with a young Christian who had been a member of the Chinese Communist Youth League, a leader of the Red Guards and also a cadre, she explained how she managed to reconcile these different roles with the teachings of the Bible. This was her reply:

"I grew up in a Christian family in the village. My grandmother, my mother, my eldest sister and younger brother are all Christians. I went with my mother to church services and Sunday School at a Baptist Church about two hours' walk away from our home. As I remember it was fun to go to church. The last time I went to church was in 1963 when my sister and I took part in the Christmas Eve celebrations. Subsequently the church was closed. During my primary four years I joined the 'Young Pioneers'. Under this atheistic influence I began to doubt the truth of the Christian faith. I felt that it was merely an old traditional belief. Several of my teachers were Christians, but they never said anything about going to Sunday services. When one of them asked me whether I was a Christian I just replied, 'My mother is a Christian. I don't know whether I am or not.' I joined the Youth League when I was in middle school and I was definitely not a Christian. After graduation I became a bookkeeper and was considered a cadre.

"At the time of the Cultural Revolution, as a committee member of the Red Guards, I was duty-bound to lead my schoolmates to struggle with others. Deep in my heart I felt uneasy especially when we had to criticise the Christian teachers. They were nice to me. I just did not have the heart to write down their 'offences'. Although I was not a believer

I saw nothing wrong in believing in religion. Because of this my schoolmates criticised me for not accusing the teachers for being religious. They suspected me of siding with the Christian teachers. All believers were classified as 'running dogs of imperialism'.

"After the Cultural Revolution I had no chance to continue at high school and was idling away the time so my mother introduced me to a Mrs. Liu who was suffering from a blood disease but who was strong in faith and a great woman of prayer. She prayed about everything great and small. At her suggestion I began to read Matthew's Gospel and she also encouraged me to commit my future to God and explained to me the difference between true faith and idolatry. 29th December 1969 was my uncle's wedding day and Mrs. Liu gave a short but moving message during the wedding feast and led us in a prayer of thanksgiving. The guests included many young Christians.

"In 1970 Father was diagnosed as having cancer. Dr. Ma's family and ours were the only Christian families in the village, which was very superstitious. Dr. Ma's treatment of my father was unsuccessful though he comforted us and prayed for Father. A year later, after a period of remission, Father passed away. My grandmother led the Christian funeral service and resisted the demands of superstitious neighbours to use heathen ceremonies. Mother took the opportunity to witness to the people who came to the funeral service.

"On 29th July 1972, the anniversary date of my father's death, I contracted acute pneumonia. During the twenty-odd days of my illness I read the Bible and prayed each day. When I read, 'But as many as received him to them gave he power to become the sons of God, even to them that believe on his name' (John 1. 12), I really believed in Him and determined to dedicate myself to His service.

"After my recovery I worked in the town and often attended the meetings in Mrs. Liu's home, along with seven or eight brothers and sisters. These meetings consisted mainly of prayers and sharing lessons of faith. Mrs. Liu often encouraged us. A team made periodic visits to various other brothers and sisters. In 1973 God led my grandmother and me to Hong Kong where we can worship and study

God's Word freely. I have not forgotten the farewell exhortation of the believers to live near to God. In Hong Kong I am studying in a seminary, hoping to equip myself to serve the Lord.

"I saved up enough money for a trip back to my native village at Chinese New Year, to repay my debt to the Gospel, and to use the personal evangelism training I had received. The comrade at the Customs examined my suitcase in which there was a Bible. He merely looked through the Bible once and put it back in the case without saying a word. My first stop was at the house of a sister named Lu—the only believer in her family. I had prayed for this family for three months. Now the whole family believed. On January 29th I spoke about God's love for mankind, and His plan of salvation, to another family and they all accepted the Lord. One sister had broken down mentally under the burden of providing for her family and concern for her children's future. When I saw her she became quite violent, but as I prayed for her she calmed down and we were able to talk together peacefully. I advised her husband to confess their sins frequently to God. Dr. Lee is a servant of God who often prays for his patients. One day his daughter-in-law invited me to their home to pray for her younger sister who was plagued by an evil spirit. Praise God! He drove out the evil spirit. The Christians in China are praying constantly for revival and for freedom to worship God. They envy me the religious freedom in Hong Kong. Before I left to return to Hong Kong a sister in Christ came to tell me she had just taken part in a retreat when more than ten young Christians had gathered together in the mountains for a week—led by Miss Wang—an older Christian. She asked me to pray for these young soldiers of Christ." [1]

[1] Other similar stories have been collected and published in a booklet, "Testimonies of Christians in China" (Christian Communications Ltd., P.O. Box 5364, Tsim Sha Tsui, Hong Kong).

CHAPTER XVI

China's International Relations

The first Europeans

Until the advent of modern means of transport in the nineteenth century, China was effectively isolated from the rest of the world geographically by the mighty mountain ranges of the Himalayas and the Tien Shan to the west, the Gobi Desert and the Mongolian steppes to the north and the wide Pacific Ocean to the east. So for centuries, in almost total seclusion, China developed her own unique civilisation and culture. Dynasty after dynasty rose and fell, century after century rolled by and "Cathay" was just a mysterious entity somewhere in "the Indies". The West knew nothing of China and China knew nothing of the West. Then in the thirteenth century a Venetian merchant family made the long, hazardous overland journey to the court of Ghengis Khan in Peking. Marco Polo was the first European ever to see China and to regale Western ears with his fabulous tales about China, Java and Sumatra and their strange peoples and customs. European explorers sailing west in the seventeenth century went in search of the land of Cathay and its riches; they thought they had found it when they reached the Americas, but what they had found was only the Caribbean Islands, which they nevertheless called the "West Indies". The Spaniard Magellan had to sail around the southern tip of the American continent and across the Pacific Ocean before discovering, not the "Indies", but the islands which he named the Philippines after King Philip of Spain. Meanwhile the Portuguese Admiral d'Albuquerque rounded South

Africa, circumnavigated the Indian Ocean and finally reached Malacca in 1517. The Portuguese later ventured further west to the "Spice Islands" and north to found the colony of Macao on the coast of south China. They also occupied Formosa (Ilha Formosa or the Beautiful Isle) for a time. Spanish friars accompanied the stately galleons from Mexico to the Philippines and Portuguese Jesuits followed their fleets to take Christianity to Goa in India, Malacca on the Malay peninsula, Ternate in the Spice Islands, Macao in China, Formosa and even to Japan. Francis Xavier was the most intrepid pioneer of them all and he planted the Cross in one exotic place after another. But it was left to Matteo Ricci, the great Jesuit scholar, to make his way from Macao to Peking to become a friend of the Emperor K'ang Hsi. Thus all the pioneers of Christianity in Asia were Roman Catholics from southern Europe.

The treaty ports

The lure of the spice trade first took the Protestant Dutch and British to the "East Indies", and with the merchant adventurers went Protestant Christianity. Until China should open its doors to European merchants and Protestant missions, the missionaries had to be content with contact with Chinese people living in Malacca, the Malay peninsula and in Batavia, the Dutch capital of the East Indies. The Chinese 'gates of brass' only yielded to foreign pressure in 1842 when Westerners first exacted the right to live and trade in five "treaty ports" along the south China coast. China's isolation had ended at last. For over a century now she has been taking her place increasingly in the world family of nations.

At first, a long-isolated, proud and cultured people were suspicious and somewhat contemptuous of the barbarians from the "outside kingdoms" and then, due to the aggressive diplomacy of the Western powers, were openly antagonistic to the "foreign devils" and all their works. Even into the late nineteenth century the conservative scholar-mandarins, headed by the Empress Dowager, were firmly opposed to the band of progressive "Reformers" at a time when the Meiji rulers of Japan were adopting a policy of full-scale westernisation. The consequence was a military defeat by Japan in 1895 when Formosa was ceded to Japan, and a China in 1979 still backward and face to face with a powerful, highly industrialised Japan.

China's debt to Christianity

It was in fact the missionaries who introduced China to Western education, culture and scientific knowledge and it was Dr. Sun Yat-sen, a Christian, who master-minded the Nationalist Revolution and the overthrow of a corrupt imperial China in 1911. And let it be repeated emphatically that the early missionaries to China did not consciously harbour any ulterior motives in their mission. With all their shortcomings, largely due to a universal ignorance of a wider world a century and a half ago, they were motivated by the love of God and believed that they were obeying Christ's command to preach the Gospel to all the people of China, and, at the same time, to share with them the material benefits and scientific knowledge of the West. The Nationalist Revolution owed much to the basic principles of Christianity and to the liberal ideals which Christian education made popular.

Communist victory

The first World War found China on the side of the Allies against Germany as was Japan. But at Versailles, the prizes of victory all went to Japan and none to China. Russia, defeated by Germany and led into a Communist revolution by Lenin, was prompt to surrender her special "extra-territorial rights" in China, "rights" which she had held in common with other European nations ever since 1842. No other power followed suit until the Second World War in 1940. Russia thus appeared to be China's only friend in the world. The Chinese Communist Party held its first Congress in secret in 1921 – the beginning of an internal conflict between Nationalists and Communists which was to culminate in the Communist victory of 1949.

The Sino–Japanese war of 1937–45 was a one-sided conflict between unequal forces. Only the victory of the Allies in the Pacific saved China from disaster. But "victory" was short-lived. Civil war was soon renewed and resulted in the crushing defeat of the demoralised Nationalist armies, despite their superior numbers, weaponry and air force, at the hands of the well-trained, well-generalled and highly-motivated Communist armies. The Communist victory placed China firmly in the camp of the Communist nations although the refugee Nationalist Government in Taiwan (recovered from Japan in 1945) continued to flourish under the protection of the U.S.A.

China joins the world

The Afro–Asian Bandung Conference of 1955, held in Indonesia, brought China for the first time to a conference table with the non-Communist but "emerging" nations of the world. By 1966, in spite of her antagonism at that time to the United Nations, China enjoyed diplomatic relations with forty-eight other states and semi-diplomatic relations with many more. In 1966, at the start of the Cultural Revolution, however, China recalled all her foreign embassies, evidently wanting to conduct her new revolution in seclusion. At the same time leftist extremists (now identified as the Radicals) destroyed the British Embassy building in Peking and also gave offence to the Russian diplomatic corps.

In 1971 a sudden and dramatic shift in policy took place. China invited American table-tennis players to take part in a tournament in Peking—the start of the so-called "ping-pong diplomacy". Prime Minister Chou En-lai was undoubtedly the man behind this move which signalled the desire of the more moderate elements in China to open China's doors and windows to the world. Chinese ambassadors gradually returned to their posts all over the world and new foreign representatives were welcomed in Peking almost weekly. In 1972 China's seat in the United Nations and on the Security Council was transferred from the Taiwan representative to the representative of the Government of the People's Republic of China. China's diplomatic activity now clearly indicated her desire to win the world's goodwill and to play a full part in the world's affairs.

China's three-world view

When the Chinese Communists came to power they saw the world in simple terms—the socialist (i.e. Communist) countries and the rest of the world. It was Communist comrades versus the non-Communist enemies. At first China quite naturally accepted the U.S.S.R. as her "big brother" and model. There was no other model. But Stalin never understood Mao and Mao was committed to quite unorthodox revolution in China. The long-standing conflict surfaced in 1960 when the break between Russia and China finally occurred. The comradely hatred persists and it may be many years before the breach between the two major Communist powers is mended. Thus China now sees the world in a different light. First of all she speaks of the two "superpowers"—the U.S.A. and the U.S.S.R. Then she groups together the industrialised bourgeois Western and European-originating nations and Japan as the "second world". Finally, the "third world" consists of the newly independent and "emerging" or "developing" nations, of which China sees herself as one and perhaps the leader.

Relations with the super-powers

A. The U.S.A.

Since 1949 both the U.S.A. and the U.S.S.R. have in turn been regarded by the Chinese as the great enemies of mankind. In the 1950s the U.S.A. was regarded by the Chinese as the world's Public Enemy No. 1—the very epitome of capitalism, imperialism and feudalism. In the Korean war Chinese and American soldiers matched their strength against each other and the Chinese were not defeated. The intervention by the U.S.A. in Vietnam aroused Chinese antagonism to an even higher pitch. But meanwhile, in 1960 Russia by her unilateral action and betrayal usurped America's unenviable position in Chinese eyes and continues to hold it. In 1972, President Nixon of the U.S.A. made a historic visit to Peking to meet Chairman Mao Tse-tung and Prime Minister Chou En-lai, who took a considerable risk in giving the invitation. The Radicals, led by the fanatical Mme. Mao, strongly opposed the visit. Mao was old and feeble. Chou was also old but mentally alert. He impressed Nixon with his brilliance and dynamism and by the remarkable extent of his knowledge of men and history, though his perspective was distorted by his rigid ideological frame of reference. In his speech at the official banquet Nixon said: "What we have said in that Communiqué is not nearly as important as what we will do in the years ahead to build a bridge across sixteen thousand miles and twenty-two years of hostility which have divided us in the past." Raising his glass Nixon concluded, "We have been here a week. This was the week that changed the world."

Following the withdrawal of American troops from Vietnam China seemed to lose her fear of the U.S.A. as a possible aggressor and now regards America as a potential ally against an aggressive Russia. The U.S.A. had yet to implement the Shanghai Communiqué of 1972, signed by President Nixon, by which the U.S.A. would extend full diplomatic relations to the People's Republic of China. Up till 1978 the U.S.A. seemed reluctant to sever her ties with the Government of "the Republic of China" in Taiwan. But China has made it crystal clear that there can be no further improvement of relations with the U.S.A. until the Taiwan question is finally settled. And, just as President Carter's national security adviser, Bryzinski, was visiting Peking, the report of a Congressional Committee which visited China at the end of 1977 favoured the recognition of China and the withdrawal of recognition for Taiwan before the end of 1978. In late December President Carter announced that this advice would be implemented. On 1st January 1979 the Stars and Stripes was lowered in Taipei and raised in Peking over the new American embassy there.

Within China, besides the debate between the by-no-means silenced ultra-leftists and the rightists in power on the subject of all-out modernisation or continued politicisation, a debate is also being conducted on how to handle China's relationships with the two super-powers U.S.A. and U.S.S.R. Teng Hsiao-p'ing may be aiming at a settlement with Russia, and it is possible that China used the Bryzinski visit to exact a higher price from the Soviet Union for a rapprochement. Clearly a re-thinking of China's foreign policy and how to handle the "super-powers" is under way in Peking.

B. The U.S.S.R.

Stalin was Mao's mentor but he never really understood the Chinese mind nor the peculiar revolutionary circumstances in China. The Russians initially under-estimated the Chinese Communists' ability to conquer China after the war in 1945 and cynically stripped Manchuria of its industrial potential. Ideologically the Russians disapproved first of an "agrarian revolution", then of the premature setting up of the communes in 1958. In that year, impatient with her bigger but younger brother, Russia took the unilateral decision to withdraw all her technicians and removed all her factories. The break was abrupt, devastating and apparently final. Kruschev's brief regime only aggravated relations between the two countries. China accused Russia of a return to "state capitalism" and of betraying Marxism–Leninism. Long-standing frontier disputes sometimes flared up into armed clashes along the Siberian border and in 1979 the Russians have a million men deployed in an offensive posture along the common frontier with China and in outer Mongolia. China never ceases to talk of Russia's threat of hegemony in Asia. Genuinely fearing a Russian attack sooner or later, China has created vast and complex underground air-raid caverns beneath Peking and all her major cities. Even without Russian technical aid since 1961 China has been able to develop nuclear power and to build medium range IBMs capable of delivering nuclear warheads. She has also taken the precaution of moving her nuclear installations away from the Russian frontier into Tibet.

China is still openly critical of the U.S.A. over certain issues but she now reserves her sharpest invectives for the U.S.S.R. Not only are there strong ideological differences, but there is the Siberian border issue and a keen rivalry throughout the world for leadership in south-east Asia, in India and in Africa. Hostility to Russia now is a main factor in China's internal policy. Moreover China sees herself as a possible victim of a catastrophic clash sooner or later between the two super-powers and a war which might bury the Chinese revolution in the rubble of her nuclear shelters. An argument raged in 1978 as to whether China's modernisation programmes would or would not speed up the modernisation of the army. In any case, even if the re-arming of the army is to take place, it will take a long time before China can stand up to Russia. So perhaps détente is preferable and both sides want it, but on their own terms. If there were to be another world war, as China predicts, China believes that "several hundred million more men will turn to socialism" and "the whole structure of imperialism will collapse".[1] The long article from which these predictions are taken argues that the U.S.A. is an unreliable ally against the Soviet Union in the light of Russia's superior military might in terms of conventional weapons. China doubts America's readiness to defend Europe and was very suspect of President Carter's apparent appeasement of the Kremlin in early 1978 before the trial of the two dissidents in July. The issue of this vital debate about China's relationships with the two super-powers may not be clear until her internal debate is finally decided.

Relations with the Second World

A. Europe

Most European states have already elected socialist governments and in France, Italy, Spain, Portugal there are strong Communist parties, though Euro-Communists do not accept the leadership of the Soviet Union and appear to favour a revised and less dogmatic variety of Marxism–Leninism. China, therefore, favours Euro-Communism and is opposed to Russian hegemony in Eastern Europe as in Asia. On principle China insists on national autonomy and the right to self-determination and so bitterly criticised the Soviet invasion of Czechoslovakia, while at the same time disapproving of Dubcek's proposed reforms. China also encourages Romania and Yugo-Slavia in their independent stand. In August 1978 Hua Kuo-feng paid visits to both countries and was outspoken against Russian imperialism, encirclement designs and hegemony aims. Albania, once a warm friend of China, is opposed to the post-Mao moderate regime and relations are very cool.

China fears Russia and her military might and never ceases to predict that another world war is inevitable. Believing that Russia will attack in the West first, China therefore heartily supports the European Economic Community and NATO as

[1] *People's Daily*, May 1978.

bulwarks against the "imperialist" designs of the U.S.S.R. and opposes "détente" as a phoney deception. It is for these reasons that Conservative pro-Europeans like Mr. Heath and Mrs. Thatcher have been warmly welcomed in Peking.

China attaches great importance to trade with the West as one means of achieving stability and of developing her own domestic economy. But her ideological insistence on "self-reliance" and her policy of incurring no internal or external debt have so far inhibited her foreign trade. In 1978, however, there were signs that China was prepared to modify these principles and policies. Large orders for plant and factories placed in the West suggest that China is making a modest use of credits and loans.

B. Japan

Japan, like the nations of Western Europe, is in the eyes of all Communist regimes, a bourgeois state and an industrially powerful one. The history of Sino-Japanese relations has given China good reason to fear Japan but in 1978, thirty years after the end of the war, a treaty of peace and friendship was at last signed between the two nations, though with the disapproval of the Soviet Union. Clearly, Japan as a near neighbour, is in a good position to supply many of China's needs and China is importing a growing volume of Japan's machine tools and industrial plant. Fortunately for China, her vast crude oil reserves and the large oil field of Taching in Manchuria mean that she can supply much of Japan's oil needs in payment for her imports from that country. But there is already a growing trade gap which is causing concern to China.

The "Nixon plan" for a Pacific Monroe Doctrine and the withdrawal of all non-Asian forces from the Pacific area could open the way for Japan to develop her own nuclear weapons capacity, even though most people in Japan are opposed to the idea. Thus the Pacific, with the U.S.A., Russia, Japan and China facing one another, all with nuclear weapons, could become the future storm centre of world politics.

Relations with the Third World

A. Asia

Geographically, China occupies a dominating position in Asia. Historically, in the thirteenth century the Mongol (Yuan) dynasty extended its empire to the whole of mainland South-East Asia and to Java as well as to Eastern Europe. Today there are wealthy Chinese communities (the "China bridge") in all South-East Asian countries, most of them originating from the southern provinces of Kwangtung, Fukien and Chekiang. They total something over twenty-two million. Some of these remain loyal to the Nationalist Government in Taiwan while the patriotism of others is centred on the Mainland of China whence they originated and where their ancestral homes and burial grounds still are.

China's policy in Asia is firmly opposed to any armed invasion of her neighbours. She insists that her armed forces are solely for defence. Long before the Communists assumed power in China, Tibet was regarded by the Chinese as an integral part of China and so the armed action taken there by the Communist Government was not, in Chinese eyes, an invasion. China, however, actively supports all struggles for "liberation" in Asian countries and gives both moral and material support to all "liberation" movements as she has done in Malaya (1945–60), in Vietnam (1945–75), in Laos (1945–75), in Campuchea (formerly Cambodia) (1945–75), in Indonesia (1950–58)—in the cases of Malaya and Indonesia unsuccessfully—and to the Philippine rebels. The domino theory may yet prove to be vindicated. Three dominoes have already fallen—Vietnam, Laos, Cambodia; others may fall—Thailand and Malaysia. The danger is there.

At first, in the fifties, the SEA countries feared China and, in an atmosphere of antagonism, they created SEATO as a defence against Communist aggression. But the Cultural Revolution spread no further than Hong Kong where it was contained. Then, in 1972, following China's entry into the United Nations, attitudes began to change. There was caution, but, realising that China was a growing power in the world, most Asian countries wanted good relations with her as well as increased trade. Now, in 1979, China enjoys full diplomatic relations with Malaysia, Thailand and the Philippines. Indonesia and Singapore recognition cannot be far off. But, since the end of the civil war in Vietnam, China's relations with that country have rapidly deteriorated and in January 1979, following Vietnam's invasion of Campuchea, China moved large forces to her border with Vietnam. Russian influence in Vietnam is strong while China has supported Campuchea in its bloody struggle to set up a Communist state. The Vietnamese occupation of Campuchea therefore precipitated a new crisis and heightened tension between Russia and China: some believe the situation could develop into a proxy war between Russia and China. ASEAN, the military alliance between SEA nations, was once criticised by China, but is now regarded as an ally against an aggressive Soviet Union.

Taiwan

Since 1945, Chinese on either side of the Formosan Strait have maintained that there is but one China and that Taiwan is an integral part of China. The "Republic of China" based in Taiwan has always professed its intention to re-assert its sovereignty and authority over the Mainland, while the "People's Republic of China" has equally demanded the recovery of Taiwan and its integration with the Mainland. The death of President Chiang Kai-shek in 1975 was the death of a world statesman and a Christian who all his life had fought against Communism. Thanks largely to fifty years of Japanese occupation and American economic aid Taiwan is today prosperous in spite of having to maintain a large, army, air force and fleet. But Taiwan's future is insecure.

Increasingly, the nations of the world have been transferring recognition of "China" to the Government in Peking. This is logical, since that Government is the only one recognised in the United Nations. When President Nixon visited China in 1972 the Shanghai Communiqué virtually pledged the U.S.A. to give full diplomatic recognition to the People's Republic of China in due course. Finally, on 1st January 1979 the American Government did establish full diplomatic relations with Peking and withdrew recognition of the refugee government in Taiwan as the legitimate government of China. China, on her part, has ceased the regular shelling of Quemoy and is making peaceful overtures to Taiwan for a rapprochement between the two vital parts of China.

In Taiwan, however, the majority of the people, i.e. four-teen million out of seventeen million (all except the refugees from the Mainland), including the Presbyterian Church of Taiwan, is in favour of independence for the island. They have no desire to be taken over by the Communist Government in Peking. Nor do they wish to be treated any longer as a colonial possession, as they feel they have been by successive rulers—the Portuguese, the Dutch, the Chinese Mings, the Japanese and finally by several million National-ist refugees from the Mainland and the refugee Government of former Nationalist China. The Taiwanese people are lobbying the United Nations in favour of a plebiscite or referendum to determine their future, which they hope would be followed by the election of an independent Taiwanese Government.

The Taiwanese issue is a thorny one. If America were to withdraw her military and naval shield, Taiwan might, as Bryzinski, President Carter's aide, warned in May 1978, "play the Russian card", possibly offering them naval and other facilities. An invasion of Taiwan in an attempt to re-cover Taiwan by force would be an immensely difficult and enormously costly operation, involving a Communist force four times the size of the well-trained and well-equipped forces in Taiwan. The Peking authorities have not ruled out this possibility, but they have declared that they want as little bloodshed as possible. The alternative is diplomacy. What can this achieve?

China's Asian relationships have far-reaching implica-tions for the future of Christianity in China. The reunion of Taiwan with the Mainland, however achieved, would bring a strong reinforcement to the struggling Church on the Main-land. Indeed Taiwan could be a strategic bridgehead for Chinese Christians to launch a new movement of witness to the Chinese people. For this the churches of Taiwan should be preparing themselves. The present cultural gulf separat-ing the two parts of China would have to be crossed and Christians in Taiwan need to be ready for a simpler life-style and also for the suffering that might result following a return to the Mainland.

B. Africa

Edgar Snow is reported to have said: "If the changes I saw in the caves of the north-west can be achieved in a few short years, then they may well reach into darkest Africa and the Andes sooner than many think." At the 1955 conference of the "emerging Afro–Asian nations" held in Bandung, Indonesia, China was invited to take part. This was her first representation at an international conference at which non-Communist states participated and it was an expression of China's desire to end super-power domination in world affairs. As a result of this conference and of Premier Chou En-lai's subsequent visit to Africa, when he made the statement, "Africa is ripe for revolution", China began to pursue a policy of seeking recognition and support among the emerging African states in order to undermine the influence of the two super-powers. Her diplomatic inexperience led to some early reverses but after the Cultural Revolution China obtained some success in relation to Tanzania. Several African states were already being assisted in their agricultural programmes by the Government in Taiwan and this aid continues.

So far, most of China's foreign aid has gone to Africa. More than thirty of the sixty countries receiving economic aid from China are African. There were early links with Ghana. Nkrumah was actually in Peking when the coup which ousted him occurred. It was in Tanzania that the Simba rebels of the Congo (Zaire) and the freedom fighters of Mozambique were trained in Mao's guerilla tactics by Chinese army experts. Mozambique's Chinese population is believed to number about two hundred and fifty thousand despite the fact that the Chinese Government long ago became critical of the way in which that country was being run. China has also given large grants for the purchase of military equipment to the National Liberation Front of Algeria and to thirteen sub-Saharan African countries. But military aid constitutes only a small part of Chinese aid; agricultural and medical aid are very popular. Forty medical teams of twenty to fifty doctors and nurses tend out-patients and set up hospitals in more than a dozen countries. Tanzania has also received a pharmaceutical factory and a gift of sports equipment from China. Mining projects in several countries are receiving Chinese help. As Chinese aid workers are paid according to local standards, the overall cost of Chinese aid is about a quarter of that provided by others.

But the greatest project that China has undertaken and carried through to a successful completion is the Tan-Zam (Tazara) railway linking Dar-es-Salaam on the east coast and landlocked Zambia. Work began in 1970 and the railway was inaugurated in mid-1976 ahead of schedule. The 1,160-mile-long railway is an outstanding engineering achievement. It cost twelve million American dollars. Thirty-five thousand Chinese, mostly PLA men, still live in work camps in Zambia. But, unlike the Russians, the Chinese maintain a low profile, have earned a high reputation for hard work and dedication, are modest about their achievement and have shown the ability to adapt to African ways. Russians, on the other hand, are generally disliked.

China was the first Communist power to move into Africa to help to overthrow all white regimes. But, when the Chinese observed the Soviet Union encircling the continent with her navies and making effective inroads into Angola and Ethiopia with Cuban support, they began to re-think their African policy. China certainly wants to see an end to domination by any super-power and to gain support for her own leadership in the Third World. She therefore seeks to help the small and medium powers. Evidence of this is seen in the United Nations where China usually votes with the African bloc. The most recent expression of opposition to Soviet "imperialism" in Africa was the intervention in the Shaba invasion of southern Zaire and the offer of naval vessels for use on the Congo River.

It is now clear that Russia and China are involved in a hard struggle to win the allegiance of African countries and the stakes are very high. China definitely uses her aid to promote development and self-reliance and rejects the production-loan formula common in other donors' schemes, believing that such is not genuine aid at all.

China may well be, up to a point, a model for developing countries to follow. But China continually insists that her revolution is not for export. It was conceived and born out of China's unique situation and owed much to her long history and culture. China urges each country to discover its own "road to socialism", though she is always ready to assist with advice and aid. It is true that those developing countries of the world whose economy is largely agricultural and where industry is in its infancy may see in China's experience pointers to solving their own economic and social problems. Certainly China has more to offer in this respect than Russia. Perhaps China's emphasis on "self-reliance" is the thing above all which many ex-colonial territories need to emulate.

Conclusion

China has not overlooked the Middle East where she is seeking diplomatic relations with Saudi Arabia, the most anti-Communist state in the Muslim world. She is, ideologically, against the state of Israel and supports the Palestinian cause. But, again, China does not wish to see Russia's influence in the region become any greater. Inevitably, China will play an increasingly important part in the future course of world history. In her present attitude, she provides a balance against Russia in favour of peace, but should there be a reconciliation with Russia, the danger of another world war would be greatly increased. We may not know what the future holds, but the Christian knows, as Dr. Stanley Jones once said, that God holds the future. "The Lord God Omnipotent reigneth!"

CHAPTER XVII

New Chairman, New Era

China's "Eight Horses" are famous in art and sculpture. 1977–8 was the "year of the horse" in the Chinese calendar. In the new era which began with the political volte-face in 1976, the new Chairman, Hua Kuo-feng, is riding a lively steed. Can he control the direction of the horse's progress? Can he even remain in the saddle? It will not be easy to move from the "great chaos" of the post-Cultural Revolution period to the "great order" which the Chairman hopes to restore. A generation of youngsters fed on ultra-leftist propaganda is still bewildered by the turn of events. The heroes of yesterday are the evil genii of today and the "demons" and "monsters" they once denounced are in the driving seat again. Was Mao as fallible as they are now asked to believe? Was the Cultural Revolution a gain or a loss? They once knew the answers, but not any longer. The China horse that the new Chairman rides is restive and needs a tight rein.

The task ahead

In July 1977 Teng Hsiao-p'ing was at last restored to office as the first Vice-premier and to all the other posts he had formerly held in 1976, including Chief of the General Staff and Vice-chairman of the Party's Military Commission, as well as a place on the Politburo. His first task was to implement the plans already outlined in 1963 and 1975 for pushing forward China's industrialisation and modernisation. At seventy-three he had a clear conception of the way ahead for China.

The Eleventh Congress of the Communist Party in August

1977 marked the consolidation of the authority of the new regime and the beginning of a new period in Chinese history. It emphasised the need for experience and expertise at all levels, a Party free of radical influence, the development of the economy and an irreconcilable struggle against the Soviet Union. Hua Kuo-feng, in a major speech, struck a fine balance between political principle and practicalities, while Teng Hsiao-p'ing urged "less empty talk and more hard work". For the time being the five members of the Standing Committee will doubtless subordinate any differences that may exist between them. The leadership certainly seems to be pursuing a compromise between ideology and economic necessity on the question of incentives.

Post-Cultural Revolution leaders

The Fifth National People's Congress, held in the spring of 1978, confirmed Hua Kuo-feng, the man from Shansi in North China, as Chairman of the Party and as Premier of the State Council, thus making him, on paper at least, more powerful than Mao ever was. For Mao never held the dual posts of Chairman and Premier. Teng Hsiao-p'ing was not, as many expected and as the people demanded, given the premiership, but large numbers of "rightists" were restored and a purge of "leftists" took place. Thousands of unrepentant radical officials were even executed. Unfortunately, in a Communist country, that is what to expect: the downfall of a leader invariably brings about the downfall of all his near subordinates, as with Liu Shao-ch'i and Lin P'iao. At the same time thousands of intellectuals who had been living for many years in "outer darkness" were reinstated and given employment where their gifts and experience are desperately needed. Maoist policies as defined by the Left are in conflict with the current pragmatic policies determined by the Chinese Communist Party and carried out by Teng Hsiao-p'ing.

The Fifth National Congress also approved a new State Constitution which lays down as a "general task" the duty of making China "a great powerful socialist country with modern agriculture, modern industry, modern national defence and modern science and technology by the end of the century". These are the "four modernisations" listed by Chou En-lai. It goes on, "The state will devote major efforts to developing science and education and to adopting advance techniques where possible. Citizens enjoy the constitutional right to education and the right to engage in scientific research."

Educational reforms

Education, as we have seen, was seriously retarded after the Cultural Revolution. Now the changes are coming along so fast that the Chinese people must be bewildered. The problems involved in a whole society shifting its priorities in such a dramatic fashion are immense. After a decade of solely political indoctrination and anti-academic education everything has changed. Even at the primary and secondary school levels politics are taking a secondary place and less time is spent on "production". The basic subjects are much what they are in schools elsewhere. New textbooks based on the latest scientific and technical materials from the West and Japan have been issued. The children are being taught for the first time to think and analyse, and that cannot be easy for them. The student who became a national hero by sending in a blank examination paper as a protest against the examination system is a hero no longer. Now he is called "an ignorant counter-revolutionary clown"! Examinations are seen as the key to tertiary education and since the competition for entry into university is extremely fierce, all students are eager to learn. In 1978 five million seven hundred thousand candidates sat for a tough competitive examination for only three hundred thousand college places. Around six hundred thousand students now attend four hundred and sixty faculties including eighty-eight teacher-training colleges, less than in 1965.

The battle against basic poverty has certainly been won but, if China is to escape from the poverty trap which still threatens and to catch up with the rest of the world, then her leaders must provide the best possible all-round education for all her people. So far only about one million students receive education beyond middle school. Hua Kuo-feng advocated five measures to revitalise intellectual life, including a ten-year school system by 1985. Meanwhile, he said that "key" schools and universities, which were once denounced during the Cultural Revolution as "pagodas for cultivating intellectual aristocrats", were essential in view of the huge task of providing good facilities for all. Preparations are under way for a massive student exchange with European and North American countries totalling possibly forty thousand. The implications for Chinese academic life are enormous.

Cultural life

For ten years after the Cultural Revolution the Chinese people, though intellectually starved, remained thirsty for culture. When reprints of classical works were authorised in the early seventies they were snapped up, almost the moment they appeared. Now, following what Ross Terrill calls "the winter blight of the Cultural Revolution",[1] some authors and poets are emerging from obscurity and the Union of Chinese Writers is again functioning. The New Year of 1977 was marked by a series of theatrical performances which included new works and some banned by the "radical four". Works by foreign authors, including Shakespeare and Dickens are also to appear in large numbers. Beethoven, once said to be a "bourgeois class" composer, and other classical composers, again find a place in orchestral concerts. A cultural "new spring" seems to be on the way.

Research is being revived in economics and the social sciences. A new Academy of Social Sciences includes institutes of philosophy, economics, literature, languages, history, archaeology, law, world religions and nationalities. The inclusion of religion is a significant development. Religion has become an intellectually respectable subject for study.

Reviving the economy

As well as getting education and culture back on the right lines, the Government's great concern was the economy.

---

[1] 800,000,000: Real China, by Ross Terrill (Penguin Books).

Three economic conferences held at the end of 1976 and early in 1977 reflected the determination to restore orderly economic development. That economic development was to be governed by the targets of the Fifth Five Year Plan (1976–80) outlined by Chou En-lai in 1975, viz. the speedy mechanisation of agriculture and the industrialisation of China by the end of the century. Hua invoked the authority of Mao Tse-tung's speech on the "Ten Great Relationships" to support the new programme which emphasised the importance of a sound agricultural base. At the same conference emphasis was placed on "proper material benefits, more attention to cost and profit, the import of new technology and a bigger role for scientists and technicians".

The new Constitution promulgated at the Eleventh National Congress of the Chinese Communist Party includes for the first time mention of the "four modernisations" and, following the Congress, the pace of change quickened all over China. A further series of high-level conferences was held on agriculture, industry, science and technology in order to alert the nation to the need to make up for lost time. The Party has always in theory been committed to a programme of industrialisation and modernisation. Modernisation was the chief appeal of Communism to the educated class. But modernisation was feared by the "leftists" as an excuse for reversion to capitalism. Now the Eleventh Congress outlined an "Economic Development Plan". A *Red Flag* article said that "It is necessary to separate 'revolution' from 'production', 'politics' from 'production', 'politics' from 'economics'" — a flat contradiction of the Cultural Revolution slogan "Grasp revolution, increase production".

The four modernisations

Four modernisations: (i) Agriculture

China's population doubled in the forty years between 1937 and 1977! Clearly there is such a delicate balance between food and population that the first consideration must be the feeding of the people. Therefore for China agriculture must always be a priority. In September 1975 a National Conference on "Learning from Tachai in Agriculture" was followed by large provincial meetings. But the differences between the purists and the pragmatists surfaced. Hua Kuo-feng then endorsed the doctrine of "putting proletarian politics in command", while Teng Hsiao-p'ing is reported to have said, "Do not be afraid of putting technology in command!" These disagreements were repeated at the local levels, but no sooner were the "gang of four" arrested in 1976 than major conferences on agriculture and industry were again arranged. The aim was to counter the influence of the "radical four" on agriculture, and to promote modern agricultural techniques. During 1977 Teng Hsiao-p'ing said to a visiting Japanese delegation: "If we are to improve our economy the first step is to improve our agriculture. If there is no agricultural advance it is impossible to advance in other areas." Agriculture accumulates the capital essential to industrialisation. The aim is to achieve seventy per cent mechanisation of all operations. The fifty thousand communes will be required to increase grain production from two hundred and eighty million tons a year in 1978 to four hundred million tons in 1985 by adding twelve new large grain-producing areas, so enabling peasant incomes to increase annually. But the most difficult task ahead for the Communist Party is to alter the traditional conservative mentality of the peasants and persuade them to accept socialist principles.

One thing, however, the Communist Party cannot do, is control the climate. In 1977 drought, which affected the whole of North-East Asia including North Korea and virtually every province of China from sub-tropical Kwangtung to northern Shansi, threatened a serious failure of the grain crop and a harvest failure would threaten the stability of the whole economy. Again in 1978 Anhwei and Kiangsu suffered their worst drought for over a hundred years. Winter drought and summer floods are a perennial problem for Chinese agriculture especially in the productive areas of the Yellow and Huai river basins.

Four modernisations: (ii) Industry

HISTORY
Chinese industry has a comparatively short history. It started in the latter part of the nineteenth century. In 1863 the first

rice-cleaning mill was established in Shanghai and the first silk filature in 1854. The first coal mine started operations in Kaiping in 1878 and the first cotton and weaving mills in Shanghai in 1890. The first iron and steel works opened in Hanyang in 1890, the first match factory in Hankow in 1894 and the first flour mill in Shanghai in 1896. Half the capital investment came from foreign sources and it was lack of Chinese capital that delayed industrial development for many years. In the present century, industrialisation carried with it all the evils of the Industrial Revolution in the West— sweated labour, child labour, lack of safety precautions and poor housing. The three main industrial areas were Anshan in Manchuria, Shanghai and Hanyang. The main products were coal, iron, steel and cotton.

China's energy resources are equal to those of the United States and the U.S.S.R. She is very rich in coal, with nine thousand million tons or one third of the world's total; China and the U.S.A. together have sixty-three per cent of the world coal resources. Exports in 1975 totalled eleven million tons. China is also very rich in oil, with possibly the third largest resources in the world after the U.S.A. and the Middle East. In 1976 total production stood at eighty-six million tonnes. Many of the fields have yet to be developed; there are about one hundred potential commercial fields and by 1980 the output could be up to two hundred million tonnes or more, especially if the offshore field in the Pohai gets into production. Japanese estimates of China's reserves are six and a half million tonnes on shore and twelve million tonnes off-shore. A huge development in the petro-chemical industry is taking place; more than fifty complete plants have been imported already from Japan and Western Europe, including Britain, and plants for producing chemical fertilisers, synthetic textiles, plastics, synthetic rubbers, etc. The production of coal increased by ninety-one per cent between 1964 and 1975 and oil by six hundred and fifty per cent in the same period. Natural gas is available in abundant supply and the electricity industry, which is still largely coal-based, is increasing its output dramatically. China also has a whole range of precious metals. Thus her industrial potential is great. By A.D. 2000 China will be the third largest energy consumer and the third largest economic power in the world, if she can maintain her annual ten per cent growth rate in gross national product.

"TWO LINE" CONTROVERSY

After 1949 China's inexperienced Government slavishly followed the Soviet model for industry, leaning heavily on Soviet advisers. The first Five Year Plan placed the emphasis on industrialisation and on heavy industry. At the Eighth Congress of the CCP in 1956, Russian-style "one man management" was rejected by the Party Committee in favour of collective leadership, a shift from "centralisation" to "democracy". In 1960 Chairman Mao approved the historic "Constitution of the Anshan Iron and Steel Company" which obtained prominence in the Cultural Revolution. Its principle was "keep politics in command". In 1962 Chairman Mao enunciated a new principle to be followed as far as China was concerned, "Agriculture as the foundation, industry as the leading factor". Economic growth hinges on the performance of the agricultural sector. In 1971 Chou En-lai told Edgar Snow that China had reached the take-off stage for industry. But, he added, "we have only just begun!"

Following years of disagreement between Russia and China, China's Soviet advisers withdrew suddenly in 1961, taking with them industrial blueprints and even whole factories. China was on her own and this led Mao to re-emphasise the need for national "self-reliance". Never again would China be beholden to any foreign power. It was no longer safe to trust anyone. Even Big Brother had let them down! The backyard steel furnaces of the Great Leap Forward were fairly useless, practically speaking; they produced only low grade pig iron. But as a visual aid and an object lesson in what everyone could do in the spirit of self-reliance they served a useful purpose. They taught the peasants the basic skills of industry. The Chinese learned the lesson well and have been putting it into practice ever since with considerable success. But, according to Edgar Snow, it took four years to pick up the pieces of the unfinished industries abandoned by the Russians.

Since Mao's 1962 directive the order of priorities has been —1) agriculture; 2) light industry; 3) heavy industry. Light industries largely serve agriculture and produce fertilisers, farm machinery, trucks, tractors, water pumps and electric generating equipment. Many such factories were moved out from the cities to the communes, though Shanghai is still the largest producer of light industrial goods. During 1964–5, as industry recovered from the Russian withdrawal, the Government undertook a radical restructuring of the major industries into twelve lines, each under centralised control. The first Five Year Plan had resulted in a thirty-one per cent growth but was cut short by the Great Leap Forward. The restructuring of industry by Liu Shao-ch'i in 1964–5 was a reversal of the Anshan Constitution. Then in 1966 followed Chairman Mao's speech "On the Ten Great Relationships" concerning relationships between the centre and the regions. The Great Leap Forward in 1969 emphasised industry rather than agriculture. But labour indiscipline led to the re-introduction by Liu Shao-ch'i of piece rates and "material incentives". These were condemned by Chairman Mao, and also caused divisions between the skilled and unskilled workers. At the Eleventh Plenum of the Chinese Communist Party Central Committee in 1966, Chairman Mao's policies again received full endorsement and the Cultural Revolution revived the Anshan Constitution as a model for industry. Many factories adopted it as a guide in 1968. The Second Five Year Plan was also cut short, this time by the Cultural Revolution, of which Chou En-lai said, "Economically speaking China has had to pay dearly for so powerful, a revolutionary movement; production, excluding agriculture, has been particularly affected".

In 1971 a fourth Five Year Plan was launched—the third never appeared. It followed the policy of "walking on two legs", i.e. encouraging both the state-run industries and the small-scale commune-run factories in rural areas. The average growth in industrial production in the following period was fifteen per cent per year. 1974 saw a record purchase of foreign technology amounting to one billion dollars in industrial plant; petro-chemical plant from Japan, steel and rolling mills from France and West Germany and automobile factories from West Germany and Japan. This policy of "using foreign things to serve China" was bitterly criticised by the Radicals on ideological grounds. In 1974 the anti-Confucius campaign coincided with the lowest recorded industrial growth rate for several years. In 1975 the leftists spoke of "a right deviationist wind blowing" and the political conflict was dividing both workers and management. The pragmatic "theory of productive forces" was opposed by the left-wing purists. Labour indiscipline was again the result. Nevertheless industrial production probably doubled between 1968 and 1975; steel production was put at twenty-four million tons, coal at three hundred and ninety million tons, electric power at 115,000 million kilowatt hours, crude oil at seventy to eighty million tons, cement at thirty-three million tons and cotton cloth at eight thousand million yards. The Radicals complained of "putting production in command"!

In 1975 on his last appearance at a National People's Congress Chou En-lai announced the new Five and Ten Year Plan to "build an independent and relatively comprehensive industrial and economic system which would enable China to catch up with the rest of the world by the end of the century". The Radicals again objected but Teng Hsiao-p'ing saw the real danger as "not daring to grasp production". He sought to de-emphasise the political struggle in order to boost production. Consequently he came under heavy fire from the Radicals and their supporters who regarded factories as battlefields in the struggle between the proletariat and the bourgeoisie. Hua Kuo-feng has admitted that, amid the confusion of policies and resultant chaos, China was in 1976 on the verge of economic collapse as industry stagnated due to sabotage by the Radicals. In Szechwan civil war became a near reality. Elsewhere many industrial plants came to a standstill and the internal state of many factories was chaotic. The "gang of four" were arrested none too soon!

FUTURE AIMS

In 1977 the New Year press published Mao's 1966 speech on "The Ten Great Relationships" which seems to support the current pragmatic approach to industry. Following an important industrial conference attended by seven thousand delegates, the first of nine such conferences, Hua announced a hundred and twenty new projects "to change the backward state of our basic industries"—ten new iron and steel complexes, ten new oil and gas fields, thirty power stations, nine non-ferrous metal complexes, eight coal mines, six trunk railways and five harbours. These are to be located in fourteen new "industrial bases" around the country. The existing heavy industry centres are at Anshan, Shanghai, Wuhan, Paotow, Chungking, Peking, Taiyuan and Penchi. The task of rebuilding China's industry began with an attempt to sort out the chronic problems of the railways where large-scale disruption had persisted for years. Industrial managers, restless under the present rigid system of centralised State control, are also seeking considerable autonomy for State enterprises, possibly after the Yugo-Slav system of worker self-management.

The present leadership knows that the task of building up China with its nine hundred and fifty million people into a powerful socialist country in less than a quarter of a century is an arduous one. It has already meant a modification of China's boasted "self-reliance" principles and her refusal hitherto to accept foreign loans which would place her in debt to foreign countries. Foreign technology is now pouring into the country and China is accepting credits with which to purchase what she needs to meet current shortages. Great Britain is providing coal-mining machinery, aircraft and aero-engines and in November 1978 signed a huge contract for the purchase by China of a wide range of military and non-military technology.

In 1977 China's steel production was probably twenty-one million tons, or eleven per cent up on the 1976 level. Indeed the figures for industrial production in 1977 showed a dramatic improvement over those for 1976. Things were even better in 1978, according to the *Financial Times*, with a continued rise in coal and oil production. The aim is to increase steel production from twenty million tons in 1978 to sixty million tons in 1985 by increasing the number of plants and coal mines. The weak links in the economy at present are coal, electric power and transport. If the problem of increasing electric power is not solved all talk of rapid development will be meaningless, said a *People's Daily* editorial in September 1977.

HIGHER WAGES

In the drive to modernise, wages have been raised for the first time in twenty years and incentives for increased work and productivity brought back. As from the beginning of

October 1977 the wages of the lower paid in China were increased between fifteen and twenty per cent, an increase which affected forty per cent of workers who come within the eight-grade work system. The total industrial labour force is only fifteen per cent of the population as compared with seventy-five per cent for agriculture. But the Government emphasised that wage increases must remain lower than the rate of increased productivity. More labour discipline and hard work were urged as the price for higher living standards—"The more you work, the more you earn!" The new slogan "It is glorious to accumulate funds for the state and shameful to lose money" seems to be a total reversal of earlier policies of ignoring profitability because that is a capitalistic motive.

Four modernisations: (iii) National defence

The oscillation between the "two lines" is seen even in the military field; the conservatives want a mechanised and professional army, free from Party control, whereas the Left have over-emphasised the role of the militia. The PLA is traditionally a partisan army, trained to defend its own territory against possible invaders. Now China faces an army of a million Russians on her northern border equipped with modern weapons and nuclear devices deployed against China. A series of conferences on defence was held in 1977 which stressed the need for China to have modern weapons. China's own limited stock of medium range ballistic missiles and nuclear warheads and obsolescent Russian-type weapons are no match for those of her potential enemies. Teng Hsiao-p'ing, the Army Chief of Staff, promises the modernisation of the army's weapons but says the expenditure on defence must not affect overall economic development. Meanwhile China is clearly interested in buying weapons, military aircraft, naval vessels and modern technology of every kind from the West.

Four modernisations: (iv) Science and technology

The Chinese leadership is fully aware that the country's economic well-being hinges on a more modern approach to science and technology with stress on properly-rewarded expertise and new techniques, if necessary imported from abroad. The principle of self-reliance does not mean blind opposition to everything foreign. This was a Radical error. In 1975 Teng Hsiao-p'ing sponsored a document called "Outline Report of the Work of the Academy of Science", which was at once denounced by the Radicals as one of the three "poisonous weeds". Now it is seen as a source of positive suggestions on promoting the highest standards in the top research organisation. Two Chinese Nobel prize winners were among the lecturers at a 1977 seminar and they urged China to engage in more scientific research. In March 1978, at a major National Science Conference, Teng blamed the Radical attack on intellectuals for the decline in research. The Government is rehabilitating many former scientists, engineers and technicians, and emphasising that intellectuals are no longer to be regarded as "bad elements"; rather, that there is no class difference between "brain" workers and "manual" workers. The press has spoken of "cherishing intellectuals in general and scientists in particular". All kinds of academics held conferences during 1977 dealing with high energy physics, developments in electronics, laser technology, geology and oil, etc. Priorities for new technology specified in a Hankow radio broadcast in July 1977 were listed as "electronics, infra-red rays, micro-waves, lasers, atomic energy and solar energy. Among new projects are a nuclear accelerator, a digital satellite communications ground station and a large high-speed computer. Groups of Chinese scientists are going abroad to study the latest techniques. 1978 posters in Peking asked why Liu Shao-ch'i had not been rehabilitated, since his colleagues were back in power and his alleged "revisionist" policies were being pursued in all fields. It is clear that the new emphasis on science and technology is helping to restore the image of Teng Hsiao-p'ing, whose 1975 document enjoyed the endorsement of Mao Tse-tung himself. In 1978 universities were enrolling more research students than at any time since 1966.

David Bonavia, writing in *The Times* in 1975 said: "The biggest question is whether the present set of priorities—'agriculture as the foundation'—can continue to seem rational or whether more attention will not have to be given to 'industry as the leading factor'. It remains to be seen whether China can re-direct its planning towards advanced industry and technology without permitting the growth of a managerial and technical élite which would turn its back on the cherished egalitarian concepts of the present leadership." This comment is still valid in 1979! The other immediate problem is to restore the concept of hard work, a virtue once very general in China. But years of radical confusion, go-slows, over-manning and working at half-steam have seriously affected China's work ethic. Can a rise in pay galvanise the work-forces into full productivity?

Foreign trade

Hitherto the People's Republic of China has not, by Western standards, been a major trading nation. Traditionally, foreign trade has only been a marginal factor in China's economic life, accounting for less than five per cent of the gross national product. It was not until 1973 that the volume of trade surpassed that of Taiwan. In spite of the great importance of trade in stabilising the economy and China's need for equipment, advanced technology and grain. China's policy of not incurring either internal or external debts has greatly restricted her foreign trade. In 1975, with about five to six thousand million pounds sterling trading balance, trade was almost stagnant and there was a deficit of four hundred million pounds. But in 1978 the Chinese Government was financing her imports by a system of "deferred payments" or by short-term commercial credits and medium-term loans. Imports have increased much faster than exports and to adjust her balance of payments China must acquire even larger credits from her trading partners, the most important of which is Japan. Imports likely are petro-chemical equipment, steel mills, electric generators and other machinery.

Trade fairs

China's annual trade fairs attract worldwide interest and in 1975 forty thousand industrial and agricultural products were on display at the Export Commodities Fair in Canton. They included light industry products, textiles and post office and telecommunications equipment in great numbers and variety. Exhibits were also shown from the two pace-setting projects—Tachai (agriculture) and Taching (oil). Oil is potentially China's largest export. At present Japan is by far the most important trading partner, importing Chinese oil and supplying industrial machinery and chemical fertilisers. In 1971 Chou En-lai told the Canadian Foreign Trade Minister that China's economy was "still rather weak, but that the seventies could see a growth in the economy". In fact, in 1974 China had an adverse trade balance, but since then there has been an average economic growth of six per cent in the gross national product per annum, which is bigger than in most developing countries and that without foreign aid. China obtains ninety per cent of its revenue from state enterprises and ten per cent from communes. The big days of China's foreign trade lie ahead as her industry develops and her relationships with the U.S.A., Great Britain and other European nations improve.

Problem of ideology

Most Chinese probably support the Government in its ambitious and long-term programme to increase production. They still feel the need to throw off the humiliation they have experienced at the hands of foreign nations and to prove that they are equal if not superior to them all. But no doubt a small section of the younger generation, indoctrinated during and since the Cultural Revolution in different ideological values, regards China's present headlong rush to industrialise as a reversion to "capitalism" and "revisionism". John Gittings, writing in *The Guardian*, suggests that "Chairman Mao may have left a time-bomb for the future quietly ticking away in the silent hearts of the younger generation who were blooded politically in the Cultural Revolution". The issue is that of how to keep balance between the demands of revolution and of production.

Life in the cities

Life in the communes has already been described. What about life in the industrial centres of China? The "new China" is studiously trying to escape from the legacy of earlier industrial development. She seeks for a method of industrialisation that avoids the problems of urbanisation. At Taching, the new oil complex in Manchuria, for example, instead of building one large city, the Government built sixty industrial-agricultural villages and a hundred and sixty-four residential areas. The Government is doing everything possible to minimise the difference between what used to be the poor and underprivileged rural areas and the prosperous, favoured cities. Light industries have been moved out of the cities and this has reduced the urban population. In 1968 fifteen to twenty-five million urban dwellers were moved to the countryside.

The eight-grade wage system operating in factories gives wages ranging from eight to twenty-seven pounds sterling a month (48 to 122 yuan). A senior specialist might earn forty pounds and a top-ranking cadre as much as sixty. Doctors, teachers and other professional class people may earn up to a hundred pounds (three hundred yuan) a month. The cost of living in Peking is about £2.40 (7.20 yuan) per month. The rationing and food-coupon system controls the movement of population and prevents a rush back to the cities. The relative distribution of population between cities and countryside is stable because people have no freedom of choice as to where they live.

Moreover China seems to be successfully avoiding the all-too-familiar "urban sickness". Few beggars, idlers, delinquents or peddlars are to be seen. The streets are comparatively safe. The cities are also clean and litter-free, though air pollution in some of them is a serious menace. Housing, too, is quite inadequate by Western standards and few dwellings are heated in winter. But rent is only about 1.80 yuan (65p.) a month. Seeing that there are no privately-owned cars in China, traffic (except for bicycles) is not a problem. At present, health care is better in the cities than in the rural areas and educational facilities and opportunities are also better. So the inequality still exists. "Intellectuals" (i.e. educated people) once regarded manual labour as degrading for people of their status. Now cadres of every rank have to attend the 7th May schools where they cultivate crops and grow vegetables by the sweat of their brows. In this way, they learn from the peasants. City dwellers enjoy a richer cultural life than the peasants, including access to parks, playgrounds, museums, lectures, concerts, television and theatre—all for small fees. However, most programmes have, until recently, been heavily larded with political propaganda. Facilities for sport are reasonably good.

Urban churches

But where do the churches and the Christians come into the picture? Christians are Chinese citizens and, as they are found on the communes, so many, no doubt, earn their living in industry, trade and in city offices. All church buildings were closed in 1966 by the Red Guards. They have not so far been re-opened and it may be that the Christians no longer want to be given back buildings which are associated with the missionary era. Now they meet as house churches, as in New Testament times, in groups of varying size. Shanghai and Nanking are known to have many such churches, as do the large southern coastal cities. Personally-owned radio receivers are much more common in the cities than in the rural areas and city dwellers are therefore better able to listen to foreign Christian broadcasts. Christians testify to the great strength and encouragement provided by the programmes of the Far East Broadcasting Company and other similar stations.

The Chinese people and the future

Given stable and wise government, undisturbed by political turmoil, China has great future prospects. Visitors to China in 1978 were impressed by the evident self-confidence and the patience of the Chinese people as a whole in spite of their fluctuating fortunes of the past thirty years. They are realists rather than romantics. Simon Leys describes them in these words: "If, despite all the stupid cruelties of politics, China still remains faithful to itself—subtle, human, so supremely civilised—it is due to them. They—the ordinary, the lowly, the anonymous—maintain China, despite the bureaucrats, and allow us not to despair for the future. They have buried twenty dynasties, they will also bury this one. They have not changed. As usual they are patient: they are not in a hurry: they know so much more than those who rule over them!"[1]

But will the "leftists" be able to stage a come-back, as Mao prophesied would happen if the "rightists" were ever again to seize power? Will there be yet another artificially-generated revolution in the series, hatched, perhaps, in one of the traditional trouble centres of Canton, Shanghai or Wuhan? Is revolutionary theory or the pragmatic pursuit of full-scale industrialisation to determine future progress? Or can China finally settle with being both "red" and "expert"? The dialectic will continue and is always in danger of erupting in open "struggle" between the two "lines" for control of the helm of the revolution. But, as the mighty vessel *Cathay* gets fully under way with her new captain and pilot, following a newly-charted course, nothing foreseeable can prevent her progress towards the destination she has determined.

[1] *Chinese Shadows*, by Simon Leys.

CHAPTER XVIII

God—and China's Future

Among the Chinese people there is a tremendous sense of destiny. Throughout Asia, historians, economists and ideologists believe that the Chinese people are on the move and that China will be playing an important role in world affairs in the future. But we must ask, will God be given any place in that future? The story of Nebuchadnezzar who boasted "Is not this great Babylon which I have built by my mighty power and for the glory of my majesty?" is a warning to every nation that fails to honour God. Nebuchadnezzar faced judgment and humiliation until he learned that "the Most High rules the kingdom of men and gives it to whom He will". God is completely sovereign in creation and in history and one day every proud and rebellious knee will bow and every boasting tongue confess that Jesus Christ and He alone is LORD.

God's sovereign purposes

But what about God's purposes for China now? It is not enough that China has experienced God's "common grace" in her liberation from hunger, oppression and superstition. That grace is intended to lead its recipients ultimately to embrace God's "special grace", which is salvation by faith in a crucified Saviour. Dr. Choan-seng Song ended his highly controversial Bastad paper with these words, "It may not be entirely wishful thinking to hope that God, the Creator and the Redeemer, will chart the course of salvation history in China in such a way that the masses of the Chinese people who found liberation from the evils of the old society may yet find liberation in truth and in God." A more positive

Christian conviction would be to assert on Biblical grounds first, that God has indeed provided salvation in Christ for all the Chinese people—a salvation entirely distinct from social revolution; and then, that each and every one has the right to hear that best of all Good News; and thirdly, that God assuredly intends to give them that opportunity. However impossible such a development may now appear, God is the living and omnipotent God with whom nothing is impossible. He will certainly act on behalf of the Chinese people in His own chosen time and in His own appointed way. His people, if they are wise, will await that moment—the "fullness of time", in the spirit of Habbakuk who wrote, "Still the vision awaits its time; it hastens to the end, it will not lie. If it seems slow, wait for it, it will surely come, it will not delay." (Habbakuk 2, 3); Later the same prophet exults: "The earth will be filled with the knowledge of the glory of the Lord as the waters cover the sea." The future of China belongs to God. But Christians who share this confidence have a demanding duty to pray. While we wait for God, may it not be that He is waiting for us to do what needs to be done, namely to pray in the Spirit with perseverance.

Encouragements to pray

For those who can discern the times there are encouraging signs in China today. China's past policy shifts have resulted in either benign freedom or outright oppression for Christians and therefore rising internationalism in China is likely to mean improved conditions for Christians. The lifting of the political repression of thirty years has already brought greater freedom. A letter from North China written in 1976 says: "The atmosphere here is greatly changed; the authorities seem to be more lenient, more permissive. Will you please send us Bible study material through the mail. We are so hungry to study God's Word." The people of China are experiencing a "second liberation", that is, a slight liberation of the human spirit, however limited as yet. There is certainly more liberty in many spheres of life as compared with one or two years ago. The people of China are showing a new intellectual curiosity and are being encouraged to use their minds. This is important if it is true that the future prospect of widespread Christian activity in China is intimately bound up with the political destiny of the Chinese people. That is why the Apostle Paul in the days of oppressive political regimes urged that "supplications, prayers, intercession and thanksgiving be made for all men, for kings and all who are in high position". (I Timothy 2. 1, 2 RSV). He saw the importance of praying for the policy-makers in every nation, whose decisions intimately affect Christians. First, because the peace which accompanies good government is beneficial for the life of the church and second, because this peace is essential for the spreading abroad of the Good News that "Jesus Christ gave Himself a ransom for all" and that "He desires all men to be saved and to come to the knowledge of the truth". The Apostle Paul clearly never doubted the universality of the Gospel and in our day the same conviction should energise our prayer for China. Christians therefore should offer thanksgiving that the prospect for a stable and progressive government in China is brighter now than ever during the past thirty years.

Straws in the wind

Another straw in the wind is the fact that, after three decades when it has been almost unmentionable and indeed seldom mentioned in the Chinese press, religion has all of a sudden re-appeared as a live issue and as a subject worthy of academic study. There were a number of references to religion in 1977–8: descriptions of temples and shrines, articles on the Dead Sea Scrolls, reference to Christian protest in South Korea and mention of the visit to China of the Christian President of Liberia. Chairman Yeh Chien-ying's speech at the Seventh Plenary Session of the Chinese People's Consultative Conference in December 1977 emphasised the need to implement positive policies towards intellectuals, the minority peoples, overseas Chinese and towards religion. Then, on 27th September 1977 an unusual article appeared in the *Kwang Ming Daily* entitled, "Study religion and criticise theology". The intention was in order to refute it, of course, for the article vigorously argued that religion and Communism can never be reconciled. Further, in April 1978, a forum on religion attended by about a hundred delegates was held in Peking. Most significant of all is the reopening of the Institute for Research on World Religions for the first time since the Cultural Revolution began in 1966. The institute has a library of a hundred thousand volumes and the director, Jen Ghi-yu says that "religious studies help to develop an understanding of history, philosophy, art, literature and political theory". He also believes that religion will not die a natural death! The deputy director is Rev. Chao Fu-san, former assistant to the Anglican Bishop of North China. One can only hope and pray that, in spite of the basic anti-religious, Marxist convictions which govern the studies, some students will, nevertheless, discover the truth of vital Christianity. In any case an era of greater religious tolerance seems likely.

Religious character of Marxism

It has been said that "Marx was never able to escape from the world of the Bible. His own thought seems all the time to move in the same realm as the prophets of the Old Testament and the eschatological expectations of the writers of the New Testament. Here is a Biblical drama in which God is the chief actor. The Marxist picture seems to be a secularised version of the same drama with the principal Actor left out." The original inspiration of Communism clearly came from Christianity. The ideals of the brotherhood of man, the rights of the humble and the community of property were first expounded in the New Testament. C. P. Fitzgerald says: "It is obvious to any observer that in China the Communist doctrine has established itself as a religion and that a great part of its success is the appeal which it makes to men of religious temperament".[1] Communism is, of course, a religion not of personal salvation but of collective improvement. Nevertheless, the Christian concepts of redemption, future bliss, struggle with evil, faith and charity are common to Communism. The emphasis on practice as well as theory and on dedicated service to the community are also significantly present both in Christianity and Marxism. Fitzgerald says again: "From Christianity Marxism has undoubtedly borrowed much, sometimes with no acknowledge-

[1] *The Birth of Communist China*, by C. P. Fitzgerald, p. 146.

ment; sometimes with a nod of recognition such as Chou En-lai bestowed upon the Protestants." If then it is true that Communism in China has had a religious character focused on Chairman Mao and justified by his semi-inspired utterances and writings, we can only imagine the religious disillusionment prevalent now that Mao Tse-tung is being cut down to size and the infallibility of his utterances is being called in question. The Mao cult is currently being attacked as a pseudo-religion which for many Chinese must be a sobering thought. If pursued the campaign could provide a great opportunity for the Gospel. In this way God is surely preparing the hearts and minds of the Chinese people to give a fresh hearing to the Gospel and to see in Jesus Christ "the way, the truth and the life". Someone has rightly said, "Without the way, there is no going; without the truth, there is no knowing; and without the life, there is no living." Professor J. C. Bennett has written, "We are witnessing the passing of Communist absolutism. Communism may even be preparing the way for more openness to the Christian faith." [1] Neither Karl Marx nor Chairman Mao have been able to find any alternative to Christianity. Jesus Christ once crucified for sinners and now alive and exercising all authority in heaven and on earth, alone has the answers to China's needs. The Lord Jesus Christ is the unique and only Saviour of men and there is no other name whereby man can be saved.

Transcendence and the human mind

The centuries have rolled by. Human society has undergone profound changes. Revolutions have altered the world order here and there, both for the better and for the worse. But today the amazing advance of technology is transforming society more rapidly than any other factor. China clearly is determined not to lag behind the rest of the world any longer. Amid the profound changes, Jesus Christ remains the same yesterday, today and forever. His message to the world is unchanged. The Gospel proclaimed by the early Church concerning salvation through Christ's death and resurrection is unchanging and requires no new interpreta-

[1] *China and the Christian Response*, ed. W. J. Richardson.

tion by the theologians. Because human minds, however brilliant, are blinded by Satan to Divine truth they need an eye-opening revelation of a transcendent God. The glory of God can only be seen in the face of Jesus Christ. It is futile to argue about whether the Chinese mind, or any other mind, has a place for transcendence. "All is of God," says the Apostle; that is, all Divine truth, to be understood, requires a personal revelation. That revelation comes to the human heart and mind as the living Word of God in the Bible is proclaimed. That Word is powerful and penetrating as a sword. And that Word is active in China today, turning men and women, young and old, from the idolatry of Marxism and Maoism to Christ.

How will the Gospel be presented?

No doubt this message was in the past sometimes imperfectly presented by witnesses from a different cultural background and therefore misunderstood. Nevertheless, the Christian Church was established. In as far as it was a Bible-based, praying Church, full of faith and devoted to the Lord Jesus Christ, it was a Church with survival potential. Today, God's witnesses in China are exclusively Chinese who are an integral part of the "people" and rooted in the culture of the new China. Many of them are young people who have been converted to Christ in spite of the fact that their whole education has been in Marxist–Maoist theory and their lives have been deeply involved in the revolutionary process. Many of the new converts were probably once Red Guards. So the Christian Church in China is undergoing a considerable change in character while clinging to the essential Christian experience. The only Good News that Christians need to share is that of God's love and forgiveness offered to sinful men. The only change they need to seek is the new birth of the Holy Spirit, which transforms men and women and makes them sons of God. The so-called "social gospel" becomes largely irrelevant in a socialised society, though Christians will still need to contend for real social justice and the supremacy of spiritual values over material values.

These Chinese witnesses clearly make their boast in the Cross of Christ alone. But not for them the mass evangelism or even the "church-based evangelism" of the West. Public preaching is out of the question, so the witness of Christians consists in a person-to-person witness, the contagious witness of lives transformed by God's power, lives of righteousness and love that speak of a peace that passes all understanding. Chinese Christians are discovering how to present the authentic Christian witness within the culture of the New China and in terms relevant to the Chinese experience. The words of Joseph Ton of Romania apply equally to Chinese Christians. "We (Christians) have a place in a socialist society. God is the one who has found the new Way and placed some of us upon it, who live in a socialist society. He has revealed Himself to us and made us His children through the new birth. We have not found Him but He has found us. We have not chosen Him but He has chosen us. Since, therefore, He chose us from within socialism it means He wants us here. The very fact that evangelical Christianity prospers here in socialism and the number of believers is increasing fast, in spite of opposition, certainly means that God is at work, at work with exceptional power. . . The divine task of the evangelical Christian living in a socialist society is to lead such a correct and beautiful life that he will demonstrate and convince that society that he and he alone is the new man that socialism seeks vainly to create." That was how a persecuted and suffering Church witnessed to Christ in the first century and history is repeating itself today in country after country all over the world.

A highway for God

Isaiah prophesied of Judah that when the time was ripe for them to return from Babylon to Jerusalem neither mountains, valleys nor deserts would bar their path. Indeed, the mountains would be made low and the desert would become a highway for God (Isaiah 40. 3). During the first hundred years of Protestant missionary work in China the acceptance of the Gospel and the growth of the Church were hindered by the complexities of the language, illiteracy, the social power of Confucianism, superstition, national insularity and pride, and by poor communications. It is highly significant that the Communists have one by one levelled these mountains to provide a new highway for God and His messengers.

At an unscheduled prayer meeting during the Congress on Evangelism in Singapore in 1968 some interesting insights were shared. Those present observed that the three languages used for the inscription on the Cross were Hebrew, Greek and Latin. And so in the first place, Hebrew was the language of the Jewish people and it was through them that God prepared the world religiously for the coming of Jesus Christ. Now in China there is little doubt that the greatest single obstacle to the growth of the Church was the Confucian family and clan system, associated as it was with ancestor worship, which Protestants, at least, regarded as idolatrous. But Confucian feudalism is condemned in the new China and the superstitious ancestor cult is discouraged, even though until recently the Mao cult took its place. Today there is an empty void. A Jesuit writer says, "The Communist occupation of China will one day be seen to be a providential preparation for the Gospel. The Chinese culture was almost impervious to the Christian Gospel. It had to be broken up and opened to new questions and new answers before the Christian message could be given a hearing. That is what Communism is doing."

In the second place just as God used Greece to prepare the world linguistically for the coming of Jesus Christ, so in a similar way God has used the Communists to unify the spoken language of China. China has five major races and at least one hundred distinct language groups, which were once a formidable obstacle to the spread of Christianity Now everyone, everywhere, thanks to the radio and universal education, both understands and speaks the common language, or *p'u t'ung hua*. Like Greek in apostolic times, the Peking dialect is now the universally used language of China, understood by all the races and in all the dialect regions of China. This must, one day, assuredly aid the spread of the Gospel. And associated with this is the dramatic increase in literacy. In 1949 most people were incapable of reading tracts or Gospel portions and few Christians could read their Bibles fluently. Today seven or eight in ten are literate and probably nine out of ten in the cities. The Chinese have become avid readers. Thus a formidable language mountain has been made low. May the day soon come, when, instead of an exclusive interest in Mao's ideology, the people of China will be hearing and reading the Word of God, which is now available in new translations and in the simplified script.

Finally, the use of Latin on the cross emphasised the power and extent of the Roman Empire, the greatest the world had ever known, whose roads and transportation system facilitated the spread of the Gospel in the first century. In China the early Christian missionaries were confronted with immensely difficult travelling conditions. They travelled by foot, by wheelbarrow, by boat, by sedan chair, on mule-back or by mule-litter. It was a slow and arduous business. Today China has a network of metalled highways covering all China, while the departure board at the Peking railway station shows destinations all over China to which express trains now run. Likewise, at Peking airport there are announcements every few minutes of the imminent departure of planes to all the major cities of China. Here surely is a literal fulfilment of the words of Isaiah's prophecy: "In the wilderness prepare the way of the Lord, make straight in the desert a highway for our God." If the Communists can in any sense be thought of as God's servants it must surely be in this sense; they have prepared the way for Chinese Christians at some future time to travel throughout China with the Word of God. In a letter from China already quoted the writer concludes, "It is time for God to work. Soon the glory of the Lord shall be revealed." Let this confidence be ours also!

The Chinese Church worldwide

The attempt to evangelise the Chinese people has a comparatively short history. That attempt got off to an unfortunate and slow start. But a hundred and thirty-five years later the Chinese Church is a worldwide Church, which is experiencing a kind of population explosion. If, in China itself, the results of a century of witness were comparatively meagre in terms of numbers and sometimes appear to have been swept away, the existence of Chinese Christian communities on every continent and in fast-growing numbers should balance any pessimism with great thanksgiving to God. Flourishing Chinese churches are found in Taiwan and in all the South-East Asian countries. These are only matched in

the quality of their membership and leadership by the numerous, large and active Chinese churches in the U.S.A. There,
in 1978, delegates representing two hundred and eighty congregations in the U.S.A. and Canada held their third North
American Congress of Chinese evangelicals. These churches
are amongst the most flourishing anywhere and are a powerful challenge to American church life. In Great Britain also
the Christian fellowships associated with the Chinese Overseas Christian Mission seem to multiply each year and are
now found in over forty of the major cities. They too often
rebuke the formality and coldness of many British congregations by their zeal in evangelism, which takes them not
only to the numerous Chinese now living in Great Britain, including Mainland Chinese students, but also to Chinese
communities in France, Holland, Germany and Scandinavia.
Everywhere new Christian fellowships are springing up.

The Congress held in Hong Kong in 1977, at which over a
thousand Chinese representing church communities all over
the world were present, was an unprecedented and historic
event. The Chinese Congress on World Evangelism
(CCOWE) is said to have marked the coming of age of the
Chinese worldwide Church. This Congress owed nothing to
missionary initiative and only a few non-Chinese observers
were present. The Chinese Church was in fact assuming the
role once played by missionaries and was itself facing up to
its own responsibilities for worldwide evangelism, both
among ethnic Chinese and in a wider context of cross-cul-
tural witness. CCOWE has set up a permanent organisation
to ensure the fulfilment of the aims of the 1977 Congress.

In 1975, after years of planning, the Chinese Graduate
School of Theology opened its doors in Hong Kong. This,
too, was the vision of Chinese theologians, themselves highly-
qualified products of British, Canadian and American theological institutions. The school has been financed almost
entirely by Chinese donors and is staffed only by Chinese
scholars—another landmark in the progress of Chinese
Christianity today. Can we not expect from this school the
kind of apologetic literature which will soon be needed in
China to refute the atheist arguments of Marxism and to
argue the truth and rationality of the Christian faith?

In thinking about the Chinese Church, therefore, we

should think of it as indivisible, inclusive of both the Church in Mainland China and the Church outside China. The affinity is both ethnic and spiritual. The time must surely come when that section of the Chinese Church abroad will be free to go to the aid of the hard-pressed section in China. In the past year or two Chinese Christians in Europe, America and in Asia have been showing a new spiritual concern for their brethren in China—that suffering remnant which is the real key to China's evangelisation. Many of them, who are professionally qualified, are eagerly awaiting the day when they can return to China to serve their country professionally and to join their fellow-Christians in a new era of Christian witness. These people are even now putting themselves through rigorous training for what they know will inevitably be a difficult and costly ministry. The moment for which they wait, suddenly, in 1979, seem much nearer.

Present activity on behalf of China

Meanwhile, what can now be done to strengthen the hand of the Church in China and to proclaim the Gospel? Here great wisdom and caution are needed, as well as "holy boldness". A few over-zealous but poorly informed, inexperienced and insensitive people could hinder the ultimate progress of the Gospel by premature and ill-judged actions. Other Asian countries provide sad examples of such activity by the few, which has provoked governments to react strongly against all Christian activity. Even Christian tourists have, on occasions, been unwise in speech and action and so jeopardised continuation of the tour itself. On the other hand tourists who know the Chinese and can speak their language have actually had the privilege of leading people to Christ during even a short tour. With the increase in tourism, more Christians will be able to witness to their guides and others as opportunities occur. Business people employed by foreign firms have also found an interested response to their Christian testimony.

Obviously the best witnesses are Chinese Christians who have relatives or business contacts in China. Since most overseas Chinese originated in the southern coastal provinces of

Kwangtung, Fukien, Chekiang and Kiangsu, it is these provinces that are most frequently visited and from which news of Christian house groups comes. More and more Chinese Christians are making use of their comparative freedom of entry to take encouragement to these groups and to take as many copies of the Scriptures to them as the customs officials allow. They also witness to non-Christians.

Some foreign Christians employed by the Chinese Government as teachers or lecturers, or studying in a university also have good opportunities to live and speak for Christ. One Chinese student, after observing his foreign room-mate's life over many months, asked him to tell him the secret, with the result that he too accepted Christ.

Present activity—radio broadcasting

When the BBC Head of Television programmes visited the People's Broadcasting Station in China in 1976 he learned that there are over a hundred million radio receivers in China, or one for every eight or nine people. Many Chinese regularly listen to the BBC and equally many, both Christians and non-Christians, listen to the programmes of the Far East Broadcasting Company, which transmits a hundred and ten programme hours per week into China in five dialects from five radio posts. These programmes are a combination of educational, English, musical and religious items. The signals from the powerful transmitter on Cheju Island in South Korea can be clearly heard all over China. Letters received show the importance of this ministry and arrivals in Hong Kong report that many Christians listen to the Christian broadcasts; some even recommend them to their friends and relatives. A Roman Catholic priest who reached Hong Kong from the Mainland had this to say: "Many Christians have only been able to preserve their sanity through these broadcasts and, due to the support of the FEBC, there is real hope for continued and expanded activity in China." For the present, the transistor receiving set and the powerful transmitters are the sole means by which the Gospel can reach "every creature" in China.

During thirty years of broadcasting to China by the FEBC, listener response was small. Then, in 1979, the Chinese people were told that the FEBC was no longer an "enemy station" and all could listen. Suddenly, the volume of letters received increased from two in December to 3,021 in March – an average of one hundred per day! Letters came from every province except Tibet and 92 per cent were from non-Christians—a further evidence of the spiritual vacuum that exists. Bibles received through the post were acknowledged with undisguised delight. Clearly large numbers of people had long been listening to Christian broadcasts, but only felt free to write after the ban was lifted.

Focus for intercession

The true believers in China today are men and women of faith. It matters not that they have no buildings in which to worship. They worship God in spirit and in truth and first-hand reports of these gatherings show them to be rich in spiritual fellowship. It is a terrible deprivation that Bibles are few. But many Christians in the past have hidden large portions of God's Word in their memories and in their hearts. Even today they are ingeniously overcoming the shortage by sharing the few surviving Bibles, by mimeographing portions for study classes and by writing down the sections which are read at dictation speed over Christian radio stations abroad. The Church in China today is a living Church, an inextinguishable light. "The darkness has not overcome it" (John 1. 4). This Church is the "sharp threshing instrument" which God is preparing for His use, the metal of which He is refining in the fires of suffering. With it He will reap the harvest among China's masses. In 1950 Dr. T. C. Chao prophesied that the Church in forty years would become the leaven of Chinese society—"the stone which the builders rejected". Bishop Otto Debelius of East Germany once predicted, "A hundred years from now people will not remember much of Communism, whose days are numbered, but the living Church will remain. Just as every other atheistic ideology had its beginning and its end, so it will be with Communism."

But a heavy obligation rests on the worldwide Church to stand with that part of Christ's Body which is in China. We, in the West, need to stand with the Church in China in humble prayer. That Church is a suffering Church. Prayer, as Hebrews 13. 1 makes clear, is powerful and effective only when we identify ourselves with those for whom we pray and put ourselves in their circumstances: "Remember those that are in prison, as in prison with them." We need to enter into their sufferings for our own good as well as theirs. Jonathan Chao has said, "The yearning for contact with the Church in China is a beautiful yearning. In that yearning the world Church confesses that she is incomplete without the Church in China. And in this desire Christians transcend sectarian, racial and political barriers. We must begin to step across those barriers and we can begin by exploring communion through prayer; by cultivating our Christian understanding of China and by putting into practice the insights of Chinese Christianity."

For what then should we pray?

1. For China's leaders and for greater liberty to be given to Christians to worship openly and to witness freely.
2. For all the Christian fellowships, large and small, throughout China and for their leaders, that they may be kept united, preserved from error, given all wisdom in relation to the authorities, kept bold in their testimony and abounding in faith, hope and love, as the Holy Spirit enables.
3. For the Scriptures already in print in the new script and available in Hong Kong to be allowed into China in larger quantities, or for permission for them to be printed in China itself.
4. For the FEBC and other Christian broadcasting stations; for well-informed script writers; for script writers in the minority languages, e.g. Tibetan and tribal languages; for improved programmes fully intelligible to hearers educated in Marxism and Maoism; for freedom to correspond with listeners; for funds to provide more powerful transmitters.
5. For the preparation of Christian literature to meet the need of a Biblically illiterate population and a deprived Church; apologetic, expository, devotional and evangelistic literature; and for the freedom to import such material into China.

6. For the large numbers of Mainland Chinese students who, in the near future, will be studying abroad in Europe and in America; that the churches may be alive to the opportunities for witnessing to them.

7. For the teachers, students, engineers, technologists and experts in many fields who will be invited to assist in China's modernisation programme, especially for Christians among them.

8. *For the early and rapid spreading of the Gospel, which is the power of God—the Good News of the world's only Saviour, among China's multiplying millions.*

A Singapore Chinese Christian writes: "I believe the basic strategy is to have men of prayer ready to evangelise China. In the last two years I have discovered a new and powerful undercurrent of prayer among overseas Chinese. Those attending this prayer meeting for China not only pray but study the situation in China, trying to understand how to spread the Gospel to those growing up in an atheistic, materialistic society. This is not just a calm, sweet fellowship but an active, serious workshop—people with a vision and a commission . . ."

"I will work" says our God, "and who will prevent it?" But who will be "workers together with God" and labourers in prayer on behalf of China and her people? Who will take up the greatest challenge to faith that the Christian Church has ever faced? Who can, like Paul, say, "I have great sorrow and unceasing anguish in my heart for I could wish that I myself were accursed and cut off from Christ for the sake of my brethren, my kinsmen by race"? Hudson Taylor from the anguish of his heart cried out, "If I had a thousand lives to live China should have them all." Have we that same spirit?

Glossary

CCP   Chinese Communist Party

KMT   Kuomintang—the Nationalist Party

PLA   People's Liberation Army

Bourgeois   Term of abuse for intelligentsia or losers in the power struggle; disgraced bureaucrats who are given a "capitalist" label.

Bureaucracy   Thirty hierarchical classes, each with special privileges and prerogatives.

Cadre   A bureaucrat, civil servant, official (originally an army term). Avoids "right" or "left" deviation. Seeks in vain for the middle way. Non-action is his best hope of survival.

Class struggle More or less fictional in a country which had almost no industrial capitalist class; people can and do have their class label changed.

Moderate   "Rightist" or revolutionary pragmatist—on the right wing of the Communist Party—places technological expertise before politics. ("Left" and "Right" are relative terms when speaking of different emphases within the Communist movement. Also used as terms of abuse in speaking of political enemies—e.g. Lin P'iao and "gang of four", who were "leftists" but were condemned as "rightists".)

Proletariat   Strictly the workers, peasants and soldiers—recently redefined to include both manual and intellectual workers.

Radical   "Leftist" or Maoist—on the left wing of the
               Communist Party—places politics in com-
               mand—favours moral incentives only—revo-
               lutionary purist.

Revisionist   One who seems to reverse the "leftist" poli-
               cies of Mao to pursue a pragmatic course.

Truth   Marxism–Leninism–Mao Thought—what is
               decided by the Propaganda Department—
               there is no such thing as an uncompromising
               and unbiased witness to truth on an intellec-
               tual or philosophical basis.

CHINA:
THE RELUCTANT EXODUS

Phyllis Thompson

*The untold story of the withdrawal of the
China Inland Mission from China*

The most significant period in the history of modern
missions was in the five years following World War II,
when the door closed on nearly one quarter of the
world's population as China, the largest 'mission field' in
the world, came under Communist government.

For over a century it had been possible, if often dangerous,
for western missionaries to enter the country and preach
where they would. By the end of 1950 all that had changed.
Most Protestant missionary societies had withdrawn
already, and now the largest, the China Inland Mission,
decided that open Christian witness in China was
impossible under Communism. The mission must withdraw.

Had the decision come too late?

The full story of the exodus, unrevealed at the time,
is told now.